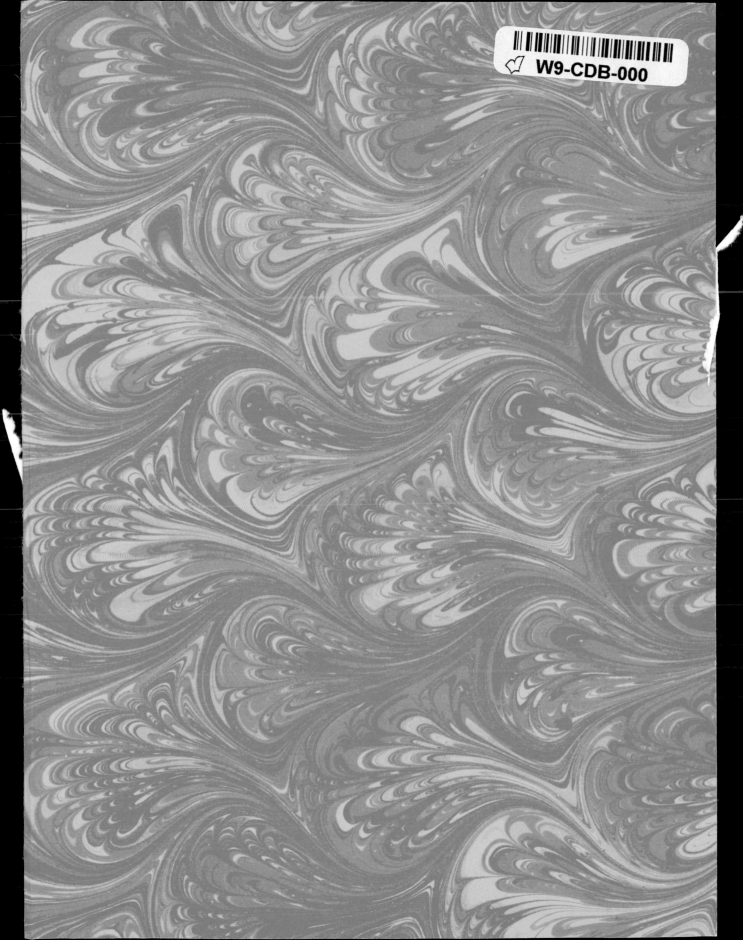

THE DARING BOOK
FOR GIRLS

Andrea J. Buchanan

The Daring Book for Girls

Miriam Peskowitz

Illustrations by Alexis Seabrook

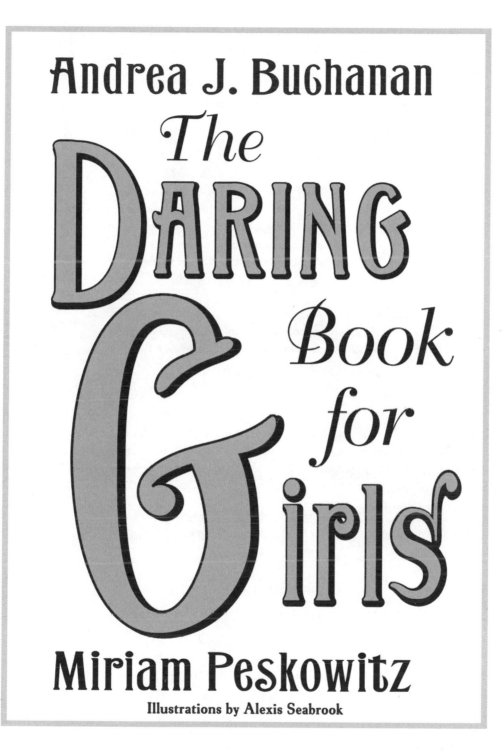

 Collins

An Imprint of HarperCollinsPublishers

To the most daring girl I know:
my grandmother Margaret Mullinix—A.B.

To my daughters, Samira and Amelia Jane—M.P.

THE DARING BOOK FOR GIRLS

HarperCollins books may be purchased for educational, business,
or sales promotional use. For information, please write:
Special Markets Department, HarperCollins Publishers,
195 Broadway, New York, NY 10007.

NOTE TO PARENTS: This book contains a number of activities which may be dangerous if not done exactly as directed or which may be inappropriate for young children. All of these activities should be carried out under adult supervision only. The authors and publishers expressly disclaim liability for any injury or damages that result from engaging in the activities contained in this book.

Illustrations by Alexis Seabrook
Designed by Richard J. Berenson, Berenson Design & Books, LLC and
The Stonesong Press, LLC

Library of Congress Cataloging-in-Publication Data
  Buchanan, Andrea J.
    The Daring book for girls / Andrea Buchanan, Miriam Peskowitz.   1st ed.
      p.   cm.
    ISBN 978-0-06-147257-2
    1. Girls—Life skills guides. 2. Girls—Conduct of life. 3. Girls in literature.   I. Peskowitz,
Miriam, 1964-   II. Title.
  HQ777 .B82 2007
  646. 70083'42—dc22
    ISBN 978-0-06-220896-5   2007031986

              18   19   20   LSCW   10

The publisher and authors acknowledge the inspiration of
The Dangerous Book for Boys for the concept and design for this book
and are grateful to Conn and Hal Iggulden for their permission.

CONTENTS

INTRODUCTION

W E WERE GIRLS in the days before the Web, cell phones, or even voicemail. Telephones had cords and were dialed by, well, actually dialing. We listened to records and cassette tapes—we were practically grown-ups before CDs came to pass—and more often than not, we did daring things like walk to school by ourselves. Ride our banana-seat bikes to the local store. Babysit when we were still young enough to be babysat ourselves. Spent hours on our own, playing hopscotch or tetherball, building a fort in our rooms, or turning our suburban neighborhood into the perfect setting for covert ops, impromptu ball games, and imaginary medieval kingdoms.

Girls today are girls of the twenty-first century, with email accounts, digital cable, iPods, and complex video games. Their childhood is in many ways much cooler than ours—what we would have given for a remote control, a rock-climbing wall, or video chatting! In other ways, though, girlhood today has become high-pressured and competitive, and girls are inducted into grownup-hood sooner, becoming tweens and teens and adult women before their time.

In the face of all this pressure, we present stories and projects galore, drawn from the vastness of history, the wealth of girl knowledge, the breadth of sport, and the great outdoors. Consider the *Daring Book for Girls* a book of possibilities and ideas for filling a day with adventure, imagination—and fun. The world is bigger than you can imagine, and its yours for the exploring—if you dare.

Bon voyage.

Andrea J. Buchanan
Miriam Peskowitz

ESSENTIAL GEAR

1. Swiss Army Knife.
A key tool for survival, exploring, and camping, it's a knife, screwdriver, and saw with tons of extras like a magnifying glass, nail file, bottle opener, scissors, and tweezers. Best of all it fits in your pocket. Clean with hot soapy water, and add a tiny drop of mechanical oil once every three blue moons.

2. Bandana.
Can be used to keep your head cool, protect your treasure, wrap a present. Tied to a stick, it can carry your treasured possessions on your adventures.

3. Rope and Twine.
A stretch of rope and a knowledge of knots will take you many places—and may also help get you out of them.

4. Journal and Pencil, with a Back-up Pen.
Life is about memories: a quick sketch of a bird or plant, a wishlist, a jot of the most important thought ever. A pad and pencil is also perfect for spying or for writing the Great American Novel.

5. Hair Band.
For when hair gets in the way. In a pinch, you can also use your bandana, or a pencil.

6. Bungee Cord.
For strapping things down on the go.

7. Flashlight.
Basic tool for sleep outs and reading under the covers late at night. A small piece of red cellophane over the lens makes ghost stories even creepier. Eventually you can graduate to a headlamp, so your hands are free.

8. Compass.
You need to know where you are, and a compass can help. Hang it around your neck along with a whistle.

9. Safety Pins.
Because they're good to have on hand when things need to be put back together, or when you want to express eternal friendship to a new pal by decorating with a few beads as a gift.

10. Duct tape.
Two inches wide and hard as nails. It can fix almost everything. Good for clubhouse construction.

11. Deck of cards and a good book.
Old standbys.

12. Patience.
It's a quality and not a thing, but it's essential so we'll include it here. Forget perfect on the first try. In the face of frustration, your best tool is a few deep breaths, and remembering that you can do anything once you've practiced two hundred times. Seriously.

Shooting Guard

Point Guard

Small Forward

Power Forward

Center

Rules of the Game: Basketball

BASKETBALL WAS FIRST PLAYED with a soccer ball and a suspended wooden peach basket when it was invented in 1891 by Dr. James Naismith at a YMCA in Springfield, Massachusetts. Girls originally shot hoops wearing Victorian petticoats, white muslin pinafores, and silk slippers. The dress code has thankfully changed, and basketball today is one of the few team sports that a girl can not only learn in elementary school but also dream of playing professionallly.

Basketball opened up to girls—real uniforms and all—in the 1970s. The United States passed a law known popularly as "Title IX" (the full name is Title IX of the Education Amendment of 1972), which said that no one, girls or boys, can be excluded from participating in school activities if that school receives federal funds. Some schools resisted, but many more decided to open up team sports to girls. As a result of Title IX, girls can now play sports at all school levels, and college women's basketball in particular has become a popular sport to watch and play.

Women's basketball made its Olympics premiere in 1996, and the American team won the gold. In 1997, the Women's National Basketball Association launched with star players, including Sheryl Swoopes, Rebecca Lobo, Lisa Leslie, and Cynthia Cooper.

WHO'S ON THE TEAM

Point Guard: She's the shortest, quickest, and best ball-handling player on the team. The Point Guard doesn't shoot much, but she is the team leader on the court and manages the plays.

Shooting Guard: She specializes in getting the ball in the basket and scoring points. She's skilled in hitting those three-point baskets from outside the line and darting to the basket for layups. Great with the ball, she can throw, dribble, and shoot in her sleep.

Center: She's the strongest, tallest, and highest-jumping player on the team. On college and professional teams, all eyes are on the Center. The Center rules the free-throw lane, and she shoots from right under the basket. She gets right into the mix, creates the space to shoot and score, and is also a major factor on defense for rebounding.

Power Forward: She grabs the rebounding ball from the other team's point, fast breaks it down the court, dribbles hard, and passes to the Center. She's also a good shooter. Actually, all the players need to be good shooters.

Small Forward: The Forward does it all. She shoots, runs, passes the ball, and scores, scores, scores. She's the ultimate player, and can substitute for anyone. '

Of course, none of this matters if you're playing a pickup game or shooting solo at the hoop in front of the house.

BASKETBALL TIPS

Dribbling: Cup your hand so that it's not your palm bouncing the ball, but the pads of your fingers. Think of a push-and-pull motion as you move your arm. Practice dribbling the ball—not too high or low—'til you can do it without looking. In a game, you won't have time to watch your hand on the ball. You'll be too busy preventing other players from taking it, and holding them at bay by stretching out your non-dribbling arm.

Passing: Throw the ball to a player who is primed to shoot, or who can protect it from the other team.

Shooting: Get your arms out in front, elbows bent. Your stronger arm holds the ball, the weaker supports it. Your hands are close together, with the fingers spread. Flick your wrist back, and push the ball into the air toward the net. Really push. For more fun, try a jump shot. Position yourself in classic ready position: two feet on the floor, legs slightly bent and shoulder-width apart, one foot slightly forward, and shoulders squared to the basket. Hold the ball with your arms and hands high and cock your wrists back. Aim for the backboard. When you shoot, stay relaxed, look at the rim, uncock your wrists—and push the ball into the air while you jump up and slightly back. The power from your legs pushes through to your arms and sends the ball high into the air toward the net. You will be able to score many more points over the outstretched hands of defenders if you can perfect this fadeaway jump shot.

Scoring: Shoot from inside the semicircle, it's two points. Shoot from outside, it's three.

If someone fouls you and you stand at the freethrow line to shoot, that's one point.

You might think that being good at basketball is about strength in your arms. Yes, but not entirely. The real strength is in your legs. The stronger your legs are, the more power you send into the ball and the easier the jump shot will be. How do you strengthen your legs? You jump. Jump everywhere: five times across the court and back, long jumps, short jumps, up and down the sidewalk in front of your house, or inside in the hallways. You are in training: jump, jump, jump.

COOL TRICKS

After you've learned to dribble (and remember the two-hundred-time rule: you can do anything once you've tried two hundred times), you're ready for tricks. Basketball is filled with show-off moves: bounce the ball under your legs, between your legs, slam-dunk the ball into the net, or pirouette away after you shoot. With a practiced flick of the wrist you can even twirl the ball on your index finger. Here are two behind-your-back moves.

Bounce behind the back: First, master the crossover dribble. Instead of the usual single-hand dribble, bounce the ball from your right hand toward the left, and then dribble with the left. Bounce the ball from your left hand and pick up with your right. Keep bouncing and dribbling back and forth. That's called a crossover. Practice until you get it. Now, try crossing behind your back. Dribble the ball with your right hand, move the ball to your right side, and bounce it behind you, picking up the dribble with your left hand.

Pass behind the back: Dribble the ball. When you're ready to catch the next bounce, reach for the ball from the side, using your full palm to sweep the ball behind you into your left hand. When you're really good at this, the ball will go all the way around the back of your body and bounce on the other side, ready for the dribble to continue from the other hand.

AROUND THE WORLD

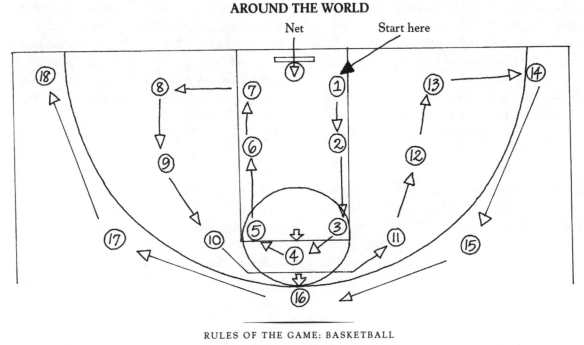

AROUND THE WORLD

This is a classic game that can be played alone or with limitless friends and is a good way to practice your shooting from different spots on the court.

With chalk or tape, follow the illustration to mark the circuit. To play, follow the numbers and shoot a basket from each spot on the free-throw line, the area between that and the three-point line, and finally, shooting from the three-point line itself.

When you make the basket, advance to the next station and shoot again. The ball is yours until you miss. If you miss, stay where you are, and pass the ball to the next player, who shoots and advances, or misses and stays put. On your next turn, shoot again until you make the basket and move ahead. The final shot must be made two times in a row or you return to the beginning. The winner is the first person to complete the circuit.

VARIATIONS
◆ Mark the court with ten stations, instead of eighteen.
◆ If you miss the ball from one spot, and miss it on the second try, return to the beginning of the circuit.
◆ Each player has her own basketball, and advances through the circuit at her own pace.

૭

Rules of the Game: Netball

JAMES NAISMITH, the Canadian YMCA instructor who invented basketball, also invented a game called netball in the United States in 1891. Netball never captured the imagination of Americans, but when some schoolteachers brought it to England, it caught on and spread like wildfire through the British Commonwealth. That's why netball now has a storied history in Australia, New Zealand, Jamaica, Barbados, Trinidad & Tobago, and India.

Fashioned as "women's basketball," netball is played with a small soccer ball. The team uniform is skirts, though in Muslim nations like Pakistan, where netball is becoming more popular, girls wear pants, and some even play in headscarves. In 1995, netball was recognized as an Olympic sport, but it has not yet been added to the roster of competition.

SOME THINGS TO KNOW

1. Netball is a game of passing. Unlike basketball, there is no dribbling. You don't bounce the ball and run full court. The netball court is divided into three zones. Players are limited to specific thirds of the court and they pass the ball quickly, from one zone to another. A player with the ball must pass to the next player within three seconds. She can pass the ball within a zone or into the next zone, but can neither skip a zone, nor throw the ball way down court.

2. A netball team has seven active positions. Each player has a particular position, one opposing player she defends against, and a specific part of the court she plays in.

NETBALL POSITIONS

Abbreviation	Position	Defends against the:	Playing Area
GS	Goal Shooter	GK: Goal Keeper	A, goal circle
GA	Goal Attack	GD: Goal Defense	A and C, goal circle
WA	Wing Attack	WD: Wing Defense	A and C, not goal circle
C	Center	C: Center	All thirds, not goal circles
WD	Wing Defense	WA: Wing Attack	C and D, not goal circle
GD	Goal Defense	GA: Goal Attack	C and D, goal circle
GK	Goal Keeper	GS: Goal Shooter	D, goal circle

3. A player with the ball cannot run. Instead, netball players perfect the pivot and move their bodies while keeping one foot planted on the court. Fouls committed against these rules, breaking the 3-second rule, or the ball going offside result in a free pass by the opposing team.

4. The basket is suspended on a ten-foot pole. There is no backboard. To make a goal, one stands within the goal circle, aims for the front or back of the rim, and shoots high, with some backspin. Oh, and no jumpshots, as at least one foot must stay on the floor. Each goal is worth one point, though a goal shot from outside the goal circle yields two points.

5. Defense players can intercept passes any way they like, but they cannot charge, intimidate, or move closer than three feet, or 90 centimeters, toward the player with the ball. Moving in too close is called obstruction, and results in a penalty pass.

6. A game has four 15-minute quarters, with 3 minutes between the first two and the last two, and a luxurious 5 minute break at halftime.

7. Netball is a no-contact sport, which means players cannot push, trip, knock, bump, elbow, hold, or charge each other. Although a player should attempt to intercept the ball while it is being passed, grabbing the ball while another player holds it is considered a foul. Breaking the personal contact rule results in a penalty pass for the opposing team, and a penalty shot should any of this—or any untoward attempt to move the goalpost—happen within the goal circle.

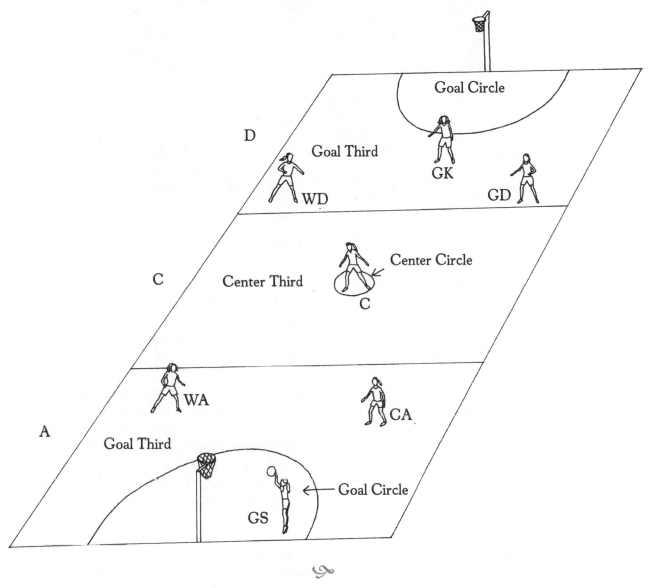

Korfball is another basketball-like game. *Korf* is the Dutch word for basket, and like netball, the korfball basket is suspended on a ten-foot pole, with no backboard. Popular in Belgium and The Netherlands, and with players in Asia, too, korfball is one of the few sports in which women and men play together; each team consists of four women and four men.

Palm Reading

ANALYZING THE SHAPE of people's hands and the lines on their palms is a several-thousand year old tradition. Once the province of Gypsies and mysterious magicians versed in astrology and perhaps even the so-called "black arts," *chiromancy* (from the Greek *cheir*, "hand" and *manteia*, "divination") is now more of a diverting amusement that can be performed for fun by anyone willing to suspend their disbelief and entertain, for a moment, the idea that a person's hand is an accurate indicator of personality.

A palm reader usually "reads" a person's dominant hand by looking at the hand's shape and the pattern of the lines on the palm. Often a palm reader will employ a technique called "cold reading"—using shrewd observation and a little psychology to draw conclusions about a person's life and character. Good cold readers take note of body language and demeanor and use their insight to ask questions or make smart guesses about what a person is hoping to know. In this way, the reader appears to have knowledge the person whose palm is being read doesn't have, and may even seem to have psychic powers.

THE IMPORTANCE OF THE HAND

As with so many things we know today, palmistry has its roots in Greek mythology. Each part of the palm and even the fingers were associated with a particular god or goddess, and the features of that area gave the palm reader clues about the personality, nature, and future of the person whose palm was being read. The pointer finger is associated with Jupiter; clues to a person's leadership, confidence, pride, and ambition are hidden here. The middle finger is associated with Saturn, originally a god of agriculture, and its appearance communicates information about responsibility, accountability, and self-worth. The ring finger is associated with the Greek god Apollo and its characteristics shed light on a person's abilities in the arts. The little finger is associated with Mercury, the messenger, and tells of a person's strengths and weaknesses in communication, negotiation, and intimacy.

Another method of reading the hand is to take note of its shape. In one tradition, hand shapes are classified by the elements: earth, air, water, and fire. Earth hands are said to have a broad and square appearance, with coarse skin, a reddish color, and a palm equal in length to the length of the fingers. Air hands have square palms with long fingers, sometimes with prominent knuckles and dry skin; the length of the palm is less than the length of the fingers. Water hands have an oval palm with long, conical fingers, and the length of the palm is equal to the length of the fingers but usually less than its width. Fire hands have square palms with short fingers and pink skin.

Other traditions classify the hands by appearance—a pointed hand, a square hand, a cone-shaped hand, a spade-shaped hand, a mixed hand—and assign personality traits to the various shapes. For instance, a person with a pointed hand appreciates art and beauty; a square hand indicates a grounded, practical, earthy person; a cone-shaped hand suggests an inventive, creative personality; a person with a spade-shaped hand is a do-it-yourself go-getter; and a mixed hand denotes a generalist who is able to combine creativity with a practical nature.

Heart line
Head line
Life line
Fate line

READING BETWEEN THE LINES

The four lines found on almost all hands are the heart line, the head line, the life line, and the fate line.

The heart line lies toward the top of the palm, under the fingers, starting at the outer edge of the palm and extending toward the thumb and fingers. This line is said to indicate both metaphoric and literal matters of the heart, revealing clues about romantic life as well as cardiac health. The deeper the line, the stronger your emotions.

The head line begins at the inner edge of the palm beneath the index finger and extends across toward the palm's outside edge. The head line is often joined or intertwined with the life line at its start, and the line itself is thought to indicate a person's intellect and creativity as well as attitude and general approach to life.

The life line starts at the edge of the palm above the thumb, where it is often joined with the head line, and extends in an arc towards the wrist. This line is said to reveal a person's vitality, health, and general well being. The life line is also said to reflect major life changes, including illness and injury—the one thing it doesn't indicate, contrary to popular belief, is the length of a person's life.

A fourth line found on most hands is the fate line, also called the line of destiny. It begins in the middle of the palm near the wrist and extends toward the middle finger. The deeper the line, the more a person's life is determined by fate. A line with breaks, changes of direction, or chains indicates a personality prone to change due to circumstance beyond a person's control.

The History of Writing, and Writing in Cursive Italics

THE FIRST writing instrument resembled the first hunting instrument: a sharpened stone. These stones were used to etch pictures on cave walls depicting visual records of daily life. Over time, drawings evolved into symbols that ultimately came to represent words and sentences, and the medium itself shifted from cave walls to clay tablets. Still, it wasn't until much later that the alphabet emerged to replace pictographs and symbols. Another milestone in the history of writing was the advent of paper in ancient China. The Greek scholar Cadmus, who was the founder of the city of Thebes and proponent of the Phoenician alphabet, was also the purported inventor of the original text message—letters, written by hand, on paper, sent from one person to another.

Some cultures lasted for many years before having a written language. In fact, Vietnamese wasn't written down until the 1600s. Two Portuguese Jesuit missionaries named Gaspar d'Amiral and Antonio Barboza Romanized the language by developing a writing and spelling system using the Roman alphabet and several signs to represent the tonal accents of Vietnamese speech. This system was further codified in the first comprehensive Vietnamese dictionary (containing over 8,000 words) by Frenchman Alexandre de Rhodes in 1651. This is why its written language uses Roman letters instead of characters like the surrounding Asian countries do.

At first, all letter-based writing systems used only uppercase letters. Once the writing instruments themselves became more refined, lowercase letters became possible. And as writing instruments improved, and the alphabet became more elaborate, handwriting became an issue. Today we have an incredible variety of things to write with—all manner of pens, pencils, markers, crayons—but the writing instrument most used in recent history was the quill pen, made from a bird feather. (Elsewhere we've included instructions for making your own quill pen.)

Before we can discuss the art of writing with a quill pen, we must talk about penmanship. Even in the age of computers a clear handwriting style is a useful and necessary skill, and drawing a row of tall and loopy As or Ps or quirky-looking Qs, twenty to a line, and making them all look font-perfect, can actually be a pleasurable act. Nowadays, when we are more likely to type than to write with a pen, cursive might seem old-fashioned. But at the time of its invention, the notion of standardized handwriting was a revolutionary idea.

The first use of cursive writing, or Italian "running hand," was by Aldus Manutius, a fifteenth-century printer from Venice, whose name lives on today in the serif typeface "Aldus." Cursive simply means "joined together" (the word has its roots in the Latin verb *currere,* to run), and one of the primary benefits of the "running hand" was that it enabled the writer to write quickly, and took up less space. But the uniform look of the script proved equally useful: in later centuries, before the typewriter was invented, all professional correspondence was written in cursive, and employees—men—were trained to write in "a fair hand," so that all correspondence appeared in the exact same script. (Women were taught to write in a domestic, looping script.)

With the introduction of computers and standardized fonts, handwriting cursive documents is no longer seen as professional business etiquette—although for invitations, certificates, and greeting cards, handwritten is still the sophisticated way to go.

Nowadays, there are several schools of thought about what nice cursive writing looks like, and writing in "a fair hand" is no longer entirely the province of men, as it originally was. Currently schoolchildren study a range of cursive, including D'Nealian, Getty-Dubay, Zaner-Bloser, Modern Cursive, Palmer, and Handwriting Without Tears. All of these styles are based on similar precepts about letter width and height, and all are designed to bring some uniformity and legibility to the handwritten word. (The Getty-Dubay team even has a series of seminars specially designed for the sloppiest of handwriters—doctors.)

Cursive Italic is a fancier way of writing

Cursive Italic

cursive that can dress up even the most mundane correspondence. Like regular cursive, the letters are connected, but Cursive Italic has a more decided slant, and the rounded lowercase letters have more of a triangular shape to them. The form also lends itself to decorative flourishes, which is why you often see Cursive Italic used for wedding invitations, menus at fancy restaurants, and the like.

Italic lettering is written at a slant of about 10° from the vertical, with your pen held at about a 45° angle from the baseline.

Aa Bb Cc Dd Ee

Ff Gg Hh Ii Jj

Kk Ll Mm Nn

Oo Pp Qq Rr Ss

Tt Uu Vv Ww Xx

Yy Zz

Victoria
Modern
Cursive

Adventure is worthwhile in itself.

In Victoria, Australia, a new style of handwriting was developed in the mid-1980s for primary schools. Now Victoria Modern Cursive is used across the country and is appreciated for its readability as well as its ease of elaboration—a few flourishes and the script is transformed from practical to fancy.

To practice, some writers like to write out their favorite poem as they work on perfecting their form. Here is a famous haiku from the eighteenth-century Japanese poet Issa that is a nice reminder of both the gradual evolution of human writing and the sometimes painstaking pace good penmanship requires.

Little snail
Inch by inch, climb
Mount Fuji!

Fourteen Games of Tag

A GAME OF TAG can be as basic or as complicated as you like: you can revel in the pure straightforwardness of one person chasing another, or liven things up by adding rules and strategy. Either way, tag requires no equipment, no court, no uniform—just someone willing to be It, and others willing to run as fast as it takes to avoid getting tagged and becoming It themselves. Here are fourteen ways of playing tag.

1. Blob Tag/Chinese Dragon Tag

In Blob Tag or Chinese Dragon Tag (also known as "chain tag," "amoeba tag," and "manhunt"), one person is It. But instead of being able to tag someone and no longer be It, the person who is It tags a player, and each player who is tagged then has to link arms with the tagger and join in as It. As more players are tagged, the link of taggers grows, making it look like a blob of people, or a Chinese dragon (hence the name). No tags count if the Blob separates. The game is over when the last player is finally tagged.

2. Freeze Tag

When a player is tagged in Freeze Tag, she must *freeze* in place immediately. Sometimes the game is played with the rule that other untagged players can *unfreeze* anyone who is frozen; the game can also be played so that the person who is It only wins when every single player is frozen.

3. Tornado Tag

Also called Hurricane Tag, Hurricane, and plain old Tornado, this variation of tag requires the person who is It to spin around like a tornado, with arms outstretched. If the person who is It tags someone without spinning, it doesn't count.

4. TV Tag

In this version of tag, your generally useless TV knowledge comes in handy by saving you from becoming It. When a player is about to be tagged by the person who is It, she can keep herself safe by touching the ground and shouting out the name of a TV show. If a player can't think of a show title before being tagged, or if she says a title someone else has already used, that player becomes It. (Another variation is to use movie titles or book titles.)

5. Shadow Tag

This game is perfect toward the end of a sunny day when shadows are long, since the main rule of Shadow Tag is that whoever is It can tag a player by stepping on her shadow.

6. Time Warp Tag

This kind of tag is played just like regular tag, except that at any point during the game play, any player (including whoever is It) can call out, "Time Warp!" whereupon all players must move in slow motion. When "Time Warp!" is called again, play returns to normal speed.

7. Line Tag

In Line Tag, which is played best on a playground or other surface with lines or painted areas on it, players are allowed to run or walk only on the lines. These can be hopscotch lines, basketball court lines, or even lines on the sidewalk—if it's a line, you can step on it. Otherwise, you're out. If a player is tagged, she must sit down, and the only player who can move past her is the one who is It.

8. Zombie Tag

The person who is It must chase after the players "zombie-style," staggering with her arms out in front of her and groaning like the undead. When the It zombie tags a player, that player also becomes a zombie. The game ends when all players have been transformed into moaning zombies.

9. Electric Tag

When a player is tagged (complete with electric-sounding "bzzt!" noises by person who is It), she must sit on the ground and become "electrified," which means that although she cannot stand up or move from her spot, she has the power of being It. The players who are not It and who have not been tagged must avoid being tagged by It and running too close to the electrified players, who are allowed to reach out and touch any player running past. Getting tagged by It or an electrified player means sitting down on the ground and becoming electrified yourself. The game continues until there is only one untagged, un-electrified player left.

10. Battle Tag

In this game, there are two players who are It: the Freezer, and the Heater. Everyone else is a Runner. The Freezer and Heater battle for control of the Runners—the Freezer wants everyone to be frozen, while the Heater wants everyone to be unfrozen. The Freezer freezes other players as in Freeze Tag, and the Heater unfreezes frozen players. The Heater cannot be frozen by the Freezer, and the Freezer cannot be melted by the Heater. The Freezer wins when all players are frozen before the Heater can get to them; the Heater wins when all players are unfrozen before the Freezer can re-freeze them; the game is over when everyone is too tired to run anymore.

11. Inverted Tag

For Inverted Tag, everything is backward. There is only one player who is Not It, everyone else is It, and the object of the game is for everyone to chase the player who is Not It and tag her. Whoever stays Not It the longest is the winner.

12. Infection Tag

In Infection Tag, the player who is It infects everyone she tags, making every tagged player become It too. The last player tagged by any of the Its becomes the first It for the next round of infection.

13. Hot Lava Monster Tag

This version of tag is similar to the game of "hot lava," where certain areas of the ground are deemed hot lava, making them untouchable. In Hot Lava Monster Tag, which is best played on a playground, the entire ground is hot lava, and the "hot lava monster" (the person who is It) is the only person who can stand on it. Everyone else must move around on the play structures, being careful not to touch the ground. Any player who touches the ground or gets tagged by the hot lava monster becomes the new hot lava monster.

14. Hide and Seek Tag

This is best played in woods with lots of places to hide. Everyone who is not It runs off while the Seeker closes her eyes and counts to 100 next to a designated tree. The Seeker calls "Ready or Not, Here I Come," and begins searching for everyone else. The goal for those hiding is to get back to touch the tree before being tagged. Those who are tagged before touching the tree are also It and join the Seeker. The last one to reach the tree or be tagged is the Seeker in the next game.

Spanish Terms of Endearment, Idioms, and Other Items of Note

TERMS OF ENDEARMENT

Mi chula
My pretty one

Querida
Darling

Hermanita
Little sister

Muñeca
Doll

FUN WORDS TO SAY

Chimichanga
(chim-ee-chahng-guh)
A crisp tortilla with a spicy meat filling.

Burro
(boo-row)
(be sure to roll the "R"!)
Donkey; stupid (*Como burro* means, "like a donkey").

Tonto
(tahn-toe)
Silly or foolish.

Chistosa
(chee-stoh-sa)
Funny; a facetious attitude.

Parangaricutirimicuaro
(pahr-rahn-gahr-ee-koo-tee-ree-MEE-kwahr-row)
The name of a town in the Southern part of Mexico; used as a nonsensical tongue-twister in much the same way as "supercalifragilisticexpiali-docious."

EXPRESSIONS

Este arroz ya se coció.
"That rice has been cooked."
(Similar to our expression, "That ship has sailed.")

De tal palo tal astilla.
"Of such a stick is the chip."
(Like our phrase, "A chip off the old block.")

No se puede tapar el sol con un dedo.
"You can't cover the sun with one finger."

Al mejor cocinero, se le queman los frijoles.
"Even the best cook burns his beans."

Porque naces en horno, ¡no quiere decir que eres una barra de pan!
"Just because you were born in an oven doesn't make you a loaf of bread!"

¡El mero, mero patatero!
"The real, real potato seller!"
(Like "The real McCoy," or "It's the real thing!")

Spanish Food

Gazpacho
A cold uncooked bread soup usually made with stale bread, garlic, olive oil, salt, vinegar, tomato, and bell pepper

Paella
A rice dish made with saffron and olive oil and usually garnished with vegetables, meat, or seafood.

Churros
Fried-dough pastry snacks, sometimes referred to as Spanish doughnuts, or Mexican doughnuts, that originated in Spain. The long fried stick, sometimes also dipped in sugar or cinnamon, gets its name from its similarity to the horns of the Churro breed of sheep reared in the Spanish grasslands.

Spanish and Latin-American Themed Books

Don Quixote by Miguel de Cervantes
One Hundred Years of Solitude by Gabriel García Márquez
Like Water for Chocolate by Laura Esquivel
Isabel: Jewel of Castilla, Spain, 1466 by Carolyn Meyer

Daring Spanish Girls

ARANTXA SANCHEZ-VICARIO

Born in Barcelona, Spain, in 1971, Arantxa Sanchez-Vicario started playing tennis at age four, following in her older brothers' footsteps. When she was 17, she won the French Open, defeating the number-one ranked player in the world, Steffi Graf, and becoming the youngest woman ever to win the singles title. (Her record was broken the next year, when 16-year-old Monica Seles won.) Arantxa gained the nickname "Barcelona Bumblebee" due her tenaciousness and her refusal to surrender points without a fight, even if it meant flying all over the court. She became the world number-one ranked singles player in 1995, competed in the Olympics three times, and over the course of her career won four Grand Slam singles titles and six Grand Slam doubles titles. She was also the first woman since Martina Navrátilová in 1987 to simultaneously hold the number one ranking in both singles and doubles. In 2007, Arantxa was inducted into the International Tennis Hall of Fame—only the third Spanish player (and the first Spanish woman) to achieve such an honor.

CRISTINA SÁNCHEZ DE PABLOS

The bullfighter Cristina Sánchez de Pablos was born in Madrid in 1972 and debuted as a bullfighter in Madrid exactly one week before her twenty-first birthday. She enjoyed tremendous international success as one of the first females in the sport ("matadoras"), performing to great acclaim at bullrings in Mexico and Ecuador as well as Spain. During her career, she earned a total of 316 cuts. She retired in 1999.

ELENA GOMEZ SERVERA

Elena Gomez Servera, born November 14, 1985, on the island of Mallorca, Spain, was the first Spanish gymnast ever to win a World Championship title, and the first gymnast ever to complete a quadruple turn in competition. She won the World Championship title in 2002, and in 2003 she won the World Cup competition in Paris on the floor exercise and the bronze medal at the Anaheim World Championships. At the 2004 Olympics in Athens, Elena reached the finals on two events and finished in eighth place in the All-Around, helping the Spanish team achieve fifth-place standing. In 2006, Elena retired from competition after suffering a back injury.

Pressing Flowers

PRESSING FLOWERS is a nice skill to have when you wish to preserve some of your favorite blossoms from your flower garden. Also, pressed flowers make nice gifts when attached to a homemade card or bookmark. We like this project because it mixes daintiness with power tools.

To make the press, you'll need:

- ❀ Two pieces of wood cut into 6″ squares.
  The wood should be ½″ to 1″ thick.
- ❀ Four bolts, 2½ to 3″ long.
- ❀ Four butterfly nuts, also called wing nuts, that fit the screws.
- ❀ Cardboard, cut to 6″ squares. These are reusable.
- ❀ Paper. While you have the scissors out, cut a supply of paper,
  same size as the cardboard. (You can also use special blotting paper.)
- ❀ Drill.

Lay one piece of wood on top of the other with the paper and cardboard in between. Drill a hole ¾ of an inch from each corner, making the hole large enough for the bolts. Drilling the wood, cardboard, and paper at the same time keeps the holes lined up together, and that's a handy tip for future projects.

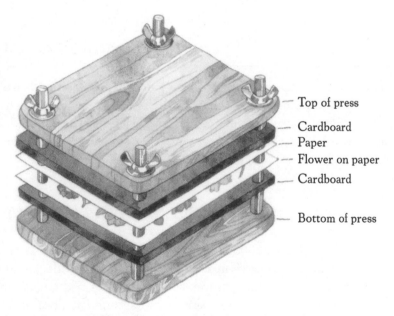

Top of press
Cardboard
Paper
Flower on paper
Cardboard

Bottom of press

To press flowers, layer in this order: bottom of the press, cardboard, paper, flower, paper, cardboard, paper, flower, and so forth. When you are done, place the top of the press over the stack. Then, tighten the bolts, and put the press away. In three to four weeks, the flowers will feel dry and rigid to the touch.

We would be remiss if we didn't mention several alternatives. One is the tried-and-true, stick-the-flower-under-a-heavy-pile-of-books method. Another, related, is the place-the-flower-in-a-random-book-on-your-shelf-and-find-it-a-year-later approach.

A more modern technique, for those who need their flowers dried fast (but not pressed), places the flower in the microwave, on a very low setting, for three minutes.

Four Square

TO PLAY, you need at least four people, and a bouncy, 8–12 inch rubber ball—a kick ball works well. Find a court on a local playground, or draw your own with sidewalk chalk, numbering each of the four squares one through four. The objective of the game is to work your way up from square number four to square number one by eliminating players in higher ranking squares.

Each player stands in a square (if there are more than four people who want to play, have the others line up behind square number one). The player in square number one serves the ball by bouncing it once and hitting it from underneath with both hands to another player in another square. The player in the receiving square keeps the ball in play by hitting it into yet another square. Play continues until a player becomes *out* through fouling the ball.

The out player leaves the game and the remaining players advance toward square number one. The new player enters the game at square number four. Players are not required to stay within their square (as long as they do not interfere with other players or step in another player's square) unless they are serving, in which case they must have at least one foot in their square.

Any of the following constitutes a foul:

♦ Hitting the ball with any part of the body except the hands.
♦ Hitting the ball with only one hand, with fingers pointing up, or with a fist.
♦ Hitting the ball more than once. before it goes to another square.
♦ Hitting a line.
♦ Not hitting a ball that bounces in your square.
♦ Holding/catching/stopping the ball.
♦ Serving without having at least one foot in your square.
♦ Stepping into another player's square.

A variation of the game is "King's Corner." In this case instead of numbered squares, the squares are "King," "Queen," "Prince," and "Princess," and the goal is to get to be King.

SPECIAL RULES

If the players agree beforehand, the game can be played with "server's rules," which means the player who serves can call special rules at the start of each round. Some of these include:

7-Up

Every player who hits the ball must shout out a number, starting with one, until the number seven is reached. The number 7, or any number ending in a 7, must be skipped, and if it isn't, the player who doesn't skip it is out.

Around the World

Anyone who has the ball may call "Around the World" at any time during the game. Once it's called, the ball must be hit from square to square in numerical order until it reaches the player who originally started it. After that, the game play returns to normal.

Backboards (also called Treetops)

Hit the ball upward into the air (instead of bouncing it once on the ground) before hitting it into another player's square.

Do Overs

A penalty-free chance to redo a play without a player becoming "out."

Friendsies

When "Friendsies" is called, players can stay in the game even if they commit a foul.

❧

Princesses Today

WHEN MOST OF US think of princesses, we conjure up fairy tales and Disney movies, lovely Cinderella or Belle in their pale blue taffeta and yellow silk ball gowns—or the ultra-pink princess merchandise pushed on girls today.

Perhaps it's a surprise to find beneath the glitter that these are real people who are princesses, and who lead very different lives than we see in the sugary movies—princesses who are comfortable wearing sensible wool suits and athletic clothes more often than fancy dresses and sparkly jewels.

Thirty-nine nations in the world still have monarchies—constitutional monarchies, which means the royal family is important, but that the real political power is in the elected parliament and the Prime Minister. Many of these monarchies include princesses, of all ages—some born into their royal family, like princesses Kako and Aiko of Japan, and some married in, like commoner Princess Mette-Marit of Norway.

However they became princesses, these real girls and women are as different from one another as any girls can be. Many do live with great wealth and privilege, true, but their lives can be quite conventional. They go to school, start businesses (like Princess Naa Asie Ocansey of Ghana, who has had a TV home-shopping show), and do charity work. Some are happy with their lives, and others struggle with their royal role, as did the late Diana, Princess of Wales, and the late Princess Leila of Iran.

Real princesses have various personalities, talents, and hobbies. Princess Maha Chakri Sirindhorn of Thailand writes poetry and short stories, plays Thai classical instruments, and also jogs, swims, bikes, and treks.

A closer look at just six modern-day princesses gives you an idea of the many ways to live a real life of royalty today—and not one of these princesses resembles Sleeping Beauty.

An Equestrian Princess

Her Royal Highness Haya bint Al Hussein—also known as Princess Haya—was born in 1974 and grew up in the royal family of Jordan. Her father is the late King Hussein, and her mother is Queen Alia Al Hussein. She attended St. Hilda's College in Oxford, England, studying politics, philosophy, and economics. She is an avid sportswoman who competes in equestrian sports (horse competitions being a popular royal pastime), including the 2000 Summer Olympics at Sydney.

In 2004, when she was thirty, Princess Haya married His Highness Sheik Muhammed, the Prime Minister and Ruler of Dubai, and moved to that vibrant city in the United Arab Emirates to be with him. In her role as princess, Haya leads many humanitarian efforts. She advocates for children's right to play and for health care, and served as the first woman ambassador to the United Nations hunger relief program.

A Champion Fighter Princess

Her Highness Sheikha Maitha bint Muhammed al-Maktum has not traveled the standard princess-and-horses route. Born in 1980 to Sheik Muhammed bin Rashid Al Maktum of Dubai and the United Arab Emirates, Maitha has fol-lowed her passion for the martial arts and is a karate champion.

Princess Maitha has won gold medals at Tae Kwon Do championships, competes in international karate championships, and was named the Arab world's best female athlete.

An Everygirl Princess

Mary Elizabeth Donaldson fits the image of the ordinary girl who becomes a royal princess. Born in Australia in 1972, she grew up on the island of Tasmania, where her father was a math professor. She played field hockey and swam, and after graduation from college, she worked for an ad agency and in public relations.

She met her future husband, Crown Prince Frederik of Denmark, at a pub in Sydney; he was in town for the 2000 Olympics. In 2004 they had a grand wedding—800 guests at the Copenhagen Cathedral—and Mary Elizabeth became the new princess of Denmark. They have since had two children: Prince Christian, born in 2005, and Princess Isabella, born in April 2007.

An Unassuming Princess

Most people know that Prince Charles is the eldest son of Queen Elizabeth, the reigning Queen of England, and know of Charles' famous late wife, Diana. However, not as many people talk of Charles' only sister, Anne—which is just how she wants it. Anne was born in 1950, and her full title is HRH The Princess Anne Elizabeth, Princess Royal, which denotes that she is the eldest daughter of the Queen.

Although she has not abdicated her royal status, she has led a very unassuming life outside the public eye. When she married, her first husband declined to take a royal title, even though it is considered common to do so. She chose not to pass on royal titles to her children, Peter and Zara, in order to protect them from the spotlight that hovers over children in the British royal family.

A Young Lady Princess
The youngest girl of the British royal line has also sidestepped the title Princess. Born in 2003 to Prince Edward (Charles' younger brother) and his wife Sophie, who are also known as the Earl and Countess of Wessex, little Louise was given the title Lady instead.

The princess title is still legally hers, and when she comes of age, she can fully adopt it if she wishes.

A Rediscovered Princess
And here's one final princess story, that of Sarah Culberson, born in 1976. Her mother and father met in college in West Virginia, fell in love, and had Sarah, but they put her up for adoption just two days after she was born. When she was twenty-two and living in San Francisco, Sarah hired an investigator to find her birth parents. She learned that her mother, a native West Virginian, had died of cancer many years before, but that her father was a royal member of the Mende Tribe in Bumpe, Sierra Leone. He was of the line of Paramount Chief, and as his long-lost daughter, Sarah was officially a princess.

Now that she has claimed her title, Sarah's life as a princess isn't about horses and galas. Sierra Leone had a devastatingly long civil war, and much of her family's village, including the school, is in shambles. Sarah has focused her efforts on raising money in the United States to send back to her tribe so they can rebuild their village and school.

Sarah Culberson

MORE LIVING PRINCESSES OF THE WORLD
From tiny babies to elderly women, representing both wealthy and struggling nations, belonging to vastly different cultures and families, the princesses in this chart show us that the fluffy pink princess stereotype is just that.

COUNTRY	NAME	BIRTH YEAR
BULGARIA	Princess Kalina *Is a vegetarian and an advocate of animal rights*	1972
DENMARK	Princess Isabella *Isabella's full name is styled Her Royal Highness the Princess Isabella Henrietta Ingrid Margrethe*	2007
ENGLAND	Lady Louise *Born prematurely at only 4 lbs., 9 oz.*	2003

Country	Name	Birth Year
ENGLAND	Princess Eugenie Victoria Helena Windsor *Had the first public christening of the royal family*	1990
ENGLAND	Princess Beatrice Elizabeth Mary Windsor *Undertakes many charity works, including visiting HIV-infected children in Russia*	1988
ENGLAND	Princess Alexandra *Refused royal titles for her children*	1936
JAPAN	Princess Aiko, also known as Princess Toshi *An avid sumo wrestling fan; began kindergarten in 2006; daughter of Princess Masako*	2001
JAPAN	Princess Kako Akishino *Rides a unicycle and is a sign language interpreter*	1994
JAPAN	Princess Mako Akishino *Did a home stay in Austria at age fourteen*	1991
JAPAN	Princess Kiko *Fluent in English and German*	1966
JAPAN	Princess Masako *Refused the prince's first marriage proposals*	1963
LESOTHO	Princess 'M'aSeeiso *The Republic of South Africa surrounds her country*	2004
LESOTHO	Princess Senate Mohato Seeiso *Lifespan in her country is decreasing from disease*	2001
LUXEMBOURG	Princess Alexandra *Related to every European monarch reigning in 2007*	1991
MONACO	Princess Stephanie *Attempted to be a pop star*	1965
MONACO	Princess Caroline *Fought in court for her privacy from news media; may become reigning sovereign of Monaco*	1957
MOROCCO	Princess Lalla Khadija *Her father pardoned prisoners in honor of her birth*	2007
MOROCCO	Princess Lalla Salma *Has a degree in computer science*	1978

Country	Name	Birth Year
MOROCCO	Princess Lalla Hasna *Is a passionate environmentalist*	1967
MOROCCO	Princess Lalla Asma *Is an advocate for protecting animals*	1965
MOROCCO	Princess Lalla Meryem *Went through a divorce in 1999*	1962
NEPAL	Princess Kritika *Her country borders Tibet, China, and India*	2003
NEPAL	Princess Purnika *Attends Roopy's International School in Kathmandu*	2000
NEPAL	Princess Himani Rajya Laxmi Devi Shah *Holds title "Grand Master of All Orders of the Kingdom of Nepal"*	1976
NORWAY	Princess Ingrid Alexandra *Second in line to her country's throne*	2004
NORWAY	Princess Mette-Marit *A rebel who met her prince at a rock concert*	1973
NORWAY	Princess Märtha Louise *Opened a school for clairvoyancy*	1971
NORWAY	Princess Astrid *Grew up with, and now helps other children with, dyslexia*	1932
NORWAY	Princess Ragnhild *Has lived in Brazil since the 1950s*	1930
SPAIN	Letizia, Princess of Asturias *Has faced a divorce and the death of her sister*	1972
SWEDEN	Princess Madeleine *Moved to New York City to work for UNICEF*	1982
SWEDEN	Crown Princess Victoria *Recovered from anorexia in the late 1990s*	1977
THAILAND	Princess Maha Chakri Sirindhorn *Has a doctorate and never married*	1955
TONGA	Princess Pilolevu *Her home country is a remote archipelago*	1952

How To Whistle With Two Fingers

MAKE A TRIANGLE with your pinkies by putting your pinkie fingertips together, palms and fingers facing towards you. Stick out your tongue and put your pinkie-tips right on the center of it, pushing your tongue strongly against your fingers where they meet. Push your tongue back into your mouth with your fingers, so that your pinkie fingers are inside your mouth up to the first knuckles. Angle your pinkie-tips slightly down, just behind your bottom teeth, and keep your tongue pressing into your fingers. Purse your lips and blow. You may have to adjust the angle of your fingers to get that sound right, but just practice and before you know it you'll be hailing cabs with your piercing two-finger whistle!

༝

Chinese Jump Rope

CHINESE JUMP ROPE—which is known in other countries by the names "American Jump Rope," "Japanese Jump Rope," "Norwegian Jump Rope," "German Jump Rope," and "Elastics"—isn't a jumping rope game in the traditional sense, with a rope that is turned for someone to jump through. Instead, the rope is static, an elastic band looped around two players' legs, while a third player jumps around it and on it in a series of moves.

To play, you'll need two people to control the rope and a third to jump. (If you're by yourself and have a pair of sturdy chairs handy, those can fill in in a pinch.) The rope-holders should stand several feet apart from one another with the rope stretched around their ankles to form a rectangular frame. The jumper begins by standing on the left side of the frame, and then jumping *in, out, over, on:*

CHINESE JUMP ROPE

25

- On *in*, the jumper jumps both feet inside the rope frame.

- On *out*, the jumper jumps up and lands straddling the rope, each foot to the outside.

- On *over*, the jumper jumps both feet to the left side outside the rope, then both feet to the right side outside the rope.

- On *on*, the jumper lands on the rope with her left foot on the left side and her right foot on the right side.

Once the jumper has successfully completed this sequence, the rope-holders raise the level of the rope to the knees. The *in, out, over, on* jumps are repeated, and if the jumper makes it through, the rope is raised to waist level. If the jumper is successful performing the sequence at that level, the rope is raised to armpit level.

Some variations:

Washies Drysies
Start standing to the left of the rope frame, which is at ankle level. With your right foot, lift the left side of the rope (the side closest to you) and, with that rope still against your right ankle, step across the other side of the rope. Then put your left foot inside the rope to make a diamond around your feet and jump left foot in front of right, feet side by side, right foot in front of left, then feet side by side. The rope is raised by the rope holders just as in *in, out, over, on.*

Diamonds
Begin as in Washies Drysies, standing outside to the left of the rope with your feet together, and lifting the elastic with your right foot, bringing it over, and stepping your left foot in to create a diamond shape. Jump up, freeing your feet from the diamond-shaped rope, and land in the middle of the ropes. Jump to right side (the side opposite from where you started) and repeat the steps on that side. Once you complete both sides, the rope can be raised.

Mississippi
This uses some of the *in, out, over, on* pattern, to the chant of M-I-S-S-I-S-S-I-P-P-I. "M" stands for jumping inside the ropes; "I" stands for jumping outside the ropes (either side); "S" stands for straddling one side of the rope (jumper alternates sides for every "S"); "P" stands for stepping on the ropes. For each letter the rope-holders chant, the jumper must perform the right jump. If she completes it successfully, the rope can be raised.

Double Dutch Jump Rope

DOUBLE DUTCH is a type of rope-skipping that uses two ropes. There are two rope-turners and usually one rope-jumper (though for added difficulty, there can be two jumpers). Each rope-turner holds the end of a rope in each hand. The ropes should be the same length, but they don't have to be the same color—in fact, having two different colored ropes can help a jumper keep track of which rope is going where. The left-hand rope is turned clockwise, and the right-hand rope is turned counter-clockwise, in an eggbeater motion. The jumper must clear both ropes as they hit the ground, jumping quickly so that it appears she is running in place.

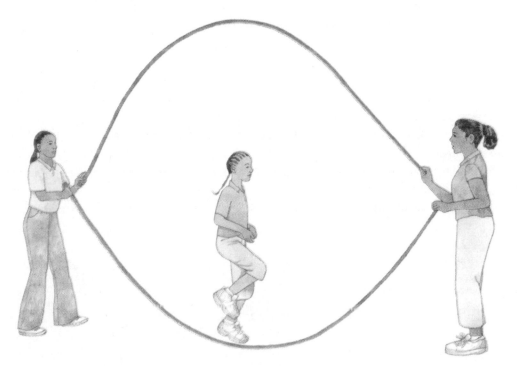

What does this rope game have to do with the Dutch? Jump rope lore has it that the game may have evolved from the twisting motions made by Dutch ropemakers as they wound ropes from hemp. With hemp around their waists and two strands attached to a wheel, ropemakers walked backward, twisting the length of hemp into rope. The runners supplying hemp to the spinners had to jump quickly over the ever-twisting ropes as the ropemakers plied their craft, turning the hemp strand over strand. It is easy to imagine how this work might have evolved into a leisure-time game for the ropemakers and their families. When Dutch settlers arrived in New Amsterdam (today's New York City), they brought the double-rope game with them, earning it the nickname "double Dutch." The game grew in popularity, especially in urban areas, but sometime after the 1950s it fell out of practice. Then, in 1973, a New York City detective and his partner revived the jump rope game by turning it into a competitive sport for city kids in fifth to eighth grades. Now double Dutch is not just a sidewalk game, but a competitive team sport played all over the world.

How To Tie a Sari
(And a Chiton)

WE DON'T KNOW when the first sari was made, but stories and artistic renderings of saris have been around for roughly 5,000 years. Saris are still worn today all over India and around the world, and the design, fabric, patterns, and wrapping styles vary depending on the region and status of the wearer.

The contemporary sari is actually a three-piece garment: the sari itself (unstitched fabric 42–49 inches in width and 5½ to 9 yards in length, usually with ornamental borders and an end piece called the *pallu,* which is the part draped over the shoulder); the petticoat, or underskirt; and the *choli,* a tight-fitting cropped shirt, also known as a sari blouse or sari jacket.

The underskirt is a fairly recent development in sari wear. It's not absolutely required, though it has practical applications: in addition to acting as a slip beneath sheer fabrics, the petticoat also provides the wearer with a waistband to tuck the cloth's edges and pleats into. Some modern sari-wearers use capri leggings instead. Most saris come with a matching piece of fabric for the *choli,* but a pre-made cropped top or tank top can be worn instead.

The most popular modern style of tying a sari is *nivi,* which is created most basically by wrapping the sari around the waist, tucking one end of it into the underskirt, and then draping the *pallu* diagonally across the chest and over the shoulder. Here are some step-by-step instructions for wrapping a sari in the *nivi* style.

Choose your 9-yard length of fabric for the sari, and put on the *choli* (a cropped top or tank top) and petticoat (full-length slip, or capri pants).

❶

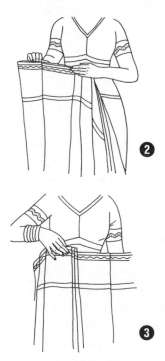

❷

❸

❹

❶ Tuck the inner top edge of the sari into the petticoat just to the left of where your belly-button is. Wrap the sari from left to right so that it goes completely around you one time, making sure that the bottom edge of the sari hangs evenly and touches the ground. Tuck that first wrap-around into the same left-of-belly-button place where you made the first tuck.

❷ Hold the tucked part of the fabric at your waist tightly and begin to make pleats. You'll be using about a yard of material for about seven to ten pleats of 4–5 inches in depth. **❸** The first pleat should lie the center of your body, and as you continue to fold, take care to keep the pleats even and straight.

❹ Hold the pleats together and make sure they line up evenly. Tuck the pleats into your waist to the left of your belly-button, making sure the folds are turned toward the left. You can use a safety pin to fasten the pleats for more security.

❺ Wrap the remaining material around your waist again from left to right. **❻** Pull the sari up diagonally with your right hand so that it fits just beneath your right armpit, then drape the material over your left shoulder so that it hangs down your back. You can pleat the material and secure it with a safety pin if you wish by pinning from inside the *choli* along the shoulder seam. Or you can wrap the *pallu* over your left shoulder, bringing it behind your back and over your right shoulder to rest in front.

Now you have a beautiful *nivi*-style sari. It might take some getting used to to walk around in. But if you can't be bothered to master the art of wearing a sari as a dress, did you know that a sari can be tied as pants?

❺ **❻**

Kachha Style

THIS SARI requires 6 yards of cloth. Starting from your left hip, wrap the sari toward the right so that it goes around your waist. Tie a knot just under your belly button using the sari edge (held with your right hand) and bunched-up fabric (from the wrapping side, held with your left hand). Once you make the knot snug, make a series of seven to ten pleats to the right of the knot. Wrap the *pallu* around yourself so that the end is centered on your back. Tuck it in all the way across your back to hold it in place. Pleat the rest of the fabric between the first pleats and the part of the sari tucked on your left hip. Tuck in the pleats at the waist, grab the bottom of your fabric and bring it back between your legs. Tuck that into your back, with or without securing it in a knot, and voila— sari pants!

The Chiton

THE SARI may remind you of another ancient style of dress involving what is essentially a large sheet—the toga. Togas were actually semicircular pieces of cotton or wool fabric measuring about 15 feet in diameter and worn wrapped around the body and draped over the shoulder. But togas were never worn by women—instead, women wore a similar but more flattering draped fabric called the *chiton* (KEE-ton).

The Doric *chiton* was a simple but elegant garment, the fabric of which depended on the season and the sensibility of the wearer. It could be worn as a dress or as an undergarment, and was constructed by drawing a rectangular-shaped cloth around the body, pinning it at the shoulders, and tying it about the waist. The most popular shade of fabric for the *chiton* was white, the better to display the elaborate embroidery or brightly colored woven patterns often used to decorate the borders. Yellow was also a favorite color, so common that the tunics were nicknamed "saffrons."

The *chiton* isn't complicated in terms of design—no sewing, no cutting—but it could be a little tricky to put on by yourself. So to assemble your own *chiton,* you'll need a length of fabric, a tie or sash to belt it, two safety pins, and a friend to help you dress.

The piece of cloth used for a Doric *chiton* should be about a foot longer than the wearer is tall and as wide as the span of her outstretched hands. A twin-sized flat sheet will most likely do, or a nice gauzy curtain.

Place the fabric on the floor and fold the top over about two-thirds of the way down. Lift up the cloth, holding it so that the folded side is facing you, and fold the fabric in half length-wise, keeping that first fold on the outside. Lay the fabric back on the floor so that the closed side of the fold is on the right, and the open side of the fabric is on the left. Use a safety pin to pin the back and front sides together along the top of the fabric about one-third of the way in. Use a second safety pin to fasten the front and back together about two-thirds of the way in. This creates two shoulder straps.

Here's where you might need a little help from your friend. Have her lift the cloth up and help you put your right hand all the way through the top, beneath the safety pins and out through the other side. Your right arm should be in the hole between the edge of the folded fabric and that first safety pin. Then put your head through the hole created between the two safety pins. The safety pins should now be resting on your shoulders. If you have a fair amount of cloth hanging open on your left side, you can wrap the back part against the left side of your body and put the front part on top of that. Then use your sash, rope, or belt to tie around your waist for the girded *chiton* look.

Hopscotch, Tetherball, Jump Rope

Hopscotch

BELIEVE IT OR NOT, hopscotch got its start not as a schoolyard game, but as a military exercise. During the early Roman Empire in ancient Britain, Roman soldiers ran through 100-foot long rectangular courses wearing full armor to help improve their footwork. Roman children drew up their own version of these courses, shortening the length and adding a scoring system, and the game of hopscotch was born.

The word *hopscotch* comes from *hop*, of course, meaning to jump, and *escocher*, an Old French word that means "to cut." The game as we know it dates back to at least 1801, and now hopscotch is played all over the world. In France, the game is called *Marelles*. Germans play *Templehupfen*, and kids in the Netherlands play *Hinkelbaan*. In Malaysia hopscotch is called *Ting-ting* or *Keteng-teng*, and in India it's called *Ekaria Dukaria*. In Vietnam it's known as *Pico*, in Chile it's *Luche*, and in Argentina and many Spanish-speaking countries, it's called *Rayuela*.

COURTS

Make your own court using chalk on a sidewalk or driveway, or by using masking tape on a floor or carpet indoors.

Traditional American hopscotch courts look something like this:

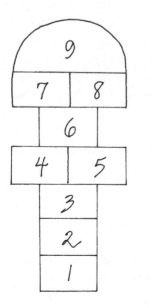 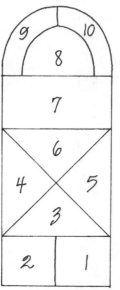 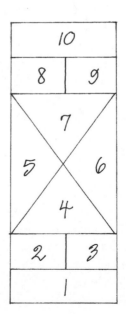 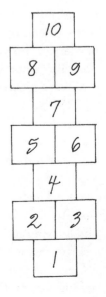

Super-old-fashioned courts had 6 boxes in a stack from 1 to 6, or 3 sets of 2 boxes:

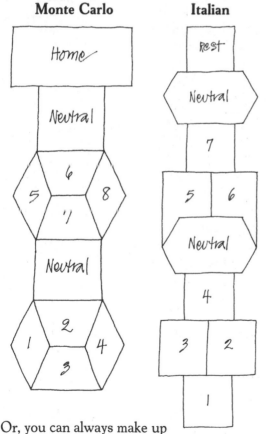

3	4
2	5
1	6

6
5
4
3
2
1

Fancier versions include the Monte Carlo and the Italian:

Monte Carlo

Home

Neutral

6

5   8

7

Neutral

2

1   4

3

Italian

Rest

Neutral

7

5   6

Neutral

4

3   2

1

Or, you can always make up your own style of hopscotch court!

RULES

Nearly every girl knows the basic rules for hopscotch, but there are some interesting variations to liven things up.

In the most basic game, the first player stands behind the starting line to toss a marker (a rock, a penny, a beanbag, a button) in the first square. The marker must land in the correct square without bouncing out or touching a line. The player should hop over the first square to the second on one foot, then continue hopping all the way to the end of the court. Side-by-side squares can be straddled, with each foot on a square, but single squares must be hopped on with just one foot. A square with a marker in it must be hopped over, and any neutral, or safe, squares may be jumped through in any manner a player wishes.

When a player gets to the end of the court, she turns around and hops back through to the beginning, stopping to pick up her marker on the way back. If she makes it to the end without jumping on a line or putting two feet down in a square, she can continue her turn by throwing the marker into square number 2 and trying again. If a player steps on a line, misses a square, falls, or puts two feet down, her turn is over. When it's her turn again, she starts where she left off. The winner is the first player to complete one course of hopping up and back for every numbered square.

VARIATIONS

A French version of hopscotch is played on a spiral court and called, because of its shape, *Escargot* (snail) or *La Marelle Ronde* (round hopscotch). The court is drawn as a big snail or shell-like spiral and then sectioned into squares, the number of which is limited only by the size of the spiral itself. In this version, each player hops on one foot to the center of the spiral and back out again. When a player

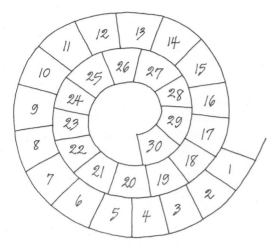

Escargot (snail) or La Marelle Ronde (round hopscotch)

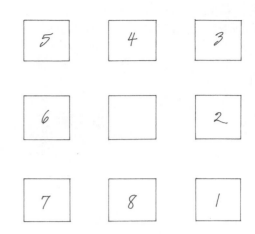

Toss-and-Reach Hopscotch

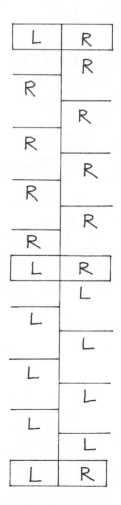

is able to complete the full circuit, she can mark one square with her initials, and from then on she is allowed to have two feet in that square. The other players must hop over it. The game is over when all squares are marked (or if no one can reach the center), and the girl who wins is the one who has her initials in the most squares.

This variation, allowing the player to initial a square, can also be adapted for the traditional version of the game. After a player has completed one hopscotch sequence successfully, jumping all the way up and all the way back, she can throw her marker onto the court, and wherever the marker lands she can place her initials. Then that square is hers, and she is allowed to have two feet in it when hopping, while the other players must hop over it. In this version, each player is only allowed to initial one square per game.

A British variation, which can be used with traditional straight courts as well as with spiral courts, involves the player holding her marker between her feet and hopping from square to square on two feet without letting go of the marker or stepping on the lines.

In Toss-and-Reach Hopscotch, a player throws her marker into the center square, then hops to each square in order. From each square, she must reach in to pick up her marker without losing her balance or stepping on any lines.

In Agility Hopscotch, the player must hop back and forth across the center line without touching any lines or losing her balance. She must hop on her left foot in squares marked L and on her right foot in squares marked R. She may rest with both feet down where the L and R are marked opposite each other.

Agility Hopscotch

Tetherball

TETHERBALL requires a fast mind and equally fast hands to send the ball spiraling around the pole for a win. This was our favorite game growing up and we'd love to see more tetherball courts—and maybe someday tetherball as an Olympic event.

At its most basic, tetherball involves a ball—similar to a volleyball but somewhat squishier—tied to the top of a 10-foot pole by a rope. Two players try to hit the ball in one direction so that the rope winds completely around the pole. (But tetherball is also fun to play by yourself—in your backyard when no one's around. You can practice and make up games for yourself, too. Like trying to duck before the ball hits you in the head.) Actual tetherball courts have a circle drawn on the ground around the pole and are divided in half. A drawn circle isn't necessary, but you should expect to need about 8-10 feet of space all around the pole, and each player should stay on her own side of the circle.

RULES

The rules of tetherball are deceptively simple: two people stand opposite each other, one person serves by hitting the ball in one direction around the pole, and the other tries to hit the ball in the opposite direction around the pole. The first player to get the rope wrapped completely around the pole is the winner.

Because the server has a big advantage (she gets to hit the ball first), players can decide to play matches instead of single games. The total number of games comprising the entire match is up to the players to decide, but the winner must win by at least two games. Another way to decrease the serving advantage is to have the player who doesn't serve choose which side of the circle she is on and which direction she is hitting.

FOULS AND VIOLATIONS

How seriously you take fouls is something that needs to be decided before the game. Fouls include:

- Stepping across the center line.
- Server hitting the ball twice at the beginning before the opponent hits it once.
- Hitting the ball twice while it is still on your side of the circle.
- Hitting the ball with any part of the body other than the hand or forearm.
- Reaching around the pole and hitting the ball.
- Catching or holding the ball.
- Throwing the ball.
- Touching the pole with any part of your body.
- Hitting the rope with any part of your body.

If you only have a few players, you can treat these fouls as mere violations and resume the game by stopping the ball and returning it to where it was wrapped when the violation occurred. The non-violating player gets to serve, and then either player can hit the ball. If a player racks up three violations, the opponent automatically wins.

If the two players commit a violation at the same time, they must do a pole drop to start the game again. Both players hold the ball with one hand, lifting it about three feet away from the pole, directly over the line dividing their two halves of the circle, and then let go of the ball at the same time. The ball should hit the pole, and then either player can hit it to continue the game.

No matter how you decide to play, the only absolute game-ender is grabbing the pole. If a player does that, she immediately loses the game.

EQUIPMENT

The Ball

A tetherball is the only piece of equipment that you must purchase specifically for the game and is similar to a volleyball, but softer. It will have either a loop sticking out of the surface or a recessed spot on the surface of the ball to attach the rope.

The Pole

The best pole for the job is a 10 to 12-foot long, 2-inch diameter steel pipe sunk 2 feet into the ground, with an eyebolt run through the pole about 4 inches from the top for attaching the rope. This may be a good time to take a field trip to your local hardware store. But with a good eye you might be able to spot a likely pole around town that will serve nicely for the game. Just remember to untie the ball and take it home with you when you are done.

MAKING A TETHERBALL COURT IN YOUR YARD

Here's your shopping list:
- 10 to 12' long, 2" diameter steel pipe
- 2' long, slightly wider than 2" diameter, steel pipe
- Eyebolt with nut (for attaching the rope to the top of the pole)
- Drill and bit capable of drilling through metal
- Concrete mix
- Tetherball
- Rope (if not included with the tetherball)

Making the court

Drill a hole through the pole about 4 inches from the top for the eyebolt, and put the eyebolt in place.

Dig a hole in your lawn, gravel driveway, or backyard about $2\frac{1}{2}$ feet deep, with a 2-foot diameter.

Pour in 6 inches of concrete and let it set.

Stand the 2-foot long pipe in the hole and add concrete around the pipe to fill the hole (it's a good idea to have something to keep the pipe in place while the surrounding concrete sets; also, the pipe should be level with the ground and should protrude just above ground level, but not so much that it sticks up enough to get nicked by a lawn mower).

Once the concrete is set, slide the pole into your concrete-and-pole base (this should be a solid, tight fit, but the long pole is removable).

Attach the rope and ball.

Jump Rope

IT'S SURPRISING to us now, since jump rope is often thought of as a girl's game, but skipping rope actually began as a boys-only activity, prohibited for females. Nowadays, though, jumping rope is for everyone. It's even a competitive sport.

Jumping rope has been a favorite game through the ages. Medieval European paintings depict children rolling hoops and jumping rope along cobblestone streets. In 1600 AD Egypt, children used vines for jump rope play. In England, jumping rope was particularly popular around Easter, when skipping took place in Cambridge and in several Sussex villages. Even today, every Good Friday in the East Sussex village of Alciston, children gather to jump rope.

TEN CLASSIC JUMP ROPE RHYMES

From the streets of Philadelphia to the schoolyards of Beverly Hills these rhymes have been passed down and around for generations. As with handclap games, you may know different versions of these. Here are some of our favorites.

1. Blue Bells, Cockle Shells
(swing rope from side to side)

Blue bells, cockle shells
Easy ivy over
(on "over," swing rope overhead and begin normal jump rope swing)

Here comes the teacher with a big fat stick
Now its time for arithmetic
One plus one is?
(jumper responds) *Two*
Two plus two is?
(jumper responds) *Four*
Four plus four is?
(jumper responds) *Eight*
Eight plus eight is?

(jumper responds) *Sixteen*
Now its time for spelling
Spell cat.
(jumper responds) *C-A-T*
Spell dog.
(jumper responds) *D-O-G*
Spell hot.
(jumper responds) *H-O-T*
(when the jumper finishes spelling hot, swing
the rope as fast as possible until the jumper
misses)

2. Cinderella

Cinderella, dressed in yella
Went upstairs to kiss a fella
Made a mistake
And kissed a snake
How many doctors
Did it take?
(start counting jumps until the jumper
misses)

3. Help

H - E - L - P

(The jumper jumps once for each letter as the
word *help* is spelled out, and the girls turn the
ropes turn faster and faster until she misses.
The letter they are on when she misses
determines what kind of jumping the jumper
must then do.)

H—Highwaters
(rope doesn't touch the ground)
E—Eyes closed
(jumping with eyes closed)
or
E—Easy over
(rope goes over slower than usual)

L—Leapfrog
(jump like a frog: crouch down,
then jump high)
P—Peppers (rope twirls quickly)
(The jumper then jumps in that style until she
misses.)

4. Ice Cream Soda

Ice cream soda,
cherry on the top,
Who's your boyfriend (or best friend)
I forgot
A, B, C, D, E, F, G, etc.
(When the jumper misses, the other players
name a boy or best friend whose name begins
with that letter.)

5. Miss Brown

I went down town, to see Miss Brown.
She gave me a nickel, to buy a pickle.
The pickle was sour so she gave me a flower.
The flower was black so she gave me a smack.
The smack was hard so she gave me a card.
And on the card it said:
Little Spanish dancer turn around.
(turn while jumping)
Little Spanish dancer, touch the ground.
(touch ground)
Little Spanish dancer tie your shoe.
(jump on one leg, pretend to tie shoe)
Little Spanish dancer, 64-skidoo.
(jump/exit rope area)

6. Not Last Night But The Night Before

Not last night but the night before,
24 robbers came knocking at my door,
As I ran out, (jumper jumps out of rope)
They ran in, (jumper jumps back in)
Knocked me on the head with a rolling pin.

I asked them what they wanted
And this is what they said:
Chinese dancers do the splits, (the jumper
does commands after each one)
Chinese dancers do high kicks,
Chinese dancers turn around,
Chinese dancers touch the ground,
Chinese dancers get out of town.
(the jumper runs out of the rope, end of turn)

7. School

School, school, the golden rule, spell your name
and go to school
(The jumper spells name and then runs out
without touching the rope. Each subsequent
turn, the jumper jumps through the grades.)

Kindergarten (jumper just runs through)
First Grade (jumper jumps once, saying "first
grade" then runs out)
Second Grade (jumper jumps twice, saying
"second grade" then runs out)
And so on, through 12th grade

(The jumper's turn ends when she misses or
once she's jumped all the way through the
12th grade.)

8. Down in the Valley

Down in the valley where the green grass
grows,
There sat (jumper's name) pretty as a rose.
Up came (a boy)
And kissed her on the cheek,
How many kisses did she get this week?

(jumper jumps and counts until she misses)

9. Policeman

Policeman, Policeman do your duty
Here comes (jumper's name), an American
beauty.
She can wiggle, she can wobble,
she can do the splits.
But I bet you five dollars that she can't do this.

(Jumper's name) jumps on one foot, one foot,
one foot, (jumper jumps on one foot)
(Jumper's name) jumps on two foot, two foot,
two foot (jumper jumps on two feet)
(Jumper's name) jumps on three foot, three
foot, three foot (jumper jumps on two feet
with one hand to the ground)
(Jumper's name) jumps on four foot, four foot,
four foot (jumper jumps on two feet with both
hands to the ground)
(Jumper's name), jump out!

10. Apples on a Stick

Apples on a stick
Make me sick,
Make my heart go
Two-forty-six.
Not because I'm dirty,
Not because I'm clean,
Not because I kissed a boy
Behind a magazine.
Close your eyes and count to ten.
If you mess up, then that's the end.
(jumper jumps and counts to 10)

Queens of the Ancient World I

Wise Artemisia

IT IS A MYSTERY what Queen Artemisia, who lived during the fifth century BC, looked like; no depictions of her survive. But the tales we know of her from the world's first historian, Herodotus, portray Artemisia as an intelligent and clever queen who bravely spoke her mind, even when no one else agreed with her. We also know she was a skillful and courageous sailor, who protected the Persian fleet during the ancient Greco-Persian Wars.

In the fifth century BC, Artemisia ruled Halicarnassus (today called Bodrum), a city nestled along a cove on the southeastern coast of Turkey's Aegean Sea. Artemisia's father and her husband had ruled the city before her. When her husband died, she became queen, as their son was too young to rule.

At this time, in 480 BC, the Persian Empire was at its zenith. Xerxes (pronounced *Zerksi*), the fourth of the great Persian kings, was in power. He had already conquered much of Asia and turned his sights toward the Greek city states and isles.

Xerxes narrowly won the battle of Thermopylae, capturing the pass to the Greek mainland, and then burned down its capital, Athens. He next headed south to take the island of Salamis, moving his battle to sea and relying heavily on the boats in his navy. He asked his allies around the Aegean Sea to send reinforcements. Loyal to Persia, Artemisia loaned five ships to Xerxes' war effort, large triremes, each with a grand sail, and powered by men from Halicarnassus rowing long oars out the sides. She herself took command.

Yet Artemisia was different from many ancient queens (and kings), whom we are told wanted only to battle. When Xerxes asked his general Mardonius to gather the commanders for counsel before storming Salamis, they all encouraged him to go ahead with the sea battle and assured him of victory. Except Artemisia. She warned Xerxes that the Greek ships were stronger than their own. She reminded him that he already held Greece's mainland with Athens and had lost many troops at Thermopylae. She contradicted all the other commanders in advising him to quit while he was ahead.

Xerxes admired Artemisia, but he decided, fatefully, to go with the opinion of the majority. The battle went wrong—terribly wrong—as Artemisia had predicted. Battle's end found the Persians watching from shore as their ships burned. Still, Artemisia kept her word to Xerxes and commanded her ship. She came under pursuit by an Athenian ship and faced a terrible decision either to be captured or to run into the Persian ships that were ahead of her.

Artemisia made the decision to save her crew, ramming one her allies' ships and sinking it in the effort to escape from the Greek ship. Some have said that she had a long-standing grudge against its commander, King Damasithymos of Calyndia. The commander of the Greek vessel chasing her turned away, assuming perhaps she was a sister Greek ship, or even a deserter from the Persian navy. The Persians lost the battle at Salamis, all the men on the Calyndian ship died, but Artemisia and her crew escaped unharmed.

After that battle, Herodotus tells us, King Xerxes again sought advice from his commanders. And again all the commanders wanted to stay and fight for the Grecian islands, except

MAVSOLÆVM.

Artemisia. Disagreeing with the group once more, the level-headed queen counseled Xerxes to consider another option: leave 300,000 soldiers behind to hold the mainland and return to Persia himself with the rest of his navy.

Artemisia reminded Xerxes for a second time that he had already torched Athens and taken the Greek city-states. It was enough. The king took Artemisia's wisdom more seriously this time, knowing she had been right before. This time, he listened to the wise woman over the majority, choosing to leave a contingent of troops in Greece and turn toward home instead of battling.

And after that? Herodotus makes a brief mention of Artemisia ushering Xerxes' sons from Greece to safety in the city of Ephesus, on the Turkish mainland. After that, we have no further information about Artemisia's life. Herodotus concerns himself with describing the next battle, and the next, and because Artemisia declines to fight, she disappears from his pages.

A small vase provides our last evidence of Artemisia: a white jar, made of calcite, that is now at the British Museum. Xerxes gave the jar to Artemisia, a gift for her loyalty and service, and he inscribed it with his royal signature. Artemesia must have bequeathed the jar to her son, and from there, it stayed a family treasure for generations. One hundred years later, another member of her royal line, also named Artemisia, built a burial monument to her husband—the Mausoleum of Halicarnassus, one of the Seven Wonders of the Ancient World. There, in the 1850s, the British archaeologist Charles Newton excavated Xerxes' gift to the first Artemisia and uncovered the final trace of the wise queen.

Knots and Stitches

A **GOOD KNOT** assures that your boat will be there when you return, your tire swing will hold, and your dog won't run into traffic. Here are a few useful knots with many everyday uses, and a few words on stitches, which come in handy for small repairs.

A piece of rope is all you need to begin. In each of our directions, "rope" means the stable or standing part of the rope. "End" refers to the part you are working with to make the knot, the working end. Make sure it's always long enough to do the job. "Bight" is another word worth knowing; it's the part of the rope that becomes the knot.

1. Stoppers

A stopper knot keeps a rope from slipping through a hole; it is the bulge at the end of a line. The most ordinary kind is called the overhand knot, or half knot. It's the knot you use to keep a thread in place when you start to sew.

Half knots are not very strong, but they are perfect for making the swing part of a rope swing. Tie four or five loose half knots near the bottom of the rope. Push them together, and tighten. They'll form a larger bulb that's perfect for sitting on as you swing. If you like, tie a half knot every few feet up the rope, for climbing or for holding on to while you do an arabesque (twisting the rope slightly around one ankle, and lifting your other leg gracefully behind you, like they do at the circus).

Safety note: For rope swings, you'll want to attach the swing to a tree branch using a stronger clove hitch or a tautline hitch. Make sure you tie the rope to a branch that extends far enough from the trunk so you can swing safely.

An alternative to the half knot is the Flemish knot, which you can also use any time you need a knot at the end of a line. It's both strong and lovely.

❶ Make a loop at the top. **❷** Cross the end in back and over to the left. **❸** Wrap the end over and into the eye of the initial loop. You should see a figure eight. **❹** Pull the end into the eye, or center, of that loop. **❺** Pull tight.

2. Loops

Once you've mastered the Flemish figure eight, you can make a loop the same way. Double up the rope or string. For hauling, tie the loop around your object, and lift or drag with the rope.

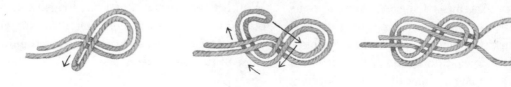

3. Bends

Bends link two ropes together. When you need to repair a string that's broken, add new length to a rope, or for any reason tie two ropes together, the square knot is what you want. Also called the Hercules knot, it was used by the Greeks and Romans as a healing charm. In *Natural History,* the Roman writer Pliny the Elder advised people to tie off their bandages with this knot, since it would heal the wound more quickly. Simple and reliable, this knot works best on twine or thinner rope, and with any ropes of equal size.

The classic formulation for a square knot is this: Left over right, right over left. Don't worry: In our experience, that's the kind of direction that makes more sense after you already know how to tie knots. So, try this: Loop A over loop B. Wrap the ropes of B over the sides of, and into, loop A. Pull.

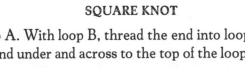

SQUARE KNOT

If you're attaching the ends of a single rope, perhaps to tie off a friendship bracelet, try this: Make loop A. With loop B, thread the end into loop A, from the back. Then weave it out the bottom side, and under and across to the top of the loop. Next, bring rope A over the top side and through the loop, so it's next to the other side of rope B.

If you need something stronger, or your ropes are different sizes, use this variation, the sheetbend knot. The green one is the thicker rope.

SHEETBEND KNOT

4. Hitches

Hitches tie an object or animal to a post, whether it's your dog at a friend's house, your horse to a tree in the shade, or your kayak to a pole on the dock while you go for a swim.

The tautline hitch is incredibly useful on camping and boating trips. Here's how to make it:

Start from the back and bring the end around the pole to the front **❶**, then over and behind the rope **❷** and into the center, or eye, and out the front **❸**. Pull the end over and behind and into the center once again **❹** and pull out the front **❺❻**. Take the end past the first two loops **❼**, and wind it over and behind and into the center **❽❾** and pull tight **❿**.

TAUTLINE HITCH

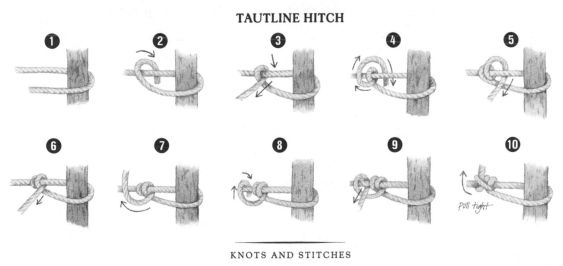

The around-the-pole hitch moves around a pole. This is perfect for a dog who doesn't want to end up tangled, twisted, and stuck with a two-inch leash.

Loop the end one turn around the pole, front to back, and bring the end under and in front of the rope. Change course and lead it toward the top.

Wrap the end again around the pole, this time back to front, and then lead the end under and through the loop.

Finally, the timber hitch helps you drag a heavy object, like a log across a field. This knot is simple and also easy to untie, an important consideration in knots. It tightens in the direction you pull in, so make sure to use that to your advantage.

AROUND-THE-POLE HITCH

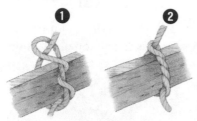

TIMBER HITCH

Wrap one turn, top to bottom, back to front. At the top, loop the end around the rope, to the left (this loop is important; the end must be wrapped around the rope it just came from). Tuck the end over, back, and around three or four times, and pull tight. The tucks must sit flat against the object for this knot to stay tight, since it is held in place by the rope's pressure against the object as you pull.

5. Stitches

There will no doubt come a time when you need to mend your gloves, replace a button that's fallen off, or sew the tear your pants suffered while climbing rocks.

Cut your thread, push it through the needle, double the thread so it's extra strong, and place a knot—a gorgeous Flemish stopper knot—at the end. You're ready. The stitches below can help you quickly mend any rip or tear that will inevitably occur in a daring life.

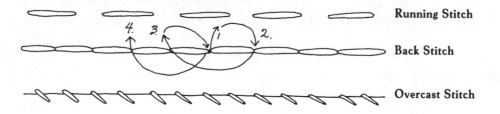

Running Stitch

Back Stitch

Overcast Stitch

Rules of the Game: Softball

SOFTBALL was invented on Thanksgiving Day in 1887, in Chicago. Tales report that the first softball game was played indoors one winter, and that it made good use of a boxing glove and a stick. Did George Hancock, an enthusiastic reporter for the Chicago Board of Trade, really draw some white lines on the floor of the gym and shout "Let's play ball!" thus inaugurating softball? We'll never know for sure, but he did become intrigued by the new batting game with the large ball, and loved playing indoors while the snow fell and the chilly Chicago winter wind blew through the fields. By the turn of the twentieth century, softball had moved outdoors, and into summertime.

Everyone plays softball, but it's still seen as a sport for girls. There's an interesting history to this. By the 1920s, women had begun to play baseball, especially at women's colleges. Several semi-professional "bloomer-girl" barnstorming teams traveled from city to city, and were incredibly popular. In 1943, the All-American Girls Professional Baseball League was established by Phil Wrigley, the man who owned the Chicago Cubs. So many American men were fighting in World War II, baseball players among them, that the rosters of men's baseball teams were empty. Like the Rosie the Riveter movement that sent many women to work in factories and gave them new experiences there, the All-American Girls Professional Baseball League opened up professional baseball to women, all in the name of the war effort, and provided entertainment to the people at home.

Some people never got used to the idea of women playing baseball. They fought against the presence of women in their sport, wanting to keep it the preserve of men and boys.

They were successful; the All-American Girls League shut down during the 1950s, and women were shuttled off to play softball instead.

Today, softball is one of only two sports that the National Collegiate Association of Athletics (NCAA) has for women only, the other being field hockey. For four years, from 1976 to 1980, women had a softball league all their own, the International Women's Professional Softball League, but it couldn't compete against the popularity of baseball. Women's softball was played at the Olympics in 1996 for the first time. The United States women's team won the gold medal, and repeated that victory in 2000. It's too bad that in 2012 softball will be dropped from the Olympic roster, along with baseball.

TO PLAY

The first rule of softball is never to apologize. This may seem an odd way to introduce a sport, but many, many girls, and women, too, find themselves saying "I'm sorry" if the ball they throw falls short, strays long, leaps out of bounds, or in any way doesn't land exactly the way they intended. Try to resist this impulse. Unless your throw inflicts actual bodily harm, never apologize for an errant throw or catch. Now you're ready to play.

Softball can be played as an organized sport, or as a pickup game with your friends. A baseball diamond is nice, but any grass field will do, as will your backyard (be careful of windows), or the street in front of your house—once the cars have been moved. In fact, curbs make terrific first and third bases. Set orange cones at the ends of your street to alert drivers that there is a game ahead.

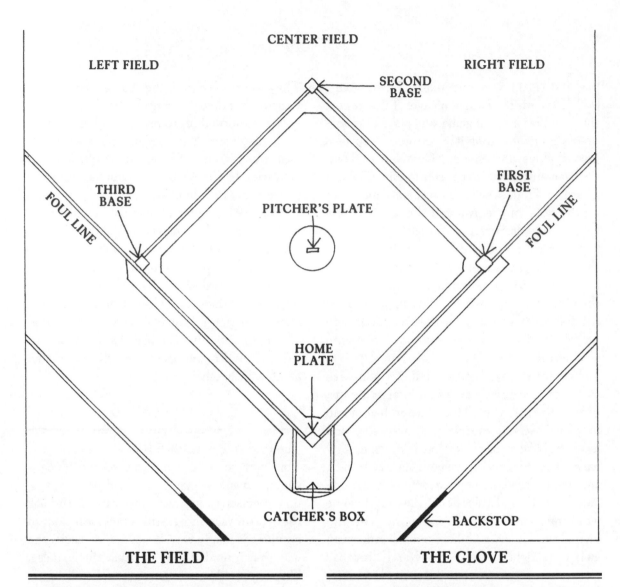

THE FIELD

The softball field is like a regular baseball field but with slightly shorter distances between home plate and the pitcher's mound and between the bases.

THE BALL

Softballs come in different sizes, but the average is nearly 2-3 inches bigger than the average baseball. You can also buy a softball that is soft enough to use without a glove, should you wish.

THE GLOVE

A leather glove molds to your hand, and is nice to have. Get a good glove, not one of those inflexible plastic gloves. A good glove is a treasure, something to toss in the sports bag for a game or practice now, and as life moves ahead, to stash in a picnic bag for any occasion where a softball game might, with luck, materialize.

A mitt is a glove with extra padding. A catcher will often prefer a catcher's mitt, since she will be catching balls at higher speeds and her hands might warrant some extra protection. Similarly, some first basewomen like to wear a mitt, as they, too, are especially prone to catch fast balls. If you become a serious softball player, with a preferred position, there are also especially large outfielder's gloves and a specific glove for pitchers. These aren't necessary for ordinary, pickup softball games.

THROWING THE BALL

Stand tall. Look forward. If you are right-handed, you will throw with the right hand and wear the glove on your left (and vice versa if you are left-handed). We will give directions for right-handers, even though lefties have a storied place in softball.

Start with the ball in your right hand, stretching your arm straight out behind you. Standing with your feet apart, one forward and one slightly back, point your forward foot—or, the foot on the side of your glove hand—in the direction the ball will go. Look where you want the ball to go, and point your glove hand at that same exact place. Your weight should be on your back leg, and as you throw, move your weight to the forward leg. Let your eyes and hand do their natural coordinating, and lob the ball overhand. Try to throw the ball right past your ear.

CATCHING THE BALL

To catch a ball thrown to you, watch it. Don't look away. The trick is to assess where it will be in the air by the time it gets to you. Think of your glove hand as an arm on a clock and follow these directions:

Pop-Ups and Fly Balls: If the ball is coming toward you from above, you want to have your glove at twelve o'clock, with the pocket facing up in the air. Watch the ball in the air, intuitively position yourself beneath where it's go-

ing to land, grab the ball, close the glove, and squeeze onto it for dear life, because it's easy to drop. The ball should be caught in the webbing of the glove, not in the palm, to ensure that it doesn't fall out.

Regular Ball: If a ball comes to you at chest level, catch with the glove in front of you, with your chest as the center of the clock. Watch it, keep your eye on the ball, glove facing out, catch the ball, and as before, squeeze that glove tight as the ball hits the webbing.

Grounders: To catch a grounder, you have to position your whole body in front the ball. Run toward it or shuffle sideways to get there. Keep your glove at six o'clock either on the ground or close to it, depending on whether the ball is simply rolling toward you or if it is bouncing as it rolls. Catch the ball in your glove and squeeze.

PITCHING THE BALL

Use an underhand toss. As in throwing, trust that your eyes, hand, and arm will work together to make it happen. Stand on the pitcher's mound, or on any old patch of grass. Visualize the strike zone: the area over the base and between the batter's shoulders and knees. The catcher's mitt serves as a good target; take a deep breath and aim there. A coach can help with different styles of pitches, but the first step is to practice the underhand motion and to figure out how to throw the ball into the strike zone.

HOLDING THE BAT AND HITTING THE BALL

Hold your hands around the bottom of the bat, throwing hand on top and catching hand right below it. Stand perpendicular to the pitcher. Here's the position: Stand with legs shoulder-width apart, knees bent, butt pushed out, bat ready—not resting on the shoulder but held over it. Swing like you are knocking all the place settings and food off the dining room table. Watch the ball, trust your instincts, and practice until you get it. It is essential to watch the ball all the way from release from the pitcher's hand to when it hits the bat. If you can master this skill, you are well on your way to being a softball superstar.

BALLS AND STRIKES

The strike zone is the imaginary rectangle extending out over home plate, from your chest to your knees. A ball is a pitch that misses the strike zone over home plate. After four balls, the batter gets a walk, a no-hits-needed free pass to first base. However, don't rely on walks to get on base. Two hundred tries and patience and you'll be able to bat that ball to the outfield easily.

A strike is a pitch that comes through the strike zone, but the batter doesn't hit the ball. Three strikes at bat, and you're out, except when you're playing with friends and you make other rules.

RUNNING THE BASES

Once on first base, your goal is to reach second, third—and home, without being tagged out. Run whenever the ball is hit, though if it's a fly ball and a player from the opposite team catches it before it touches the ground, run back to your base. You can steal bases, which means running even when the ball isn't hit, as long as the pitcher seems distracted enough not to throw the ball to the upcoming base and immediately render you out.

PLAYING THE GAME

One team is up at bat. Everyone on the team gets a number for the batting order. The second team is in the field. Their pitcher pitches the ball, and the rest of the team fields the bases and outfield, hoping to prevent the team at bat from scoring. After three outs, teams switch. Each team tries to get on base, run home, score more points than the other team, and win. One point per run. Softball games have seven to nine innings, or you can just play until everyone's tired.

After an agreed-upon number of innings or time, the team with more points than the other wins. Alternately, each team and player just tries to have fun, and no one keeps score. That's a good tradition too.

෴

KICKBALL

It would be unforgivable to end a discussion of softball without mentioning its red-ball cousin, kickball. Kickball uses the same diamond, same positions, and the same general rules, except you can also throw the ball at the person to get them out, and there are no gloves or bats. Just pitch the ball, kick the ball. Kickball aficionados say the best strategy to get on base is to kick the ball on the ground to avoid easily caught pop-ups.

Caring For Your Softball Glove

A NEW GLOVE is a beautiful thing, but the secret truth is that an already broken-in glove is a lot easier to play with as the leather has already been softened.

If you do have a new glove and need to break it in, don't worry; you can do it, it just takes a while. Start by putting it on your hand, and with the other hand, toss a softball at it, over and over. Use your glove daily. Play catch with a parent or friend. Play toss-and-catch against a solid brick wall or a pitchback. Walk up and down the street tossing a ball into your glove. Your goal in breaking in the glove is to soften the leather and create a pocket for the ball. Your glove is properly broken in when you close the mitt and the thumb and pinkie come together and touch.

Some people get kind of crazy about glove break-in: One time-honored suggestion involves putting the glove down on the street and running over it with a car. It's possible to bang at it with a rubber mallet (though make sure it's off your hand when you do). Some softball players store their glove with a ball in the pocket, held in place by a rubber band. Hardcore softball fanatics put the ball in the glove; wrap it very tightly with string, making sure the pinky side is tucked beneath the thumb side; and stow the whole package under the foot of their parents' mattress for a week or two.

When the days get colder and softball season is long gone, it's time to rub the smallest amount of conditioner into your glove. You can use official glove conditioning oil, or home remedies like Vaseline or foam shaving cream. Just a little bit, really—less is more when it comes to glove oil. Start at the bottom of the pocket and massage the oil toward the top. Find a cozy spot on the top shelf of your closet to store your glove until next softball season. Enjoy the winter.

Playing Cards: Hearts and Gin
A Short History

EARLY PLAYING CARDS are believed to have originated in China, where paper was first invented, as a form of paper dominoes. The earliest references to playing cards in Europe featuring decks with four suits date from 1377. Cards back then were very expensive, as they were hand-painted, and they looked quite different from the design of cards today.

The earliest cards from China had designs recognizable to players of Mah Jong: coins, or circles; and bamboo, or sticks. On their way from China to Europe, cards passed through the Islamic empire, where they gained cups, swords, and court cards. Once in Europe, the generic court cards evolved into depictions of actual kings, knights, and other royalty—hence the name "face cards." The Italian, Spanish, German, and Swiss cards did not include a queen—and in fact, even today, they still do not.

The basic familiar design of the cards—with hearts, diamonds, spades, and clubs, and court cards of Jacks, Queens, and Kings—came from France, and with the invention of woodcuts in the 14th century, mass-production became possible, making the French cards popular all across Europe. Cards became popular in America as well, and Americans began refining card design around 1800.

It was an American invention to create double-headed court cards, so that the kings, queens, and jacks never needed to be turned upright; to index the cards by placing the number and suit in the corner for easy reference; to varnish the surface of the cards for easier shuffling and durability; and to round the corners, which always seemed to get bent over anyway. It was in America, too, that the Joker was born, as a part of a card game called "Eucher," or sometimes "Juker." The Joker became an opportunity for satire—depicting popular political figures as jesters or clowns—and for advertising, which savvy marketers had already plastered on the back of the cards.

There are hundreds of games that can be played with cards. Here are two popular and fun games for four or two people: Hearts and Gin.

HEARTS

Hearts is a trick-taking game for four players in which the object of the game is to avoid winning tricks (a set of cards) containing Hearts or the Queen of Spades. Hearts began its life in Spain around 1750 in a game called Reverse, the point of which was to lose tricks, not gain them. Eventually, about 100 years later, Reverse fully morphed into the game we know today as Hearts.

"Tricks" are rounds of play in which each player puts a card face up on the table, and the player with the highest card wins all the cards—also called "trick-taking." But the real trick in this trick-taking game is that in Hearts, players want to avoid winning tricks, because the lowest score wins.

Hearts uses a standard 52-card deck. Aces are high, and there is no trump suit. To start, the dealer deals the cards clockwise so that all players have 13 cards each. Each player then chooses three cards to pass: on the first hand, the cards are passed to the left; on the next hand, the cards are passed right; on the third hand, cards are passed across; and on the fourth hand, no cards are passed. Cards are passed stacked face-down, and players must choose and pass their cards to the correct player before they can look at the cards passed to them.

The player who has the 2 of Clubs goes first and must "lead," or put down, that card. The play goes clockwise, with all the other players following suit (putting down a card of the same suit), if possible. That means each player must put down a Clubs card—if a player doesn't have any Clubs in this first hand, she can play any other card except for a Heart or the Queen of Spades. The player with the highest card takes the trick (stacking the cards face down next to her) and starts the next round. After the first trick, a Heart or the Queen of Spades can be used if a player doesn't have a card in the suit being led. Hearts can only be led (that is, be the first card in a trick) after a Heart has been "broken"—played on a trick where a player couldn't follow suit.

Play continues until all the cards have been played. Then you add up the points for each player. Each Heart card gets 1 penalty point, and the Queen of Spades gets 13 penalty points. The game is over when at least one person has 100 points or more, and the winner is the player with the lowest score.

But there is one last "trick" to be played in Hearts: a player can do something called "Shooting the Moon." That is when one player takes all the point cards (all Hearts and the Queen). The player who does this has her points reduced to zero, and everyone else automatically gets 26 points added to their score.

GIN RUMMY

This two-player card game is said to have been created by a man named Elwood T. Baker, who was inspired by an 18th-century game called Whiskey Poker. Gin rummy became popular in America in the 1930s, when Hollywood stars began playing the game in much the same way that celebrity poker is played today.

To play the game, you need a standard 52-card deck, and a pen and a pad of paper to keep score. You also need to know a bit of card talk to understand the game.

GIN VOCABULARY

Combination
Two cards of the same rank, such as 2-2; or consecutive in the same suit, such as 2-3 of Clubs.

Count
The point value in a hand after deducting the total melded cards.

Deadwood
Cards that are not a part of any meld.

Gin
Ten melded cards.

Knock
To end the round.

Layoff
Getting rid of deadwood by incorporating it into the other player's melds, so that it is not counted.

Meld
Either a sequence or a set.

Sequences
A group of three or more cards of the same suit in consecutive order, such as 3-4-5 of Spades, or 8-9-10-J of Hearts.

Sets
A group of three or four cards of the same rank, such as 3-3-3 or J-J-J-J.

TO PLAY

Decide who will be the dealer. The dealer then deals 10 cards to each of the two players and places the remaining cards in a stack between the players. Another card is placed face-up, next to the deck, to create a discard pile.

The goal of gin is to try to get your 10 cards grouped in melds—sequences of cards (three or more cards of the same suit in order) or sets of cards (three or four cards of the same value). Before you take a turn, check to see if you have any melds, or any groups of cards that could easily turn into melds.

Each turn involves taking a card and discarding a card. The player who goes first draws a card from the deck. Now she must discard, choosing a card from her hand that is least likely to become part of a meld. High-point cards, like face cards, are good to discard if you can, since getting rid of them decreases your deadwood (the cards that are not part of any meld). Aces are low in this game: face cards are worth 10 points each, Aces are 1 point, and the other cards are equal to their numerical values (a 2 card of any suit is worth 2 points, a 3 card is 3 points, etc.).

When a player discards, the card must be placed face-up on the discard pile. The other player then has a turn, and she can draw from either the deck or the discard pile. Continue taking turns until a player "knocks," or until only 2 cards remain in the deck (in which case the hand ends in a draw).

Knocking is when a player ends the round, and is signaled by a player literally making a knocking sound on the table. A player can only knock if she has 10 points of deadwood or less. If you have 0 points of deadwood, also known as "going gin," you must knock. Otherwise, you don't have to knock unless you want to—even if you have 10 points in deadwood or less, you can keep playing to try for gin or for a lower point count.

When you decide to knock, rap once on the table, lay down your cards face up, and add up your deadwood. The other player then lays down her hand and separates her deadwood from her melds. If she has any deadwood that can be incorporated into your melds, she can "layoff"—that is, give them to you for your meld so they cannot be counted as her deadwood. After that, add up her total remaining deadwood. Subtract your deadwood from the other player's deadwood, and the answer you get is your score for this hand.

If you have 0 points of deadwood, you must knock and call "gin." You get a 25-point bonus for gin, on top of the points for the other player's deadwood (which she cannot layoff in this case).

If you knock and it turns out the other player has less deadwood than you, you get no points—but the other player scores not only the total of your deadwood minus hers, but 25 bonus points as well. That is called "undercutting."

After the cards have been counted and points totaled, gather up the cards, shuffle, and deal the next hand.

Keep playing until one of the players reaches 100 points. Each player receives 25 points for each hand she won, and the player who reached 100 points first gets an extra 100-point bonus. The winner is the player with the most points after all the bonuses have been added.

∽

South Sea Islands

THE SOUTH SEA ISLANDS are rich with history, lore, and fantastical beauty, and are a tropical adventure paradise.

One famous visitor to these remote islands was Pippilotta Delicatessa Windowshade Mackrelmint Efraim's Daughter Longstocking, otherwise known as Pippi, the spunky fictional heroine of the Pippi Longstocking books. In one adventure, red-haired Pippi's pirate father, the swashbuckling Efraim Longstocking, capsizes his boat, The Hoptoad, on a South Sea Isle (the fictional Kurrekurredutt). The locals pronounce him their leader, calling him Fat White Chief. And when Pippi comes to visit with her friends from Sweden, they call her Princess Pippilotta.

Well, that was the 1940s. It has gone out of fashion to barge onto native islands like that, expecting to become the princess and chief, in fiction or in reality. Today, were you to land on a South Sea Island (whether because your own pirate ship takes water in the Pacific, or because the tunnel you were digging from your backyard to China went slightly askew), here are some contemporary and historical details you'll want to know.

FASCINATING FACTS

The South Sea Islands are part of the geographical area called Oceania. This includes more then 10,000 islands in the Pacific Ocean. Some are mere specks of rock in the ocean. Others, like Hawaii, Australia, and New Zealand, are large and well known. The islands are divided into four groups: Australasia, Micronesia, Melanesia, and Polynesia.

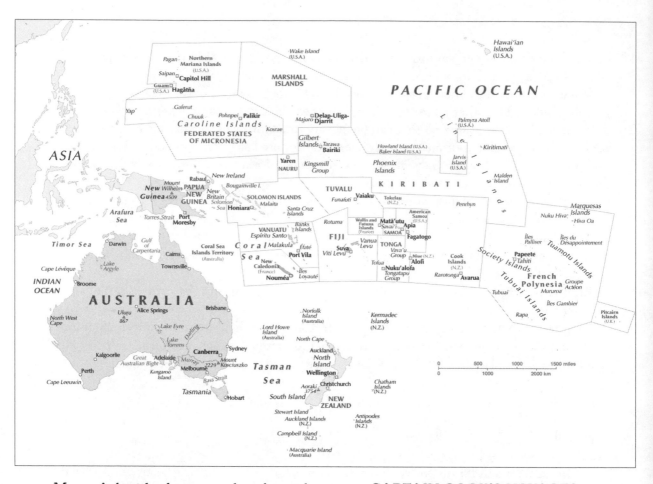

Many of the islands are coral reefs—with villages built on the delicate skeletons of live coral. Some formed from the once-hot lava of underwater volcanoes, which eventually rose to the water's surface.

Additional islands are atolls—that's a narrow circle of land surrounded by ocean, with a lagoon in the middle. Atolls are the result of coral that has grown on top of a volcanic island that over the years and, with changing water levels, has sunk back into the sea. Still others are archipelagos, long chains of islands scattered over an expanse of water.

A good number of the islands are actually territories of far-away nations like the United States, France, and the United Kingdom. A few, like Fiji, the Marshall Islands, Pelau, and Vanuatu, are independent.

CAPTAIN COOK'S VOYAGES TO THE SOUTH SEAS

The famous English explorer Captain James Cook made three voyages through the Pacific islands between 1768 and 1779. Cook was the first European to see Tahiti, to sail around New Zealand, and to set foot in Australia.

A Tahitian man named Omai guided Cook through the islands during his first voyage. Cook brought Omai back to England with him and, on his third and final voyage to the islands, he returned Omai to his home.

Cook left from Tahiti, heading north and then east to the Americas, where he mapped the west coast and tried, unsuccessfully, to find passage back to England through the Bering Strait. He died in Hawaii in 1779.

PAUL GAUGUIN AND THE SOUTH PACIFIC

Perhaps you have seen French artist Paul Gauguin's vivid paintings of village scenes, huts, and the spiritual life of South Sea Island people, in his trademark oranges and lush greens. Gauguin (1848-1903) embraced these islands. On his last legs as a failed businessman, he left his Danish wife Mette and their five children (forcing them to live with Mette's family to make ends meet) and boarded a ship for the South Pacific. There, he dreamt, he could escape the conventions of European life and the Impressionist school of art, which he found confining.

In Tahiti and the Marquesas Islands, where Gauguin lived the rest of his days, he painted his now renowned images of island life. Gauguin found himself at odds with the European governments established on the islands; it turns out he couldn't really escape Europe after all. The colonial government sentenced him to prison, but he died of illness at the young age of 54, before he could serve his time. Gauguin is buried on the Marquesas Islands, and his work earned fame and fortune only after his death.

WAR BATTLE ON THE SOLOMON ISLANDS

During World War II, the key battle of Guadalcanal took place in the Solomon Islands. The Japanese were using several of the Solomon Islands as bases, hoping to intercept ships between the United States, Australia, and New Zealand. The Allies (the United States and its partners) wanted these islands for their own bases, and to stop Japan's growing control in the South Pacific.

From August 1942 to February 1943, United States marines and allied forces fought Japanese troops in and near the Solomon Islands. The Allies' victory at Guadalcanal was a major turning point in the war against Japan.

Tahitian Women on the Beach by Paul Gauguin

EASTER ISLAND AND THE MOAI STATUES

Deep in the Pacific Ocean sits Rapa Nui, two thousand miles from its nearest neighbors, Tahiti and Chile. Rapa Nui, also known as Easter Island, is famed for its haunting—and huge—human-like stone carvings, the Moai, who stood guard around the whole circle of the island's coast for a thousand years.

The first European to discover Easter Island was the Dutch explorer Admiral Roggeveen, who landed with his caravan of three ships, the *Eagle,* the *Thienhoven,* and the *African Galley* on Easter Day in 1722 (hence the island's English name). They were neither the first nor the last explorers to reach this outpost, as the Polynesians had been there since 400 AD and other Europeans such as Captain Cook were on their way.

Cook visited Rapa Nui/Easter Island in 1774, on the second of his three voyages to the South Sea. He brought along the artist William Hodges, who was transfixed by the Moai statues and made oil paintings of them. A century later, several hundred villagers helped roll two of the Moai statues onto the British ship *HMS Topaze.* The statues were brought back to England and presented to Queen Victoria.

The queen made a place for them in the British Museum, where, in Room 24, you can see them today.

In 1888, Chile claimed Easter Island, and transformed it into a giant sheep ranch. The Chilean colonists crowded the native islanders into the small village of Hanga Roa and confined them with a stone wall, even taking some islanders as slaves. Life went from bad to worse. Some natives tried to escape the island in raft-like fishing boats, facing near-certain death on the high seas.

And the remaining statues? In the 1950s Norwegian archaeologists docked at Easter Island, fascinated by reports and pictures of the mysterious Moai. (Once again the history of the South Sea Islands intersects with far-off Scandinavia!) They found the Maoi in sad disrepair. Invaders had taken some, and the rest had been pushed to the ground when missionaries converted the island to Christianity in the 1890s.

Over time, the archaeologists restored nearly 250 of the Maoi statues—some weighing several tons and standing thirty feet tall—hoisting them back onto their ancient stone platforms, each one-half mile from the next, where they circle the mysterious, stark, now treeless island once again, and look out to sea.

EXOTIC NAMES FOR ADVENTUROUS PLACES

The South Sea Islands have amazing native names that paint mental pictures of this faraway world of ethereal beauty: Giao, Hatuti, Rapa Nui, Bora Bora, Makatea, and Tongal; Fanafutti, Olosega, Fatu Hiva, Mangareva, and many more.

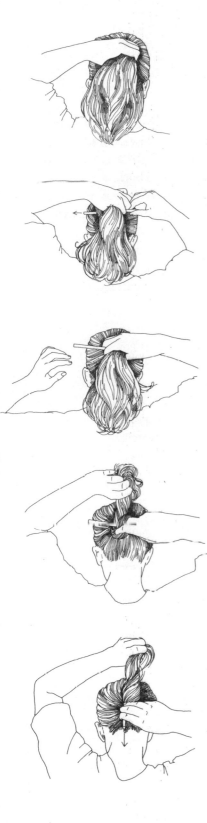

Putting Your Hair Up With a Pencil

PERFECT for when you're on the run, in the midst of a project, or otherwise adventuring and too busy to fuss with your hair. This skill is best practiced on hair that is at least shoulder-length long; otherwise, a quick ponytail with a rubber band is your best bet.

We're using a pencil, but you can really use anything that's handy and stick-shaped—a toothbrush, a fork, a chopstick. Just make sure to have the sharp side of the implement pointing up, and you'll be good to go. (We're also assuming a righty here, so if you're a lefty, reverse the rights and lefts in the directions.)

First, find a pencil.

Gather your hair into a tight, high ponytail with your hands—you don't need to use a rubber band.

Hold your hair with your left hand, and with the right, grab your pencil, sharp side pointing down.

Turn the pencil sideways, then slide it, end-side first, through your hair just next to your left hand that's creating the base of your pony tail.

Change your grip with your right hand so that you are grabbing both the pencil and your hair, and with your left hand, pull the ponytail down, loop it behind the pencil, and pull the end of the ponytail straight up.

Shift the pencil, turning it clockwise so that the sharp end is down and the eraser end is up. Push the end-side of the pencil down a bit so that just a small part of it sticks out.

Flip the pencil over by lifting the sharp side up and pushing the end side down. Keep pushing until the end part pokes through the underside of your hair.

Cartwheels and Back Walk-Overs

Doing a Cartwheel

PULLING OFF a cartwheel is easy enough. But looking good while doing one is the real trick. To really nail the master cartwheel you need to practice your form and presentation. First imagine a line on the floor in front of you—if you're outside, and a piece of chalk is handy, you can draw one; if you're inside with access to masking tape, you can tape one. This line is the track you'll follow as you cartwheel. Also, bendy, collapsing elbows are the bane of a good cartwheel, so try to imagine when you raise your arms overhead that they are straight, strong rods, with no pesky bending places.

Everyone who cartwheels has a favorite side, or favorite leg. For these instructions, we'll assume you're cartwheeling on the left, with your left leg in front, and with your arms up by your ears. (If you're cartwheeling on the right side, with your right leg in front, just switch the lefts and rights in the following directions.)

❶ Start out standing in a lunge—your front leg (the left) bent slightly at the knee, your other leg straight. Lunging will give you some leverage when you push off your front leg onto your hand.

❷ Reach out and down with your left arm, pushing off with your left leg and kicking up your right leg so that your weight transfers to your left hand. Your momentum should be propelling you into the cartwheel at this point, as your right hand is placed on the ground.

❸ Go with your momentum, passing through a momentary handstand, and land your

❶   ❷

right foot on the ground. **4** Then, as you stand up, put your left foot on the ground, finishing in a lunge with your arms up, just the way you started.

Try it a couple of times, and keep in mind the rhythm of the cartwheel as you touch your left hand, then right hand, then right foot, then left foot on the ground. If you can pace yourself with that "hand, hand, foot, foot; one, two, three, four" rhythm, you'll be well on your way to smooth, easy cartwheeling.

TAKING IT TO THE NEXT LEVEL

Once you've got this down, try doing a cartwheel one-handed—just don't put that second hand down! This will mean kicking your legs over a bit harder than with a two-handed cartwheel, but once you get the hang of it you'll be windmilling with the best of them.

TIPS
✔ Make sure you have enough room!

✔ Keep your stomach sucked in to help support your whole body.

✔ Aim for keeping your legs straight and your toes pointed.

✔ Starting in a lunge is a good way to practice, but once you're secure with it, you can also try cartwheeling from a run and hop approach. It is also easier to do multiple cartwheels in a row using the momentum of a full running approach.

3

4

Doing a Back Walk-Over

If you can go into a back-bend from a standing position, you can most likely do a back walk-over. Before trying a back walk-over, it's a good idea to practice back-bends, making sure your arms are strong enough not to collapse when you land your hands on the ground. Otherwise you'll land on your head, and while that may appear amusing to onlookers, it won't feel that way to you. If you haven't done a standing back-bend or a back walk-over by yourself before, don't try it alone—have an adult help you by holding your waist as you go over.

❶ Start standing up, with plenty of room behind you. If you're right-handed, put your right leg in front, toe pointed. If you're left-handed, lead with your left leg. Put your arms up and look straight ahead. Your arms should be straight and solid, like in cartwheel, and they should be right up against your ears. They should also stay right there through the entire move. You can look up at your hands, but try not to tip your head back.

❷ Begin bending backwards, keeping your leading leg pointed out in front of your other leg.

❸ When your hands touch the ground, push up through your supporting leg.

④ Kick over with your leading leg into a kind of split handstand.

⑤ After you pass through the split handstand, your leading leg should come down first, then your other leg. **⑥** Stand up straight, with your arms still up by your ears, finishing in the same position in which you started.

TAKING IT TO THE NEXT LEVEL

Once you can do a back walk-over with ease, mix it up by landing in a split instead of on your feet. Just slide that leading leg down and through your arms instead of placing it on the ground to finish the move.

④   ⑤   ⑥

TIPS

✔ Squeeze those arms next to your ears.

✔ Use a wall to help you practice. Lie down on the floor with your feet close to the wall and go into a bridge. Push down from your shoulders onto your hands so that the weight is off your feet, and walk your feet up the wall. From there, kick into a handstand. Once you've got the hang of that, kick all the way over to standing.

Weather

Signs, Clouds, Vocabulary, and Famous Poems About the Weather

⇒ WEATHER SIGNS ⇐

METEOROLOGISTS use Doppler radar, weather balloons, satellites, and computers to give fairly accurate predictions of what the weather will be like in the near future. But even before we had computerized weather forecasts, we had ways to interpret and predict the weather. Generations ago, people passed down their knowledge about weather signs through rhymes and sayings they taught to their children. As it turns out, those rhyming proverbs based on the observations and wisdom of sailors, farmers, and other outdoorspeople are grounded not only in experience but also in science. So if you're out camping, or hiking, or traveling on foot in nature, far away from technology, you can use some of that lore to determine a fairly reliable reading of the weather. Here are some of the most well known rhymes about weather signs.

"Red sky at night, sailor's delight. Red sky in morning, sailor's warning"
The various colors of the sky are created by rays of sunlight that are split into colors of the spectrum as they bounce off water vapor and dust particles in our atmosphere. When the atmosphere is filled with lots of dust and moisture, the sunlight coming through it makes the sky appear reddish. This high concentration of particles usually indicates high pressure and stable air coming in from the west, and since weather systems usually move from west to east, that means you'll have good weather for the night. When the sun rises in the eastern sky looking red, that indicates a high water and dust content in the atmosphere, which basically means that a storm system may be moving in your direction. So if you notice a red sky in the morning, pack your umbrella.

"Ring around the moon, rain or snow soon."
You may have noticed some nights it looks like there's a ring around the moon. That halo, which can also form around the sun, is a layer of cirrus clouds composed of ice crystals that reflect the moon's light like prisms. This layer of clouds are not rain or snow-producing clouds, but they sometimes show up as a warm front and low pressure area approaches, which can mean inclement weather. The brighter the ring, the greater the chance of rain or snow.

"Clear moon, frost soon."
When the moon sits in a clear, cloudless sky, lore has it that frost is on its way. The weather science behind the saying explains that in a clear atmosphere, with no clouds to keep the heat on earth from radiating into space, a low-temperature night without wind encourages the formation of frost. When clouds cover the sky, they act as a blanket, keeping in the sun's heat absorbed by the earth during the day.

"A year of snow, a year of plenty."

This one seems a bit counter-intuitive, but in fact a season of continuous snow is better for farmland and trees than a season of alternating warm and cold weather. When there's snow throughout the winter, that delays the blossoming of trees until the cold season is fully over. Otherwise, the alternate thawing and freezing that can come with less stable winter weather destroys fruit-bearing trees and winter grains.

"Rainbow in the morning gives you fair warning."

Rainbows always appear in the part of the sky opposite the sun. Most weather systems move from west to east, so a rainbow in the western sky, which would occur in the morning, signifies rain—it's giving you "fair warning" about the rainstorm that may follow. (A rainbow in the eastern sky, conversely, tells you that the rain has already passed.)

⊙ CLOUDS ⊙

THE TERMS for categorizing clouds were developed by Luke Howard, a London pharmacist and amateur meteorologist, in the early 1800s. Before this, clouds were merely described by how they appeared to the viewer: gray, puffy, fleece, towers and castles, white, dark. Shortly before Howard came up with his cloud names, a few other weather scientists started devising cloud terminology of their own. But it was ultimately Howard's names, based on Latin descriptive terms, that stuck.

Howard named three main types of clouds: cumulus, stratus, and cirrus. Clouds that carried precipitation he called "nimbus," the Latin word for rain.

Cumulus is Latin for "heap" or "pile," so it makes sense that cumulus clouds are recognizable by their puffy cotton-ball-like appearance. These types of clouds are formed when warm and moist air is pushed upward, and their size depends on the force of that upward movement and the amount of water in the air. Cumulus clouds that are full of rain are called cumulonimbus.

Stratus clouds are named for their layered, flat, stretched-out appearance, as "stratus" is the Latin word for layer. These clouds can look like a huge blanket across the sky.

Cirrus clouds are named for their wispy, feathery look. "Cirrus" means "curl of hair," and looking at cirrus clouds you can see why Luke Howard thought to describe them that way. These clouds form only at high altitudes and are so thin that sunlight can pass all the way through them.

Nimbus clouds, the rain clouds, can have any structure, or none at all. If you've seen the sky on a rainy day and it looks like one big giant grey cloud, you'll know what we mean.

☙ WEATHER VOCABULARY ☙

Air pressure
Here's a fun fact: air is actually a fluid. Like other fluids, it has internal pressure due to the force of Earth's gravity. Measured at sea level, the air weighs 14.7 pounds per square inch. Air pressure gets lower with increasing altitude.

Alberta Clipper
A fast-moving snow storm originating from the Canadian Rockies and moving quickly across the northern United States, bringing with it gusting winds and chilly Arctic air.

Barometer
An instrument measuring atmospheric pressure, which can predict weather changes.

Chinook
A type of warm, downslope wind in the Rocky Mountains, usually occurring after an intense cold spell, and capable of making the temperature rise by as much as 40°F in a matter of minutes.

Humidity
The amount of moisture in the air. You've probably heard the expression, "It's not the heat, it's the humidity"—meant to convey that the oppressive moisture in the air is what makes hot weather so uncomfortable. But even in the driest, hottest desert, there is always some water vapor in the air. There are two ways to measure humidity: Absolute humidity and relative humidity. Absolute humidity is the percentage of moisture actually present in the air, while relative humidity is absolute humidity divided by the amount of water that could be present in the air. Relative humidity is what people are complaining about when they say, "It's not the heat, it's the humidity"—because relative humidity indicates the amount of sweat that can evaporate from the skin.

Mean Temperature
The average of temperature readings taken over a specified amount of time.

Wind
Wind is the air in natural motion, a current of air moving along or parallel to the ground. We can feel the wind, and see the effects of wind, but we can't see the wind itself—except as it appears in meteorological pictures, as in the swirling spirals we see on weather maps when a hurricane is present. The way the wind blows depends on the atmosphere around it: in the presence of high and low pressure, the wind blows in a circular pattern, clockwise around a high pressure cell and counterclockwise around a low.

FAMOUS POEMS ABOUT WEATHER

Who has seen the wind?
by Christina Georgina Rossetti (1830-1894)

Who has seen the wind?
Neither I nor you:
But when the leaves hang trembling
The wind is passing thro'.

Who has seen the wind?
Neither you nor I:
But when the trees bow down their heads
The wind is passing by.

Fog
By Carl Sandburg (1878-1967)

The fog comes
on little cat feet.

It sits looking
over harbour and city
on silent haunches
and then moves on.

I Wandered Lonely As A Cloud
by William Wordsworth (1770-1850)

I wandered lonely as a cloud
That floats on high o'er vales and hills,
When all at once I saw a crowd,
A host, of golden daffodils;
Beside the lake, beneath the trees,
Fluttering and dancing in the breeze.

Continuous as the stars that shine
And twinkle on the milky way,
They stretched in never ending line
Along the margin of a bay:

Ten thousand saw I at a glance,
Tossing their heads in sprightly dance.

The waves beside them danced; but they
Out did the sparkling waves in glee:
A poet could not but be gay,
In such a jocund company:
I gazed and gazed but little thought
What wealth the show to me had brought:

For oft, when on my couch I lie
In vacant or in pensive mood,
They flash upon that inward eye
Which is the bliss of solitude;
And then my heart with pleasure fills,
And dances with the daffodils.

The Cloud
By Percy Bysshe Shelley (1792-1822)

I bring fresh showers for the thirsting flowers,
From the seas and the streams;
I bear light shade for the leaves when laid
In their noonday dreams.
From my wings are shaken the dews that
    waken
The sweet buds every one,
When rocked to rest on their mother's breast,
As she dances about the sun.
I wield the flail of the lashing hail,
And whiten the green plains under,
And then again I dissolve it in rain,
And laugh as I pass in thunder.

I sift the snow on the mountains below,
And their great pines groan aghast;
And all the night 'tis my pillow white,
While I sleep in the arms of the blast.

Sublime on the towers of my skiey bowers,
Lightning, my pilot, sits;
In a cavern under is fettered the thunder,
It struggles and howls at fits;

Over earth and ocean, with gentle motion,
This pilot is guiding me,
Lured by the love of the genii that move
In the depths of the purple sea;
Over the rills, and the crags, and the hills,
Over the lakes and the plains,
Wherever he dream, under mountain or stream,
The Spirit he loves remains;
And I all the while bask in Heaven's blue
    smile,
Whilst he is dissolving in rains.

The sanguine Sunrise, with his meteor eyes,
And his burning plumes outspread,
Leaps on the back of my sailing rack,
When the morning star shines dead;
As on the jag of a mountain crag,
Which an earthquake rocks and swings,
An eagle alit one moment may sit
In the light of its golden wings.
And when Sunset may breathe, from the lit
    sea beneath,
Its ardors of rest and of love,

And the crimson pall of eve may fall
From the depth of Heaven above,
With wings folded I rest, on mine aery nest,
As still as a brooding dove.
That orbed maiden with white fire laden,
Whom mortals call the Moon,
Glides glimmering o'er my fleece like floor,
By the midnight breezes strewn;

And wherever the beat of her unseen feet,
Which only the angels hear,
May have broken the woof of my tent's thin
    roof,

The stars peep behind her and peer;
And I laugh to see them whirl and flee,
Like a swarm of golden bees,
When I widen the rent in my wind built tent,
Till the calm rivers, lakes, and seas,
Like strips of the sky fallen through me on
    high,
Are each paved with the moon and these.

I bind the Sun's throne with a burning zone,
And the Moon's with a girdle of pearl;
The volcanoes are dim, and the stars reel and
    swim
When the whirlwinds my banner unfurl.
From cape to cape, with a bridge like shape,
Over a torrent sea,
Sunbeam proof, I hang like a roof,
The mountains its columns be.
The triumphal arch through which I march
With hurricane, fire, and snow,
When the Powers of the air are chained to
    my chair,
Is the million colored bow;
The sphere fire above its soft colors wove,
While the moist Earth was laughing below.

I am the daughter of Earth and Water,
And the nursling of the Sky;
I pass through the pores of the ocean and
    shores;
I change, but I cannot die.
For after the rain when with never a stain
The pavilion of Heaven is bare,
And the winds and sunbeams with their
    convex gleams
Build up the blue dome of air,
I silently laugh at my own cenotaph,
And out of the caverns of rain,
Like a child from the womb, like a ghost from
    the tomb,
I arise and unbuild it again.

Lemon-Powered Clock

A | **PAIR OF LEMONS** and a quick trip to the hardware store is all you need to convert natural chemical energy into electric power.

Alessandro Volta invented the battery in Italy, in 1800, combining zinc, copper, and an acid to create energy. A common lemon can provide acid (as do potatoes, which you can use if there's no lemon around), and you can rig one to run your own digital clock.

WHAT YOU NEED

1. A battery operated digital clock without a plug. It can use two AA batteries, or a round battery. Depending on the connections, you have to rig the wires in different ways, but that's where the fun starts.
2. Two fairly large galvanized nails. Nails are measured in length (in inches) and in diameter (with designations of 3d, 6d, 8d, 10d, and the like). We used a 16d, $3\frac{1}{2}$ inches—a solid nail. Galvanized nails are a must and we'll explain why below.
3. Copper wire. Uncoated wire is easier. If your wire comes with a coating, use a wire stripper to remove an inch or two of the covering.
4. Three electrician's clips.
5. Two lemons, or one very large lemon cut in half.

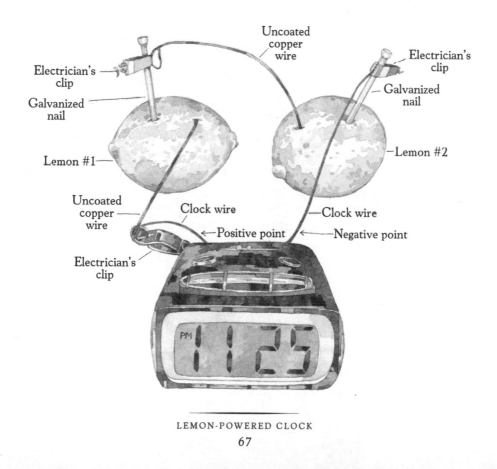

WHAT YOU DO

In five simple steps, here is how you run a digital clock on a lemon.

Step One: Place the lemons on a plate, or any flat surface that can serve as the base for the clock. Push one nail into each lemon and then, as far away from the nails as possible, also push in a strand of copper wire. Label your lemons one and two. What you're going to do now is create a closed circuit, so energy can flow from the lemon into the clock and back again.

Step Two: Open up the clock's battery compartment. Depending on your clock, there are two AA batteries, or a single battery that looks like a button. Remove the battery (you'll be replacing its energy, believe it or not, with the lemon-nail-and-copper concoction you've just created). Notice that the positive and negative points are marked as such.

Step Three: On lemon number one, use the electrician's clip to connect the copper wire to the positive point in the clock. This may be a challenge; in some cases it is easier said than done.

    If you can't connect your wire to the positive point in the battery compartment, you'll need to remove the clock's plastic backing and open up the clock. An adult should help with this, and remember, once you take the clock apart it may not go back together. Inside, you'll see that the positive and negative points are connected to wires on the inside of the clock. You can remove the wires from the back of the battery compartment, and then use them to make your connections. If you have a two-AA-battery clock, and inside you find two positive wires, make sure you connect your copper wire with both. Once you've figured this out, the rest is a breeze.

Step Four: On lemon number two, connect the nail to the clock's negative point. You may need to move the lemon into a new position so you can clip the nail to the clock.

Step Five: Link the copper wire from lemon number two to the nail sticking out of lemon number one. You'll see now that you've made an entire electrical circuit, from clock, to lemon, to the next lemon, and back to the clock. If all has gone well, the clock now works, because just under one volt of electricity is coursing the circuit.

If the clock does not work, make sure all connections are secure, and then double-check the directions. If several months from now the clock stops, replace the lemons, or the nails, and it should begin ticking once again.

WHY IT WORKS

1. The nail has been galvanized, which means it was coated with zinc to help resist rust. The lemon contains acid. This acid dissolves the zinc on the nail. In chemistry terms, this means that the zinc loses an electron and becomes a positive force. (If you haven't already read the

chapter about the Periodic Table of the Elements, now's a good time to do so.) The moisture in the lemon functions as an electrolyte, a fluid that conducts electrons—if you will, a swimming pool for electrons.

2. The electron shoots out of the zinc, through the lemon, to react with the copper on the wire. The copper gains an electron and becomes a negative force. The exchange of electrons is a chemical reaction. It creates chemical energy, or charge. All that charge needs is a circuit.

3. The electron exchange buzzes around the circuit you built—zinc/nail to copper wire to clock to copper wire to nail to lemon to copper to zinc/nail to lemon, and so on. That's the transfer from chemical energy to electricity, and it gets the clock going as well as any manufactured battery.

⚬⌇

❄ Snowballs ❄

SNOWBALLS MAY NOT BE ALLOWED in schoolyards, but this shouldn't stop you from holding a neighborhood snowball fight when school gets canceled because of a big storm. When a snowball fight breaks out, everyone must agree to some ground rules, such as no ice, and all snowballs must always be aimed well below the neck.

There are four basic kinds of snow.

Powder. Likely to be seen on very cold days. It has low moisture content and lots of air. Skiers love it, but not snowball fighters, because it's too dry to pack well.

Slush. No one likes slush; this mushy, melty waterlogged snow is horrid for snowballs.

Ice. Snow that has melted and refrozen. Leave it alone. You don't want to be hit by it, and you don't want to throw it. Ice hurts, and it wrecks the fun.

Snowball Snow. Made in weather that hovers around the freezing mark. You know it when you see it. The snow is airy yet firm, and when you roll some between your hands it sets into a ball that nearly leaps into the air.

To make a snowball, scoop enough snow to fill your hands. Push in, and rotate both hands around your snowball. Pack it. Smooth it. Add more to make it bigger. It's your choice to stockpile, or make them as you go.

After hours playing in the snow, head inside to warm up, but not before you've filled a pan with fresh snow. Bring it inside, where maple syrup—somewhat mysteriously—has been warmed on the stove by a thoughtful parent (to 230° Fahrenheit, if one uses a candy thermometer). Pour the maple syrup in ribbon patterns over the snow, and enjoy Snow Taffy.

Every Girl's Toolbox

WITH TOOLS you can make stuff, and that is a powerful feeling. You can help your grandfather finish that dollhouse he's been tinkering with for years. You can make a swing for the backyard, a bench for your clubhouse—or make the whole clubhouse.

Experiment with wood, nails, screws, hammers, screwdrivers, and drills. After a while, you'll start to think in tools and materials, and you'll see how screws and nails hold wood together. Then you'll begin to come up with your own projects. Trial and error are the best teachers, and it doesn't take long to feel comfortable.

VISITING THE HARDWARE STORE

Before we turn to the basic tools, a word on hardware stores. You might be intimidated by them, as many people are. Especially those antiquated-looking, small hardware stores, with their dusty shelves filled to the brim with unfamiliar, scary-looking objects, usually guarded by men who are burly and possibly gruff.

Fear not, we are here to tell you. Said hardware stores mark the entrance to a world in which you can create and repair anything imaginable. And the hardware store's burly guardians? The truth is, they may look gruff, but usually they're very nice, and they love to problem-solve and to find the perfect nail or wire for you. Ask for help when you're matching bolts and nuts. Get their advice on what kind of drill bit will attach a wood plaque to the stone wall outside your house. They'll show you where to find hardware store exotica, and they know fix-it secrets you'll never learn in books.

Besides, many of them have daughters, too, and you can bet they've taught their girls a thing or two about what to do with a hammer and a box of nails.

CREATING YOUR TOOLBOX

Every girl needs her own toolbox. You can get a decent toolbox, with a latch and an organizing tray, for as little as ten dollars. Here are the basics to fill it with.

1. Safety Glasses
These are an absolute must when hammering, drilling, or sawing.

2. Claw Hammer
The flat side of the hammer bangs nails into wood; the V-shaped claw side pulls them out.

To hammer, grip the handle solidly, near the bottom. Hold a nail with your thumb and forefinger, and tap it in to the wood, gently, until it stands on its own. Then move your fingers away and hammer harder, from your forearm (that is, don't use your entire arm), and keep your wrist straight. Keep your eye on the nail, and trust your eye-hand coordination.

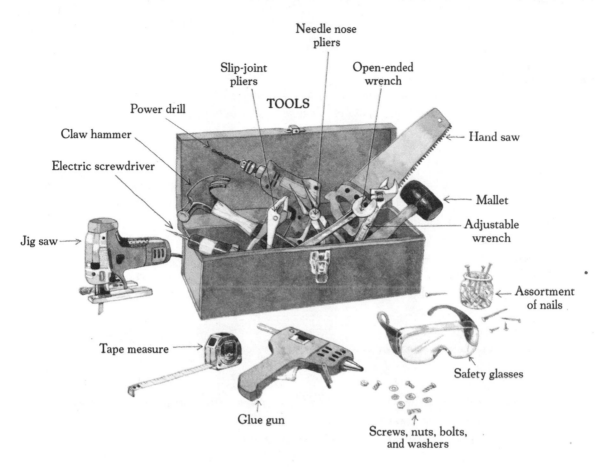

Needle nose pliers · Slip-joint pliers · TOOLS · Open-ended wrench · Power drill · Hand saw · Claw hammer · Electric screwdriver · Mallet · Adjustable wrench · Jig saw · Assortment of nails · Tape measure · Safety glasses · Glue gun · Screws, nuts, bolts, and washers

3. Nails

The measurements for nails derive from the British custom of selling 100 nails for a certain number of pennies. Nails are thus described in pennyweights, except the resulting abbreviation is not p, but, oddly enough, d, in reference to an ancient Roman coin, the denarius.

Once upon a time you could walk into a store in Yorkshire and purchase one hundred 1½-inch nails for 4 pence, and because of that, they are now labeled 4d nails. Much of the world, it must be said, uses the metric system for a more systematic and reasonable way to measure nails.

4. Screwdriver

The screwdriver not only gets screws where they're going and takes them out, it can be used in a bazillion creative ways to do almost anything. Try a 6-in-1 screwdriver (which has six changeable heads). To get jobs done faster, we recommend a battery-operated screwdriver.

5. Screws

Screws and bolts live in those mysteriously thin cabinets in the back aisle of the hardware store, along with their friends, bolts, nuts, and washers. Tighten a nut on a bolt to keep things ultra-secure. A washer—that's a flat circular object that slips on the bolt between the nut and the surface—protects the surface and helps tighten the nut.

Remembering the saying "righty-tighty, lefty-loosy" will help you recall which direction to turn a screw.

6. Wrench

Wrenches tighten and untighten the nuts that go at the end of bolts. They come in the open-end (fixed size) variety, and the adjustable. A small set of open-end wrenches, or one adjustable wrench, should start you off well.

7. Pliers

For gripping objects, like a stuck faucet, get a versatile groove-joint pliers. Also handy is a needle-nose pliers to grab small objects, like wire. It often has a little wire cutter built in (peek at the intersection of the handles and you'll find it).

8. Glue Gun

When you can't use screws, bolts, or nails, a glue gun saves the day, and is quite fun to operate. A small one should do, and don't forget plenty of glue sticks to melt in it.

9. Tape Measure

A 16-foot retractable tape measure that can lock in place is a good start.

10. Saw

A saw is not for the very young, of course, but it's a necessity for cutting wood to size and making shapes. A handsaw is a flat hand tool. A modern jigsaw is a power tool, activated by a trigger. All power tools are extremely dangerous if they are not used exactly as specified in their instructions, and you should always have adult supervision when operating them.

Hold long strips of wood on a sawhorse (a beam connected by four legs); cut small pieces of wood off the edge of a work table. Be careful, ask for help, and, as always, use your safety glasses.

11. Drill

To drill, start with an awl or center punch (hand tools that look like small spikes) to make an indentation in your surface so the drill bit won't slip. Bits are the small cutting pieces you fit into your drill for each project.

A battery-operated power drill is very handy. It will come with a basic set of bits, or you can get a set if it doesn't. There's an art to matching up the right drill bit to the size of the hole you'll need for the screw. If you know the size of the bolt or screw, that helps. Otherwise, the best we can tell you is to peer closely at the sizes and when in doubt try the smaller bit first. Experience will make it all the more clear.

* * *

Once you have your own toolbox, you might begin to truly love the hardware store. You'll stand for hours looking at the display of unique drill bits to make holes in metal, brick, plastic, or stone; at the sander attachment that can remove paint or brush wood's rough edges clean; at the buffer that smoothes it to perfection. You'll handle each one carefully, and after much deliberation with the burly hardware store guy about the pros and cons of each, take some home to try out on a project of your own imagination.

Going to Africa

TRAVELING TO DISTANT COUNTRIES and experiencing different cultures is extremely daring. It can sometimes be disorienting at first, as you adjust to the language barriers and foreign foods and customs, but the rewards often more than make up for the challenges. A well-planned trip to Africa offers incredible history, mind-blowing sights, and once-in-a-lifetime adventures. Before you go, make sure to read up on the facts, like the ones below.

ALGERIA
Declared independence in 1962 from France
Languages: Arabic, French, Berber dialects
Adventures: The 400,000 palm trees of the Sahara oasis town of Timimoun, and El-Oued, the Town of a Thousand Domes

ANGOLA
Declared independence in 1975 from Portugal
Languages: Portuguese, Bantu, and other African languages
Adventures: The Calendula waterfalls

BENIN
Declared independence in 1960 from France
Languages: French, Fon, Yoruba, and six other tribal languages
Adventures: Elephants and baboons at the Pendjari wildlife park

BOTSWANA
Declared independence in 1966 from the United Kingdom
Languages: English, Setswana, Kalanga, Sekgalagad
Adventures: Chobe game park

BURKINA FASO
Declared independence in 1960 from France
Languages: French, African languages
Adventures: Wild elephants at Nazinga Reserve

BURUNDI
Declared independence in 1962 from Belgium
Languages: French, Kirundi, Swahili
Adventures: Drumming in Gitega, Bujumbara, a port on Lake Tanganyika

CAMEROON
Declared independence in 1960, from French administration of a United Nations trusteeship
Languages: English, French, 24 African languages
Adventures: The Royal Palace at Foumban

CAPE VERDE
Declared independence in 1975 from Portugal
Languages: Portuguese, Crioulo
Adventures: The fishing village of Tarrafal

CENTRAL AFRICAN REPUBLIC
Declared independence in 1960 from France
Languages: French, Sangho, African languages
Adventures: The rainforest surrounding M'Baïki

CHAD
Declared independence in 1960 from France
Languages: French, Arabic, Sara, over 120 languages and dialects
Adventures: Prehistoric cave paintings in the Ennedi desert

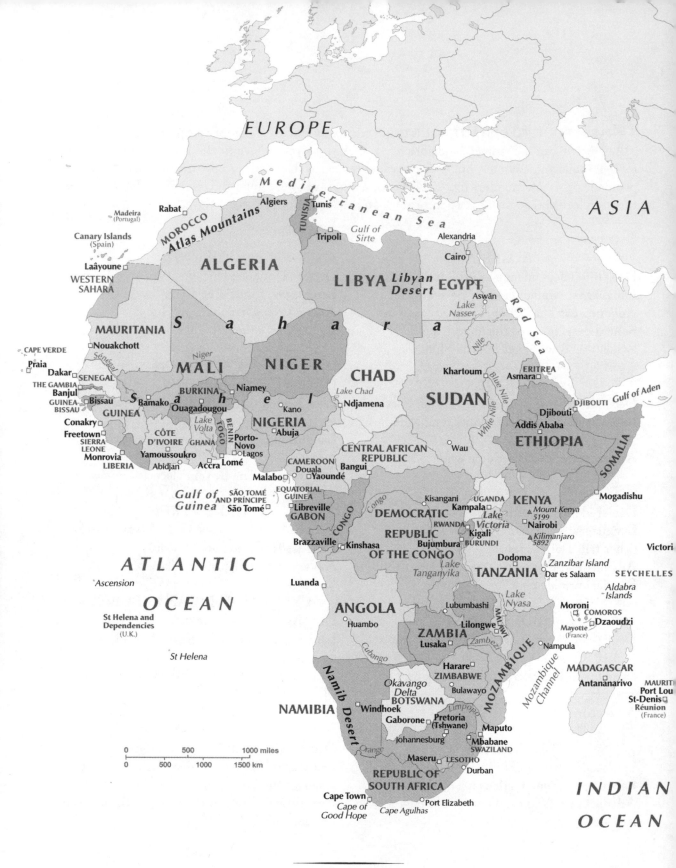

COMOROS
Declared independence in 1975 from France
Languages: French, Arabic, Shikomoro
Adventures: The active volcano at Mount Karthala

REPUBLIC OF CONGO
Declared independence in 1960 from France
Languages: French, Lingala, Monokuluba, and Kikongo
Adventures: Hundreds of gorillas, elephants, and monkeys at Odzala National Park

DEMOCRATIC REPUBLIC OF CONGO
Declared independence in 1960 from Belgium
Languages: French, Lingala, Kinguana, Kikongo, Tshiluba
Adventures: Pygmy chimp orphanage at the Chutes de Lukia

CÔTE D'IVOIRE (IVORY COAST)
Declared independence in 1960 from France
Languages: French; 60 native dialects, of which Dioula is most widely spoken
Adventures: Stained glass windows at the Cathédrale Notre-Dame-de-la-Paix

DJIBOUTI
Declared independence in 1977 from France
Languages: French, Arabic, Somali, Afar
Adventures: Tadjoura, Djibouti's oldest town

EGYPT
Declared independence in 1922 from the United Kingdom
Languages: Arabic, English, and French
Adventures: Ancient Egyptian pyramids

EQUATORIAL GUINEA
Declared independence in 1958 from Spain
Languages: Spanish, French, pidgin English, Fang, Bubi, Ibo
Adventures: Beaches with black volcano sand

ERITREA
Declared independence in 1993 from Ethiopia
Languages: Afar, Asmara, Tigre, Kunama, Tigrinya, other Cushitic languages
Adventures: The ruins of the old town of Koloe, in Qohaito

ETHIOPIA
Ethiopia has been independent for at least 2,000 years.
Languages: Amharic, Tigrinya, Oromigna, Guaragigna, Somali, Arabic, other local languages, English
Adventures: The caves of Sof Omar

GABON
Declared independence in 1960 from France
Languages: French, Fang, Myene, Nzebi, Bapounou/Eschira, Bandjabi
Adventures: The river rapids in the Okanda region

THE GAMBIA
Declared independence in 1965 from the United Kingdom
Languages: English, Mandinka, Wolof, Fula
Adventures: Cruise through the Abuko Nature Reserve and see crocodiles, monkeys, birds, and antelopes

GHANA
Declared independence in 1957 from the United Kingdom
Languages: English, African languages such as Akan, Moshi-Dagomba, Ewe, Ga
Adventures: 600 butterfly species at Kakum National Park and a walkway 98 feet above the forest floor

GUINEA
Declared independence in 1958 from France
Languages: French, and each ethnic group has its own language
Adventures: Malinke music on the streets of Conakry, and Les Ballets Africains

GUINEA-BISSAU
Declared independence in 1973 from Portugal
Languages: Portuguese Crioulo, African languages
Adventures: Winding streets of the old Portuguese quarter of Bissau

KENYA
Declared independence in 1963 from the United Kingdom
Languages: Kiswahili, English, African languages
Adventures: The Gede Ruins, a Swahili village abandoned in the 12th century, and baobob trees

LESOTHO
Declared independence in 1966 from the United Kingdom
Languages: Sesotho, English, Zulu, Xhosa
Adventures: Ancient rock shelter paintings in Malealea

LIBERIA
Settled in 1847 by freed African slaves from the United States of America
Languages: English and about 20 ethnic group languages
Adventures: Firestone Plantation, the world's largest rubber plantation; and the forest elephants and pygmy hippos at Sapo

LIBYA
Declared independence in 1951 from Italy
Languages: Arabic, Italian, English

Adventures: The ancient Greek architecture of Cyrene

MADAGASCAR
Declared independence in 1960 from France
Languages: Malagasy and French
Adventures: Parc National de Ranomafana and its 12 species of lemur

MALAWI
Declared independence in 1964 from the United Kingdom
Languages: Chichewa, Chinyanja, Chiyao, Chitonga
Adventures: Mt. Mulanje for some of the best hiking in Africa

MALI
Declared independence in 1960 from France
Languages: French, Bambara, numerous African languages
Adventures: The Mosques of Timbuktu

MAURITANIA
Declared independence in 1960 from France
Languages: Arabic, Pulaar, Soninke, French, Hassaniya, Wolof
Adventures: Chinguette is the seventh holiest city of Islam

MAURITIUS
Declared independence in 1968 from the United Kingdom
Languages: Creole, Bhojpuri, French
Adventures: Tamarin Waterfalls

MOROCCO
Declared independence in 1956 from France
Languages: Arabic, Berber dialects, French
Adventures: Fès el-Bari, the largest living medieval city in the world

MOZAMBIQUE

Declared independence in 1975 from Portugal
Languages: Emakhuwa, Xichangana, Portuguese, Elomwe, Cisena, Echuwabo, other Mozambican languages
Adventures: Wimbi beach and its spectacular coral reefs

NAMIBIA

Declared independence in 1989 from South Africa
Languages: English, Afrikaans, German, Oshivambo, Herero, and Nama
Adventures: Bubbling hot springs at Fish River Canyon

NIGER

Declared independence in 1960 from France
Languages: French, Hausa, Djerma
Adventures: Climb the minaret of the Great Mosque for a view of Agadez

NIGERIA

Declared independence in 1960 from United Kingdom
Languages: English, Hausa, Yoruba, Igbo (Ibo), Fulani
Adventures: Visit the Shrine of Oshuno, the River Goddess, in the sacred forest

RWANDA

Declared independence in 1962 from Belgium
Languages: Kinyarwanda, French, English, Kiswahili
Adventures: Rare mountain gorillas at the Parc National des Volcans

SAO TOME AND PRINCIPE

Declared independence in 1975 from Portugal
Languages: Portuguese
Adventures: Snorkel at Logoa Azul and see the giant baobob trees

SENEGAL

Declared independence in 1960 from France
Languages: French, Wolof, Pulaar, Jola, Mandinka
Adventures: Three million birds migrate from Europe to the Parc National des Oiseaux du Djoudj

SEYCHELLES

Declared independence in 1976 from the United Kingdom
Languages: Creole, English
Adventures: At Valée de Mai, the Seychelles black parrot and the rare *coco de mer* palm trees

SIERRA LEONE

Declared independence in 1961 from the United Kingdom
Languages: English, Mende, Temne, Krio
Adventures: Dive to underwater shipwreck sites and coral in the Banana Islands

SOMALIA

Declared independence in 1960 from the United Kingdom
Languages: Somali, Arabic, Italian, English
Adventures: Las Geel has Neolithic rock art paintings in caves and shelters

REPUBLIC OF SOUTH AFRICA

Declared independence in 1910 from the United Kingdom, and again in 1994 from minority white rule
Languages: Afrikaans, English, IsiNdebele, IsiXhosa, IsiZulu, Northern Sotho, Sesotho, Setswana, SiSwati, Tshivenda, Xitsonga
Adventures: Cable cars to the top of Table Mountain; Robben Island, where Nelson Mandela was once imprisoned, now a national monument

SUDAN

Declared independence in 1956 from Egypt and the United Kingdom
Languages: Arabic, Nubian, Ta Bedawie, Nilotic dialects, Nilo-Hamitic, English
Adventures: Ancient hieroglyphics and pyramids in Meroe

SWAZILAND

Declared independence in 1968 from the United Kingdom
Languages: English, SiSwati
Adventures: Safari through the Mlilwane Wildlife Sanctuary to see zebras and giraffes

TANZANIA

Declared independence in 1964, as the merger of Tanganyika and Zanzibar
Languages: Kiswahili or Swahili, English, Arabic
Adventures: Scale mysterious Mt. Kilimanjaro, the tallest peak in Africa

TOGO

Declared independence in 1960 from France
Languages: French, Ewe and Mina (South), Kabye and Dagomba (North)
Adventures: The Grand Marché market in Lome with its famous female merchants; the fortified villages in the Tamberma Valley, built in the 1600s by people fleeing the slave traders

TUNISIA

Declared independence in 1956 from France
Languages: Arabic, French
Adventures: The ruins of ancient Carthage

UGANDA

Declared independence in 1962 from the United Kingdom
Languages: English, Ganda, Luganda, Swahili, Arabic
Adventures: The bustling city of Kampala, and the mountain gorillas of the Impenetrable Forest

ZAMBIA

Declared independence in 1964 from the United Kingdom
Languages: English, Bemba, Kaonda, Lozi, Lunda, Luvale, Nyanja, Tonga, 70 other African languages
Adventures: Victoria Falls

ZIMBABWE

Declared independence in 1980 from the United Kingdom
Languages: English, Shona, Sindebele, numerous dialects
Adventures: The ruins of Great Zimbabwe, near Masvingo

Bandana Tying

THE WORD *bandana* has a global history. It comes from the Sanskrit *bhandhana,* which means tying. The word was absorbed first into Portuguese (in the sixteenth century, Portugal had conquered the cities of Goa and Bombay, now called Mumbai, on the western coast of India). From Portuguese, the word entered English. We can thank Indian languages for an assortment of English clothing words, such as cashmere (from the northern region of Kashmir), cummerbund, bangle, khaki, pajama, and dungaree.

Bandanas are often sold under the nondescript name "All Purpose Cloth," or APC. A bit of a boring moniker, perhaps, but, oh, so true. A bandana can be a belt, or a blindfold for Blind Man's Bluff. With a needle and thread, two or more can be sewn together to make a shirt or skirt.

You can wrap it loosely around your neck, cowboy style, pull it up over your nose and mouth for a disguise, or use it to dress up your pet. Best of all, you can wrap found treasures or lunch in an APC, then attach it to a long stick and sling it over your shoulder when you head out to see the world.

Bandanas are an excellent way to cover your hair, too, while playing lacrosse or hiking on a hot day, and they make perfect headbands.

To tie a bandana around your head, fold it in half to make a triangle. Place the long edge on your forehead, however low or high you want (you'll likely experiment with this, and try different possibilities). The cloth will fall lightly over your hair. With your hands, smooth it toward the back, push the tip of the triangle toward the nape of your neck. Then draw the ends over it, and tie (use your square knot).

You'll probably want to pull the triangle portion of the bandana into place, so it's smooth against your head, and so the corners don't stick out the sides.

If your head is larger, or if your mom or dad wants to wear one, instead of folding the cloth in half, merely fold one corner toward the opposite corner, and go from there.

To turn a bandana into a headband, fold in half to make a triangle. Start folding in, from the tip of the triangle toward the long edge, till you're left with the size headband you want to wear. Wrap around your head and tie in the back.

Five Karate Moves

KARATE BEGAN in the fifth century BC as a set of mind-strengthening exercises. Legend says that it was brought to a small forest temple in China by a Zen Buddhist monk named Bodhidharma (Bo-dee-darma) who, amazingly, had walked there all the way from India. Below are five basic moves that are fun to do with friends. To learn more and to take karate more seriously, look for a professional instructor in this and other martial arts.

Front Kick

Back Kick

Front Kick

The front kick is Karate's most powerful kick. Bring your left knee up to waist level, then extend the rest of the leg straight out. Your right leg should be firmly grounded to balance the kick, and your arms should be held close to your chest. Try the quick-surprise front kick, and then try a slower but more forceful variation.

Back Kick

Stand in a comfortable position facing forward. Your right leg is your kicking leg. Bend your left non-kicking leg just a little bit to give your body extra support and balance. Look over your right shoulder. Find your target. Bend your right knee, aim your heel in a straight line toward your target, and kick your foot high behind you. Your eyes are very important in this kick. Keep looking at your target while you kick back, extending your leg. Pull your leg back in the same path you used for your kick. Alternate kicking leg.

Knife Hand, or
Classic Karate Chop

Open your hand and turn it so your thumb faces the ceiling and your pinky faces the floor. Extend your fingers forward and away from you. The fingers should lightly touch. Let your thumb fall into the palm of your hand, and bend the top of the thumb downward. Arch the hand slightly backward. Raise your hand above your shoulder. Swing diagonally downward across to the other side of your body aiming to strike your target with the part of your hand that's just below your pinky.

**Knife
Hand**

**Punch
and
Pull**

Punch and Pull

Face forward with your feet shoulder-width apart. Keeping your right leg straight, lunge forward with your left leg, bending at the knee. Push your right arm forward in front of your body, with your hand in a downward-facing fist. Your left arm stays back, at your side, with your left hand in an upward-facing fist. Now, punch forward with the left arm and twist the wrist so that when this arm fully extends forward, your fist faces down. While the left arm punches, the right arm comes to rest at your side, with hand in an upward-facing fist. Alternate punches.

The Lunge Punch

Face forward, with your feet shoulder-width apart. Place your left leg in front of the right, and bend your knee into a lunge. Keep your right leg straight. This is called front stance. Step forward with your right foot into a powerful lunge, and as your right foot lands forward, punch forward with the right hand. To add power, at the same time you punch the right fist forward, pull your left hand back to your left side in an upward-facing fist. Pull your punching hand back to lunge again, alternating sides, or to switch to another move.

**The
Lunge
Punch**

The Daring Girls Guide to Danger

FACING YOUR FEARS can be a rewarding experience, and pushing yourself to new heights will inspire you to face challenges throughout life. Here in no particular order is a checklist of danger and daring. Some you should be able to do right away, but a few you might need to work up to:

1 Ride a roller coaster. The biggest roller coaster drops in America include the Kingdom Ka at Six Flags Great Adventure in New Jersey at 418 feet; the Top Thrill Dragster in Ohio at 400 feet; and Superman: The Escape in California at 328 feet. But the scariest coaster ride in America is still the Cyclone in Coney Island. Built in the 1920s, this comparably small metal and wooden ride packs an unbelievable punch with sudden drops and hairpin turns.

2 Ride a zip line across the canopy of a rain forest. A trip to Costa Rica offers incredible adventures, including "flying" across the roof of the world 200 feet off the ground with distances between trees of up to 1,200 feet. Many outdoor centers around the country also offer zip line courses.

3 Go white-water rafting. Most people think looking at the Grand Canyon from the rim down is scary, but a true act of daring is to take a white-water rafting trip down the stretch of Colorado River that cuts through it. Some trips even include a helicopter ride for an extra dose of danger!

4 Have a scary movie festival in your living room. Some good ones are *The Exorcist, Jaws, Alien, The Shining,* and Alfred Hitchcock's classic but still frightening *Psycho.* But don't blame us if you can't go sleep without wondering what's under the bed.

5 Wear high heels. This may not sound so dangerous, but without practice you can fall or twist an ankle. For your first time in heels, borrow someone else's, and make sure to start on a hard surface like wood. Once you're feeling steady on your feet, give carpeting a try. If you can wear heels on a thick carpet, you can do anything. Eventually, if it's a skill you want to learn, you'll be able to run, jump, and do karate in three-inch heels.

6 Stand up for yourself—or someone else. It's scary to feel like you're the only one who doesn't agree, but when something's wrong, a daring girl speaks up, for herself or someone who needs an ally. Summon your courage and raise your voice—real bravery is feeling the fear and doing it anyway.

7 Try sushi or another exotic food. California rolls do not count. For the true daring girl try some *natto* (fermented soy beans) or *escargot* (snails).

8 Dye your hair purple. Sometimes the scariest thing is just being a little bit different, even for a day. There are many hair dyes that wash out after a few weeks—so you can experience what it would be like to have a lime-green ponytail without having to wait for all your hair to grow out to change it again.

French Terms of Endearment, Expressions, and Other Items of Note

FRENCH TERMS OF ENDEARMENT

Ma petite chou
"My little cabbage." Can be used romantically to mean "my darling," or said to a younger person ("my little one.")

Bonjour ma petite chou, t'as passé une bonne journée?
"Hello my little cabbage, did you have a good day?"

Ma puce
"My flea"

Bonne nuit, ma puce!
"Goodnight, my flea!"

FUN WORDS TO SAY

Pamplemousse
(Pom-pel-moose) grapefruit

Aubergine
(Oh-bear-jean) eggplant

Chantilly
(Shan-tee) whipped cream (or a kind of lace)

Gros
(Gross) big

Dodo
(Doe-doe) a baby's naptime

Coucou
(Coo-coo) Hello there!

EXPRESSIONS

Avoir un chat dans la gorge
To have a cat in your throat. (Like the expression, "I have a frog in my throat.")

Revenons a nos moutons.
Let's get back to our sheep. (Meaning, return to the subject at hand.)

Oui, quand les poulets auront des dents.
Yes, when chicken have teeth. (Like the expression, "When pigs fly!")

WHAT TO ORDER AT A RESTAURANT

Bonjour, Monsieur. Puis j'avoir un croque monsieur avec une salade verte? Et aussi un coca s'il vous plait?
Hello, sir. May I please have a grilled ham and cheese sandwich with a green salad? And a Coke, please.

BOOKS WITH A FRENCH SETTING

Madeline
by Ludwig Bemelmans

The Little Prince
by Antoine de Saint-Exupery

Eloise in Paris
by Kay Thompson

Hunchback of Notre Dame
by Victor Hugo

The Count of Monte Cristo
by Alexandre Dumas

Joan of Arc

One life is all we have and we live it as we believe in living it. But to sacrifice what you are and to live without belief, that is a fate more terrible than dying.—Joan of Arc

JOAN WAS BORN around 1412 in the small town of Domrémy in France, on the border of the provinces of Champagne and Lorraine, to Jacques d'Arc and Isabelle Romée. She grew up helping her father and brothers work the land and helping her mother, a devout woman, tend the house.

The year she turned twelve, she became convinced that there was something special about her—a destiny she alone could fulfill. She began hearing the voices of St. Michael, St. Catherine, and St. Margaret, whom she believed had been sent by God to inform her of her divine mission to save France. So compelled was she by the urgency of these voices that by the time she was fifteen she cut her hair, began dressing in a man's uniform, and took up arms.

France and England were deep into the Hundred Years' War at this point. At that time in

history, the two nations were not as separate as they are now, and there was a battle raging over who should be king of the general area. By 1429, Henry VI of England was claiming the throne and the English occupied Paris and all of northern France. Joan had two missions, thanks to the voices that guided her: to recover her homeland from English domination and reclaim the besieged city of Orleans; and to see the dauphin of France, Charles VII, crowned king. She left her home, without telling her parents, and appealed to the captain of the dauphin's army, telling him of her divine mission. He initially dismissed the notion of a fifteen-year-old girl having the leadership capacity to head his forces. However, her persistence and clarity of vision ultimately convinced him, and she went on to convince the dauphin as well that she was on a mission from God meant to save him and restore France. After being examined by a board of theologians, she was given the rank of captain and allowed to lead men into battle.

She was seventeen when she led her troops to victory over the English at the battle of Orleans in May 1429. She rode in white armor and carried a banner bearing the likenesses of her three saints. She organized her army of men into professional soldiers, and even required them to attend mass and go to confession. So formidable was her leadership that it was said when her troops approached, the enemy fled the battlefield. But by far her most innovative act was instilling among her people a sense of nationalism and patriotic pride: she was one of the first leaders to consider England and France as separate countries, with separate cultures and traditions that were worth fighting to preserve.

Due in great part to Joan's leadership on the battlefield, Charles VII was crowned king of France on July 17, 1429 in Reims Cathedral. Her victory, however, was short-lived: she was captured by the Burgundians in 1430 while defending Compiegne, near Paris, and was sold to the English. The English turned her over to the court at Rouen to be tried for witchcraft and crimes against the church. Though the witchcraft charge was dismissed (on the grounds that she was a virgin), she was accused of perpetrating crimes against God by wearing men's clothing. After a fourteen-month trial, during which she never strayed from her insistence on the divinity of her voices and the absolute rightness of her calling, Joan was convicted and burned at the stake in the Rouen marketplace on May 30, 1431. Her last words were, "Jesus! Jesus!" She was nineteen years old.

Almost twenty-five years after her death, Pope Callixtus III reopened the case at the request of Inquisitor-General Jean Brehal and Joan's mother Isabelle Romée. Joan was vindicated as a martyr and declared an innocent woman on July 7, 1456. It was nearly 500 years after her death that she was canonized as a saint, on May 16, 1920, by Pope Benedict XV. Joan of Arc is now recognized as the patron saint of France.

The story of a girl guided by voices to change the world has proved irresistible to storytellers and artists from the time of her death to the present day. She continues to serve as an inspiration to daring girls everywhere.

Making a Willow Whistle

YOU WILL NEED

◆ An 8″ straight, smooth, round willow twig
◆ A Swiss Army knife
◆ Water

Find a willow twig that is straight and round, without any side branches, less than an inch thick, and about 8 inches long.

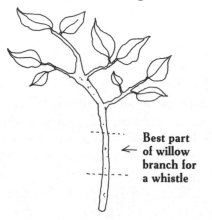

Best part of willow branch for a whistle

Using your Swiss Army knife, cut one end of the willow twig at an angle to make the mouthpiece. Then cut just the end of the pointy tip off to make it a little blunt.

On the top side of the twig, the side opposite your angled cut, carve a small notch in the willow, starting just past the point where your angled cut ends.

Just more than halfway down, cut a ring around the twig, taking care to cut just the outer layer of bark and not all the way through the wood.

Wet the twig (from the ring to the mouthpiece) with water, tap it gently with your knife to loosen the bark, and then carefully twist and pull the bark off. Try not to rip, tear, or break the bark, because you'll need to put it back on the twig. Dunk it in water to keep it moist until you need it again.

Go back to the notch you made on the top side of the twig, make it deeper, and cut it some more so that it extends down the length of the twig towards the end that still has bark on. The length and depth of this notch is what determines the pitch of your whistle. Carve off just a sliver of wood from the upper surface of the mouthpiece to make it totally flat.

Dip the bark-less end of your twig into a glass of water and slip the bark back on.

Now all you have to do is blow! It may take a few tries or alterations to get it right, but keep at it and you'll have your willow whistle blowing.

A dried-out willow whistle can be revived with a thorough soaking in water, but you might want to keep it wrapped in a damp towel so that it doesn't dry completely.

Periodic Table of the Elements

T HE **MYSTERIOUS** Periodic Table of the Elements holds up to 118 squares with numbers and abbreviations that are, really, the secret code to how the universe works. In these squares rests the true story of how elements combine to create chemical reactions and electricity and the tantalizing mechanisms of life itself.

A scientist named Dimitri Mendeleev of Siberia published *The Periodic Table of the Elements* in 1869 (beating another European scientist to fame by just a few months). Mendeleev listed all the elements that scientists knew at that time—63, but he had figured out the pattern of those elements, which had gaps, and predicted there were actually 92.

Mendeleev was correct in his prediction of elements in the gaps. And we now know, in fact, that there are 111 natural elements, along with seven (slightly controversial) elements made in the laboratory. Our chart shows 109 of them.

Some elements—like silver, gold, tin, sulfur, copper, and arsenic—were known in classical antiquity, and native peoples of the Americas knew about platinum. Others were discovered during Europe's Age of Science, or more recently. Six elements are the core of life as we know it: phosphorous and sulfur (the main components of DNA), carbon (the most abundant element in the universe), hydrogen, oxygen, and nitrogen. Women scientists have discovered several elements:

Element	Abbreviation/ Atomic Number	Discovered By	Date
Polonium	Po/84	Marie Sklodowska Curie	1898
Radium	Ra/88	Marie Sklodowska Curie with her husband Pierre Curie	1898
Rhenium	Re/75	Ida Tacke-Noddack with her colleagues Walter Noddack and Otto Carl Berg	1925
Francium	Fr/87	Marguerite Catherine Perey	1939

WHAT IS AN ELEMENT?

Elements are basic pieces of matter, composed of a single unique kind of atom. There is nothing that's not made of elements.

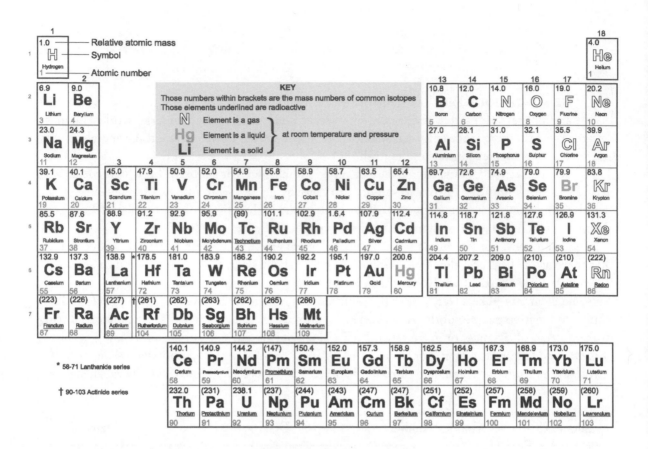

WHAT IS AN ATOM?

An atom is the basic structure of everything. A group of atoms is called a molecule, and molecules form everything we know, sense, live in, and touch.

WHAT IS IN AN ATOM?

Protons, neutrons, electrons, quarks, and gluons, none of which are visible to our eyes, unfortunately. Protons are in the atom's nucleus and carry a positive charge. Each element has a unique number of protons. In fact, the protons determine the order of the elements in the chart. Os, or Osmium, is not the random 76th element, it has 76 protons—hence its place on the chart. The number of protons in an atom never changes. Hydrogen, H, always has 1 proton. Aluminum, Al, always has 13. The proton number distinguishes one element from the others and accounts for each element's character and behavior. Neutrons also are in the nucleus, and carry a neutral charge. Both protons and neutrons break down into quarks, and quarks are held together by gluons.

Electrons have a negative electrical charge and they orbit around the nucleus. The sharing of electrons between atoms creates bonds. In metals, the movement of electrons can generate electrical current.

WHAT DO THE ABBREVIATIONS AND NUMBERS IN EACH BOX MEAN?

The top number is the relative atomic mass, or how heavy the element is. This is measured in atomic mass units, or amu's. One amu weighs about one trillionth of a trillionth of a gram.

The letters are the atomic symbol, or abbreviation, of each element. B stands for Boron.

The atomic number, at the bottom, tells how many protons are in the nucleus.

WHAT DO THE COLUMNS AND ROWS STAND FOR?

Mendeleev observed that some of the elements behave similarly. He organized the elements into columns, according to eighteen family groups, such as gas or metal. He organized the rows according to the pattern of atomic numbers, or number of protons, known as the seven periods.

❧

Vinegar and Baking Soda

SCIENTISTS across the globe have studied and debated the concept of acid-base reactions since the 1700s. This chemical reaction can get quite complicated, but it's easy to understand the basic idea and use your knowledge straightaway for everyday projects. All you need is a trip to the supermarket (or your own pantry) for two ingredients: vinegar and baking soda.

ACID-BASE BASICS

Acids corrode and dissolve things. They work by releasing hydrogen bubbles. Vinegar is a medium acid. On the pH scale, which measures the "potential of Hydrogen," it ranks 3 or 4 on a scale of 1-7.

Bases cancel out acids. Another word to know, science-wise, is alkali, which is a base that can be dissolved in water. Baking soda is a base, or at least it acts like a base, which is good enough for us. Together vinegar and baking soda, acid and base, can tackle many a small task—and some bigger projects, too.

EVERYDAY VINEGAR USES

Vinegar corrodes and dissolves, it has a repellent smell, and it counteracts things that act as a base. Use it to:

Treat skin irritations. Certain itches, like poison ivy and mosquito bites, and pains like jellyfish stings and sunburns, act as bases, so vinegar will counteract them. Mix vinegar half and half with water and spray directly on skin, or soak in towels for compresses. (Apple cider vinegar smells a bit better than white, if you prefer.)

Get rid of rust. Take rusty hand shovels and other items, dip them in a bowl filled with vinegar, and leave overnight. You can do this to shine pennies, too.

Remove sticky goo. For stubborn stickers or the like, soak a cloth in vinegar, then drape it over the sticky area for a few hours.

Repel mosquitos and ants. Apply it to your body with a cotton ball as a mosquito repellent. Leave a cup of it open to persuade ants to camp somewhere other than your family kitchen.

Counteract stink. Put smelly things in a half-and-half mixture of water and vinegar overnight. Or, if something stinky happens in your family car, leave a bowl of vinegar in there overnight to capture the smell.

EVERYDAY BAKING SODA USES

Baking soda neutralizes acidic things, and can act as an abrasive for scrubbing. You can use it to:

Soothe bee stings. Apply a baking soda and water paste to a bee sting (which acts as an acid) to neutralize it. Now, if your sting is from a wasp or yellow jacket (which actually act as bases), you'll want to treat those stings with vinegar on a cotton ball.

Remove stains. If you get food coloring on your hands, scrub them with baking soda and water. However, if that food coloring gets onto your clothes, you'll want to soak those in vinegar.

Calm animal smells. If you're stink-sprayed by a skunk, mix hydrogen peroxide (available at all pharmacies) with baking soda and some liquid dish soap—that works like a charm. Similarly, if your dog smells, sprinkle her all over with baking soda, rub it in, and brush through her hair.

Brush teeth. Mix baking soda with water into a thick paste (without the unnecessary extras in toothpaste).

Extinguish fires. Baking soda, when heated, emits carbon dioxide, which can smother small flames. That said, if you see fire, shout quickly for the nearest adult, and call 911 immediately.

WASHING THE CAR

You can forgo expensive non-eco-friendly store-bought cleaners for our two wonder products instead.

Before you start washing, sprinkle baking soda through the car's interior to remove odors. Vacuum it up when the outside washing is done.

For the car body, grab a bucket, and pour in $^1/_2$ cup of vinegar for every gallon of water; scrub car with a big sponge.

For windows, mirrors, and interior plastic, mix 2 cups of water and $^1/_2$ cup vinegar in an empty spray bottle. You can add up to $^1/_4$ cup of rubbing alcohol and, to make it look fancier, one drop each, no more, of blue and green food coloring. Instead of rags, use newspapers to clean and shine windows.

VOLCANO PROJECT

In an old soda bottle, pour a little more than a $^1/_2$ cup of vinegar, and a little more than a ½ cup of dishwashing liquid. Add red food coloring, if you wish, for a lava effect.

Make a foundation from a piece of cardboard. Stick the bottle onto that with tape. Then build up a volcano around it. Mound up old newspapers, leaves, or whatever material you have on hand. Once it attains a mountain shape, cover the whole thing with a large sheet of foil, crimping it a bit so it looks volcano-like.

For the eruption, measure 1 heaping tablespoon of baking soda. Wrap it in a small piece of paper towel or pour it straight in. Either way, when you deposit the baking soda, the concoction will erupt before your eyes. It's very second grade, but always fun, no matter what your age.

Here's the chemistry behind the volcano: vinegar is acidic acid, baking soda is sodium bicarbonate, a base. When they react together they produce carbonic acid, and that decomposes very quickly into water and carbon dioxide. The foaming bubble explosion is the carbon dioxide gas escaping.

Rules of the Game: Bowling

IN THE 1930s, a British archeologist named Sir Flinders Petrie discovered items in an Egyptian grave that appeared to have been used in an ancient version of the game we know today as bowling. By his estimation, bowling is a 5,000-year-old game. In the Middle Ages in Britain, bowling was so popular—and distracting—that King Edward III was said to have outlawed it, so that his troops could keep focused on honing their archery skills for battle. Bowling's first mention in American literature was by Washington Irving: his Rip Van Winkle is awakened by the sound of "crashing ninepins." In 1895, Americans established the American Bowling Congress to regulate the rules of the game and establish national bowling competitions. They forgot to include women, however, so in 1917 women bowlers rectified that by forming the Women's National Bowling Association. Today bowlers all over the world compete and play for fun with friends. Here are some rules for playing and scoring the game.

HOW TO KEEP SCORE

There are ten frames in the game, and each bowler is given up to two opportunities to try to knock down all ten bowling pins in each frame. The object of the game is to have the highest score. The pins knocked down on a player's first attempt are counted and recorded on a score sheet. (The score sheet has a place for each players name, and next to that ten boxes, one for each frame of the game. At the top of each box are two squares, which is where the scores for each of the two balls thrown per frame are recorded. At the far right is a larger box, which is where the total score for all ten frames should go.) If there are still pins left standing, the bowler then has a second try at knocking them down, and the number of pins knocked down on her second try is recorded. Her score is the pins from the first roll, plus the pins from the second roll; the resulting amount is then added to any previous score. Scores continue to accumulate as each bowler takes her turn until all ten frames have been played by each of the bowlers.

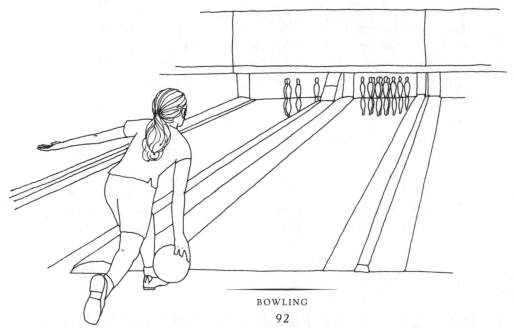

BONUS SCORING

When a bowler rolls a strike or a spare, she gets bonus points. Both a spare and a strike are worth 10 pins, but how they are scored actually depends on what the bowler does in the next frame. With a spare, marked by a "/" on the score sheet, you add ten to the number of pins knocked down in your next attempt. With a strike, marked by an "X" on the score sheet, you add ten to the number of pins knocked down in your next *two* attempts.

If you bowl a spare in the tenth frame, you get an extra ball. If you bowl a strike in the tenth frame, you get two extra balls. If you happen to bowl a strike in the tenth frame, and then score a spare with your two extra balls, you're awarded a score of 20 for the tenth frame, and your game is over. If you bowl a spare in frame ten, and then a strike with your additional ball, you get a score of 20 for frame ten, and your game is over. If you bowl a strike in the tenth frame, and then get two additional strikes with your two extra balls, you get a score of 30 for the tenth frame, and your game is over.

BOWLING TERMINOLOGY

Approach
This 15-foot-long area is where bowlers start. The approach ends at the foul line, which marks the start of the bowling lane. Your feet cannot cross the foul line, or even touch it, not even after you've released the ball.

Average
This is the sum of all a bowler's games divided by the number of games played.

Bowling shoes
These are shoes with special soles to help a bowler glide across the floor during her approach. Street shoes are not allowed on bowling alleys.

Clean Sheet
This means making all the spares in the game.

Dutch 200
Scoring spare-strike-spare-strike for the entire game, resulting in a score of 200.

Foul
The foul line separates the approach from the start of the lane. When a bowler steps on or over the foul line, she doesn't get the score for that attempt. A foul is marked on the score sheet with an "F."

Frame
Each game of bowling consists of ten frames for each bowler, who has two chances to knock down the ten pins in each frame.

Lane

The narrow stretch where the ball rolls toward the pins. Lanes are usually about 60 feet long and 42 inches wide. Gutters, two lower rounded areas alongside the lane about $9\frac{1}{2}$ inches wide, are there to catch balls that stray to the left or right. When a ball rolls into the gutter, it's called a "gutter ball" and gets zero points.

Open Frame

This is when a bowler fails to knock down all ten pins in both tries.

Perfect Game

A perfect game is when a bowler scores twelve strikes in a row in the same game. The resulting score is 300, the highest possible score for a bowler in any one game.

Pin Deck

The place where bowling pins are set at the end of the lane. The pins are set a foot apart from each other to form a 3-foot triangle. Pins, which are 15 inches tall, are usually made of wood and plastic, and weigh about $3\frac{1}{2}$ pounds. The widest part of the pin is called the belly.

Sleeper

When you have a spare with one pin standing directly behind another, the back pin is called a "sleeper."

Spare

If one or more pins are standing after a bowler's first try, the bowler gets a second chance to knock all the pins down—a "spare" shot. If the bowler knocks the rest of the pins down on her second try, she has made a spare. A spare is marked on the score sheet by a slash (/).

Split

This is when two or more pins remain standing with a gap between them. A split that is left can be marked on the score sheet by drawing a circle around the pin-count for that frame.

Strike

This is when a bowler knocks down all ten pins on her first try. When a bowler gets a strike, her score goes up by 10, and in addition the score of her next two turns gets added to the strike score. A strike is marked on the score sheet by an X.

Turkey

Getting three strikes in a row. Each "turkey" (group of three strikes in a row) is worth 30 pins a frame.

Queens of the Ancient World II
Salome Alexandra of Judea

SALOME'S STORY is a tale of diplomacy, of managing the constant challenges of royal leadership, and of resisting attacks from outside armies as well as from members of her own family. She is remembered as the last independent ruler of her country, Judea, during the period just before the countries of the Mediterranean were conquered by Rome.

Salome Alexandra was born in 140 BC. Not much is known of her girlhood. Her Judean name was Shelamzion, which is translated as Salome. Her Greek name was Alexandra, after Alexander the Great, who brought his Greek armies to the region nearly 200 years earlier. Like many people of her time, Salome lived amid her family and clan and spoke their language, Aramaic. She was also versed in the Hellenistic culture and Greek language that united the many lands around the Mediterranean Sea, including the nearby empires of Egypt and Syria.

From what historians can piece together, it seems Salome Alexandra first married in her late twenties. Her choice of husband—Aristobulus, the eldest son of the native ruler of Judea—led her both to royal life and to the beginning of her family problems. Aristobulus was intensely ambitious. When his father the king died in 104 BC, he willed the country to Aristobulus' mother. But his eldest son would have none of it. He imprisoned his mother, starved her to death, and jailed three of his brothers.

In this brutal way, Judea became his, and Salome became the reigning queen. Just a year later, though, Aristobulus died of a mysterious disease. As Salome performed the proper funeral rites over him, she learned that he had bequeathed the kingdom to her.

Salome was faced with another complicated decision: should she rule by herself or share the throne? She released the three royal brothers from jail and chose the eldest of them to be king and high priest. His name was Alexander Janneus. She married him and continued her life as queen.

Her second husband, Alexander, was a tough man to live with. He was mean tempered and he drank too much. He was fond of raiding and pillaging nearby cities, and he was cruel to his own people. He reigned for twenty-seven years. The historian Josephus tells us that as much as the people hated Alexander, they adored Salome, and considered her wise, kind, strong and reliable, decent, fair, and a person of good judgment. It's possible that during Alexander's long rule, the people didn't rise to overthrow him because they loved Salome so much.

In 76 BC, Alexander was on his deathbed. He called Salome close and bequeathed the kingdom to her, returning the favor she had granted him twenty-seven years before.

Alexander presented Salome with a plan: "Conceal my death until, under your command, the soldiers will have won this battle we are now fighting. March back to the capital Jerusalem and hold a Victory. I have oppressed many people, and they now hate me. Make peace with them. Tell them you will include their leaders as advisors in your government.

Finally, when you return to Jerusalem, send for the leading men. Show them my dead body and give it over to them. Let them defile it, if they wish, or honor me with a proper burial. The choice will be theirs. And then, they will support you." Quite a beginning for the new reigning queen.

<hr />

As queen, ruling from her palace in Jerusalem, Salome faced immediate challenges from her family once more, this time from her two grown sons. Salome anointed her oldest son, Hyrcanus, a quieter and more private sort of man, to be high priest. Hebrew religious law forbade women from overseeing the Temple and performing the animal sacrifices, so although she was queen, she couldn't be high priest, as her husband had been. Her younger son, named Aristobulus after Salome's first ruthless husband, was a much bigger problem. Like his father, he was very ambitious. He wanted Salome's throne from the start. Soon he would rise against her.

True to her promises and King Alexander's plan, Salome delegated the domestic affairs and a good deal of the power over the nation's religious life to the elders of Judea. This helped to end the civil war that had simmered under her husband's rule, during which he had killed a great many of the elders' group. Still, the remaining elders wanted revenge. Before Salome could stop them, they slit the throat of one of Alexander's ringleaders, Diogenes, and set out to find more.

The ambitious son Aristobulus used the growing violence to threaten his mother's reign. After the revenge killings, Aristobulus led a delegation of men to Salome's throne. They demanded she put a stop to the killings. If she could do so, they promised they would not avenge the recent murders. They would keep the country from descending into a spiral of violence. In return for keeping the peace, Aristobulus demanded his mother give him several of the family fortresses strung throughout the desert from Jerusalem to the Jordan River.

Salome negotiated a deal. She kept the majority of the fortresses for herself, including those that housed her royal treasure, but she gave a few to Aristobulus. Seeking to push him far from her capital, she dispatched him on a small military mission to Damascus.

<hr />

As Salome dealt with the situation at home, another problem was brewing outside of Judea. The country's northern neighbor, Syria, was very weak. The Seleucid dynasty that had once controlled the entire region was in its last days. Taking advantage of this weakness, King Tigranes of Armenia descended on Syria with a massive army of a half million soldiers, quickly taking over Syria's cities. Tigranes trapped the Syrian queen, Cleopatra Selene, in the city of Ptolemais, on the Mediterranean coast.

Ptolemais was not far from Salome's city of Jerusalem. Terrible news of the siege reached Salome quickly, as did the rumor that Tigranes planned to march on Judea next. Salome knew that despite her large army of mercenaries and native soldiers, she could not beat Tigranes.

Rather than ready her troops for war, Queen Salome took a different stance. She sent her ambassadors to meet with King Tigranes, and sent along with them many camels loaded with extraordinary treasure. Tigranes agreed not to attack. Luck was on Salome's side, because another army had begun to attack Armenia. Instead of marching south toward Jerusalem, Tigranes had to turn north to defend his own people back home.

That episode, and the years of strife leading up to it, wore Salome down. She was over seventy, and her health was beginning to fail. She had outlived two husbands, she faced attacks from outsiders, and her youngest son continued to undermine her authority from within.

Sensing her final frailty, Aristobulus planned a coup. He had been angry that Salome negotiated a peace with King Tigranes. Had it been up to him, he would have led their soldiers to battle. He knew she was near death, and he suspected that she would bequeath the throne to his older brother, who was already the high priest.

Secretly, Aristobulus left the family palace in Jerusalem. He rode his horse through the countryside, and at each city and village he asked the people to foreswear their allegiance to Queen Salome and pledge their loyalty to him.

Salome gathered her last ounce of strength and decided to take harsh action against her son. She imprisoned his wife and children—much as her first husband had done to his relatives. She stashed them in a fortress next to the Temple where Hyrcanus was high priest, but she knew her time was running out. She gave Hyrcanus the keys to the treasury and directed him to take command of her army.

Salome Alexandra died soon thereafter, in 67 BC, before Aristobulus could strike against her. She was seventy-three, had reigned for nine years as her people's only independent queen, and she died a natural death. Salome took part in no great battles. She commanded no stunning ships on the sea. She merely did her best to keep the peace at home and to keep stronger armies at bay.

Queen Salome was so admired that for many generations, hers was one of the two most popular names that Judean people would give to their baby daughters (including one infamous Salome who appears in the New Testament). She couldn't have known that she would be the only Judean queen, and that this era of independent states was about to end.

In the year Salome died, across the sea in Italy an empire was growing. The Roman general Pompey was fighting the pirates who controlled the Mediterranean. He cleared them out and made it safe once again to cross the vast waters by boat. By 64 BC, Pompey forged his soldiers into battalions and started his eastward trek. He took control of Syria later that year, and of Judea the year after. Soon, all of western Asia was under Rome's hand, and the era of Queen Salome the diplomat was a distant memory.

Secret Garden

IN *THE SECRET GARDEN*, by Frances Hodgson Burnett, the orphaned Mary is sent to live with her uncle at Misselthwaite Manor. Mary takes to roaming the grounds, and one day she finds a mysterious, ivy-covered wall. A robin leads her to the key that reveals, behind the wall, an abandoned garden. Once in, Mary learns that the "small, pale green points" emerging beneath the cover of weeds are bulbs on their way to becoming "sweet-smelling" things, and that February's dead roses return to life by Spring. Mary befriends the local boy Dickon, who knows the mysteries of the natural world and can talk to animals. Together they bring the secret garden back to life. In Mary and Dickon's spirit, you can create a garden of your own, secret or not. Here are two ideas for working your own patch.

❀ A BULB GARDEN ❀

The secret garden at Misselthwaite teemed with all kinds of bulbs, and your garden can, too. First, you must know that the essence of gardening is good soil, planting in sun or shade (depending on the plant's needs), and water. Find a space in your yard, till the soil, add nourishments like compost and old leaves to the soil, then plant.

In the Fall, plant bulbs six inches or so down, in good soil. Choose a variety of bulbs: crocus, daffodils, tulips, and gladioli. Then add several kinds of lilies; even though they are not officially bulbs, they are part of the same plant family, *Liliacaeae*. These will bloom in succession from early Spring through mid-Summer. Nearby, in the Spring, you might plant peas, cherry tomatoes, and other pick-as-you-go vegetables, for when you're outside playing and need to nibble.

❀ A SUNFLOWER HUT ❀

If you already have an outdoor fort of your own, add flowers or vegetables, like a bustle of orange tiger lilies or a line of hardy Black-eyed Susans. Tall plants such as a stand of joe-pye weeds or butterfly bushes provide excellent cover.

You can also grow sunflowers into a hut. In Spring, plant sunflower seeds in a circle or square (or any shape you wish). Leave some unplanted space for a doorway. Dig a one-foot wide planting area according to your plan, and add mulch till the soil is rich and ready.

Plant sunflower seeds, two to a hole, in holes one foot apart. As they grow, prune away the weaker seedling. In between the sunflower seeds, plant morning glories. They will tangle their way up the sunflower stalks and give your hut more privacy and a blur of color.

Water daily and pull any weeds that grow nearby. When the sunflowers are tall, weave rope or twine through them. Find a way to pull the rope over and across until the sunflower tops come together to create the roof of the hut. Tug gently, though, so the sunflowers won't pop off their sturdy stems.

Friendship Bracelets

FRIENDSHIP BRACELETS can be very simple or extremely intricate, but at heart they're just colorful embroidery floss woven into lovely patterns, to be given to dear friends. Originally part of Native American life, particularly in Central America, these handwoven bracelets became popular in the United States in the 1970s—and not just for girls. President Bill Clinton sported one in the first televised interview of his post-presidential years.

The slender **Snake Around the Pole** is the easiest friendship bracelet to make.

1. Cut two strands from different colors of embroidery floss, using a bit less than one yard.

2. Hold the two strands together. Tie a knot at one end, leaving 2 inches above the knot. Use a safety pin to attach it to your pants or the arm of a sofa (if you do that, make sure your parents won't mind a tiny hole). Some people use tape, but it can come off and mess up the pattern. You can also use a clipboard, putting the knot just under the clamp **Ⓐ**.

3. Separate the two strands. Take the left and cross it on top of the right, making the shape of a number 4 **Ⓑ**. Then loop the left strand under the right and bring it through the opening created by the "4" shape **Ⓒ**.

4. This forms a knot that you will pull tight by sliding it toward the big knot at the top. Repeat this with the same string for as long as you want this color. When you're ready to change colors, just take the right-hand strand and move it to the left.

5. With this new left-hand strand of the second color, repeat steps 3 and 4 until you're ready to switch colors again, or until you're done with the bracelet.

6. Finish with another big knot, and leave enough room to tie the bracelet around your friend's wrist.

**SNAKE AROUND
THE POLE**

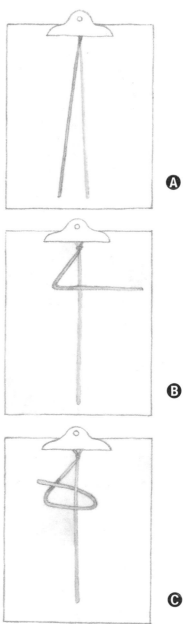

Ⓐ

Ⓑ

Ⓒ

For a heftier and more colorful **Snake Around the Pole,** use four colors, with two strands of each color. Knot the strands together, and attach to a hard surface. Follow the directions for the first Snake Around the Pole, but twist the knot around seven other strings instead of only one. Tighten each knot by pulling it toward the top. Repeat for as long as you want that color, then switch to the next. Continue until you're done. Knot to finish.

The flatter, wider **Candy Stripe** is a different kind of knot bracelet. With the string on the left, you'll tie a knot around each strand one at a time, moving to the right. All this knotting can be a bit tedious—which shows your true devotion to the friend who gets the bracelet! Once you get the hang of it, though, you can knot a friendship bracelet practically without looking.

1. Cut three strands each of three colors, about one yard long. Tie a knot at the top, leaving two inches above the knot. Attach the strands to a hard surface, like a clipboard, or use a safety pin to attach it to your pants. Separate the strands by color **Ⓐ**.

2. Start with the leftmost strand and make the "4" shape over top of the strand directly to its right. Bring the left strand back through the opening created by the "4" shape, and slide it to the top, pulling the knot tight **Ⓑ**. Repeat for each of the other strands, moving left to right, always using the leftmost strand to make the knot. When all eight knots are done, the strand will be at the far right, where it should stay.

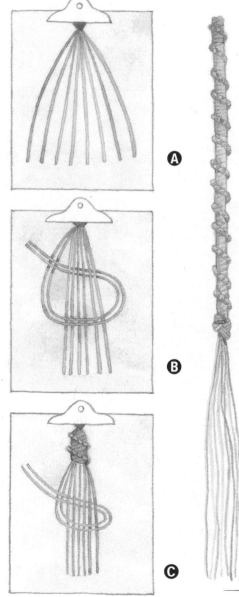

Ⓐ

Ⓑ

Ⓒ

Ⓓ

SNAKE AROUND THE POLE 2

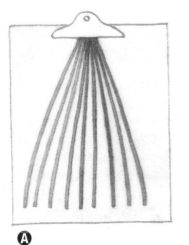

A

B

C

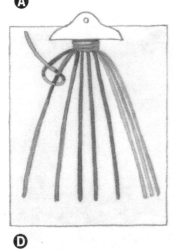

D

E

CANDY STRIPE

3. Take the strand that is now the leftmost **C**, and start knotting across the strands, as in step 2. As before, when it reaches the far right, let it rest, and allow the new leftmost strand to make a new row of knots **D**. The key to success is to make sure you make all the knots very tight, and push each finished row tightly to the top.

4. Repeat the process until you are done **E**. Leave room at the end, tie a knot, and then fasten it with care onto a friend's ankle or wrist.

Slumber Party Games

THERE IS USUALLY not much slumber involved in your typical slumber party. Instead, pajama-clad girls stay up into the wee hours talking, watching movies, playing games, telling stories, having pillow fights, and giggling. It's a chance for girls to enjoy the bonding element of playing together as a group, and revel in subverting the normal evening routine—sleeping in the living room together instead of in bed, alone; staying up well past bedtime; being awake in the dark telling scary stories. It's a time for mystery and daring, as illustrated by some of the most popular slumber party games played by girls over the years.

Bloody Mary

Who was Bloody Mary?

There are many different stories of who the real "Bloody Mary" was. The Bloody Mary of slumber party fame has been linked to Queen Mary Tudor of England, who gained the nickname of "Bloody Mary" when she had more than 300 people burned at the stake during her reign because they would not follow her Roman Catholic faith. She is also sometimes confused with Mary Queen of Scots (Bloody Mary Tudor's cousin), who in fact may have been instead the subject of a much more benign children's tradition: the nursery rhyme "Mary, Mary, Quite Contrary." In other versions, Bloody Mary is also thought to be the ghost of "Mary Worth," a supposed witch killed in the Salem Witch trials, though no historical record of a person by that name exists. The most far-fetched version of the story is rooted in the legend of a woman named Elizabeth Bathory, a sixteenth-century countess who was rumored to have killed girls and then bathed in their blood to retain her youth. Her name wasn't Mary, obviously, but the nickname she earned, "The Blood Countess," may contribute to her confusion with the Bloody Mary of countless slumber parties. The most mun-

Queen Mary Tudor of England

dane story associated with the Bloody Mary myth is that Mary was a local woman who was killed in a car accident; her ghostly visage features a horrible facial disfiguration she received in the crash. No matter which story you decide to go with—and there are merits to each of them—the basic method of summoning the restless spirit of Bloody Mary is the same: a darkened room, a mirror, and the chanting of her name.

Why the mirror? "Mirror, mirror on the wall, who is the fairest one of all?" is probably the most familiar rhyme about the magical divination possibilities of your own reflection. Indeed, girls in ancient times were encouraged to eat a red apple and brush their hair at midnight in front of a mirror, whereupon they would be rewarded with a glimpse of their future husbands (the red apple and the mirror both figure prominently in the Snow White story we know today). Other rituals involving a mirror required spinning around a certain number of times or looking over your shoulder, the end result being, again, the revelation of whom you might marry. Even today we have less binding versions of these chanting rituals and superstitions—think "he loves me, loves me not" to see if someone likes you, or the twisting of an apple stem while chanting the alphabet to discover the first initial of the person you like best. What does this have to do with Bloody Mary? One of the variations of the Bloody Mary chant was "Bloody mirror, bloody mirror." This, combined with the idea that you were supposed to discover who you were going to marry by looking in the mirror, plus the gruesome legends of various Marys

who were bloody themselves, easily evolved into the "Bloody Mary" game we know today.

How to Play

Go into the bathroom, or another darkened room with a mirror. Holding a flashlight beneath your chin so that it lights up your face in a ghostly way, close the door and turn off all the lights. Stand in front of the mirror and chant "Bloody Mary" thirteen times to summon the spirit of Bloody Mary. Ideally this should be done alone, but you can take your friends in there with you for moral support—which you may indeed require, since the legend is that if you get to the thirteenth chant of her name, Bloody Mary will appear in the mirror and either reach out to scratch your face, pull you into the mirror with her, or scare you to death. However, some people believe Bloody Mary isn't always cruel: they say if you're lucky, you'll just see her face in the mirror, or she'll appear and answer your questions about the future. And even if no face appears in the mirror, there are other ways Bloody Mary can make her presence felt—a scar or cut that wasn't there before, a window slamming shut, or other eerie happenings. Ultra-daring girls can play this game with one crucial variation: turning off the flashlight and summoning Bloody Mary completely in the dark.

Truth or Dare

How to Play

Truth or Dare, the essential sleepover party game, goes by several different names. Sometimes it is called "Truth, Dare, Double-Dare," and there is also a variation called "Truth, Dare, Double-Dare, Promise to Repeat."

In its most basic version, "Truth or Dare," players take turns choosing between a truth or a dare, and must either answer a question or perform a dare determined by the other players. The questions can be as embarrassing as you like, and the dares as risky as you can imagine—but neither should ever be harmful. First, because the game is supposed to be fun, and second, because what you ask or dare may come back to haunt you when it's your turn to choose. In "Truth, Dare, or Double-Dare," the players have a choice between telling the truth when asked a question, performing a minor dare, and performing a bigger dare. In "Truth, Dare, Double Dare, Promise to Repeat," there is the added choice of promising to repeat something—usually embarrassing—in public later.

It's a good idea to set some ground rules before you play so that nobody gets her feelings hurt or gets in too much trouble: nothing that would get a girl in hot water with her parents, nothing that requires going outside or bothering people not involved in the game. The other basic rule is that once you agree to tell the truth, perform a dare or double-dare, or repeat something embarrassing in public later, there is no chickening out. If you refuse to do what's asked of you, you're out of the game.

Examples

Truth: You have to answer a personal question. This can be something like: What's your deepest darkest secret? What was your most embarrassing moment? When was the last time you brushed your teeth? What superpower do you wish you had?

Dare: You have to do an easy dare, such as "Act like a chicken for thirty seconds," "Wear your underwear on your head the rest of the night," "Do ten push-ups," or "Act out a dramatic death scene."

Double Dare: A bigger or more embarrassing dare, such as "Kiss a stuffed animal with sound effects," "Try to pick your nose with your big toe and then wipe it on somebody," "Sing the national anthem at the top of your lungs," must be done.

Promise to Repeat: If you don't want to tell the truth or perform a potentially humiliating dare, you can choose "Promise to Repeat," which requires you to promise to repeat something embarrassing in public later, like agreeing to include the word "stultifying" in every sentence you say to your mom the next day.

Light as a Feather, Stiff as a Board

How to play

Have one person lay on the ground, while four to six others gather around her. The players should place the index fingers of both hands underneath the person lying down, and then, with eyes closed, everyone begins to chant, "Light as a feather, stiff as a board." After twenty chants or so (or whatever number of chants you agree upon ahead of time), the players start raising their arms, lifting the person and seemingly levitating her above the ground.

One variation is to play this game as a call-and-response story. The player next to the person's head begins the story with, "It was a dark and stormy night." Each player (except the one lying on the ground) repeats the phrase one at a time, and then the player at the head continues, "It was cold and the road was icy." Everyone repeats, then the head player says, "The car she was in spun out of control." Everyone repeats, then: "And when they found her." Everyone repeats, then: "She was light as a feather." Everyone repeats, then: "And stiff as a board." These last two sentences are repeated by the group several times, and then the entire group begins chanting "Light as a feather, stiff as a board" and lifting up the person who is lying down.

Is Your Slumber Party Guest Really Levitating?

The "Light As A Feather, Stiff As A Board" slumber party game has its roots in a long tradition of unexplainable, seemingly miraculous feats of weightlessness. Levitation, from the Latin word *levis,* or "light," means to float into the air, and numerous religions, from Christianity to Islam, have stories of levitation by shamans, mediums, saints, and those demonically possessed.

Saints who levitated were said to possess a luminous glow. Among the reported levitators was Saint Teresa of Avila, who levitated while in states of rapture in the 1680s and is usually painted with a bird, signifying her ability to fly; St. Edmund, around 1242; St. Joseph of Cupertino who astonished the Church with his flights in the 1600s; Catherine of Siena in the late fourteenth century; and St. Adolphus Liguori in 1777. Reports of levitation in more recent times include Father Suarez in 1911 in Southern Argentina, and, also at the beginning of the twentieth century, the Passionist nun Gemma Galgani. The Christian saints, priests, and nuns generally attributed their levitation to states of rapture or ecstasy that were beyond their control, while in Hinduism, Buddhism, and other Eastern traditions, levitation was presented as a skill that could be accomplished through spiritual and physical training. Levitation, like all things otherworldly, turned demonic in the Middle Ages, where rather than being a signal of a person's divinity and proximity to God, it was seen as a manifestation of evil generated by demons, ghosts, or witchcraft. The nineteenth-century Spiritualism movement in America, with its interest in séances, ghosts, poltergeists, and other spooky things, helped give levitation a boost once again. But in modern times it's mostly understood to be a magic trick, a phenomenon based in real-world explanations and techniques. Still, as anyone who has seen David Blaine—or played "light as a feather, stiff as a board" at slumber parties—can attest, it's entertaining, even when you're pretty sure it's not real.

Making a Cloth-Covered Book

YOU WILL NEED

- Two pieces of $6^{1}/_{2}" \times 9^{1}/_{4}"$ cardboard
- A needle or embroidery needle and thread
- Fabric (about $16" \times 12"$)—an old dress, T-shirt, or pillowcase works well
- Eight pieces of $8^{1}/_{2}" \times 11"$ plain white paper (for a longer book, you can use more paper)
- 1 piece of fancy or colored $8^{1}/_{2}" \times 11"$ paper
- Wide packing tape and regular tape
- A ruler
- Fabric glue
- 12" ribbon
- Scissors

Fold the plain paper and the fancy paper in half. If the fancy paper looks different on the front than it does on the back, fold it so that the "front" side is on the inside. Put the folded plain paper inside the folded fancy paper, like a book. Then use your needle and thread to sew the papers together in two places, about an inch and a half from the top and an inch and a half from the bottom.

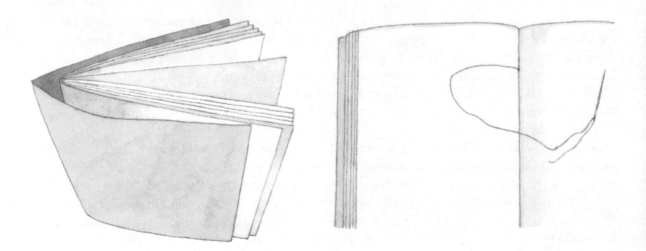

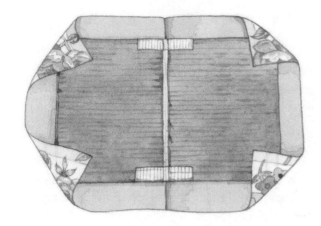

Cut your fabric to about 16 inches by 12 inches and lay it out, wrong-side facing up. Place the two pieces of cardboard in the middle of the fabric, leaving about a quarter of an inch between each piece. Tape the cardboard pieces together and maintain the quarter-inch separation. Coat the back of the cardboard lightly with fabric glue and then glue the cardboard to the cloth. Fold and glue each of the corners first and then fold and glue the fabric on each side. You can use tape to secure the fabric if necessary; just make sure the tape doesn't stick up close to the outer edge. Now you've made the fabric book cover.

Cut your 12-inch ribbon in half. Use your ruler to find the center of the left side of your fabric cover and glue the end of one ribbon there (starting about two inches from the end of the ribbon). Try not to overglue, but also try to make sure you glue right to the very edge so that the ribbon is firmly attached. Secure with tape. Do the same thing on the right side of the cover with the other ribbon.

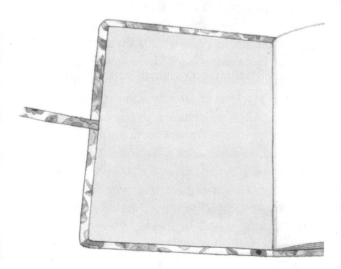

Open your papers and place them in the middle of the cardboard and fabric so that the fold of the paper is right in the center of the tape between the cardboard pieces. Using the fabric glue, glue the outer paper (the fancy paper) to the inside of the cover and let it dry. Once dry, tie the ribbon to close your book. It's not as secure as a lock and key, but it's a pretty way to keep safe your handmade journal, should you choose to use it as a secret diary.

Pirates

THERE HAVE BEEN women pirates throughout the ages, from Queen Artemisia to female Vikings to modern-day women pirates in the Philippines. Many of the stories about female pirates are just that: stories made up showcasing women pirates who are merely fictional. But there are several women pirates whose stories are verifiable, and who really did live and (in some cases) die a pirate's life on the high seas.

CHARLOTTE BADGER

Charlotte Badger was a convicted felon when she was sent to Australia from England. She was found guilty of the crime of breaking and entering when she was eighteen years old and sentenced to seven years deportation. She sailed to Port Jackson, Sydney, aboard the convict ship *The Earl of Cornwallis* in 1801 and served five years of her sentence at a factory, during which time she also gave birth to a daughter.

With just two years of her sentence left, she was assigned to work as a servant to a settler in Hobart Town, Tasmania, along with fellow prisoner Catherine Hagerty. In April 1806, Charlotte, her daughter, Catherine, and several male convicts traveled to Hobart Town on a ship called *Venus*. When the *Venus* docked at Port Dalrymple in June, the convicts mutinied, and Charlotte and her friend Catherine joined in with the male convicts to seize control of the ship. The pirate crew headed for New Zealand (even though nobody aboard really knew how to navigate the ship), and Charlotte, her child, Catherine, and two of the male convicts were dropped off at Rangihoua Bay in the Bay of Islands.

Charlotte and her compatriots built huts and lived on the shore of the island, but by 1807, Catherine Hagerty was dead, and the two men had fled. The *Venus* had long since been overtaken by South Sea islanders, who captured the crew and then burned the ship. Charlotte and her child stayed on Rangih-oua Bay, living alongside the Maori islanders. Twice she was offered passage back to Port Jackson, and twice she refused, saying that she preferred to die among the Maori.

What happened to Charlotte after 1807 isn't entirely clear. Some stories have her living with a Maori chieftain and bearing another child; in other stories the Maori turned on her, prompting her and her daughter to flee to Tonga; still other stories eventually place her in America, having stowed away on another ship. Whatever happened to her, she was quite possibly the first European woman to have lived in New Zealand, and one of New Zealand's first women pirates.

ANNE BONNY AND MARY READ

Anne Bonny, born in Ireland around 1700, is by all accounts one of the best known female pirates. She was disowned by her father when, as a young teen, she married a sailor named James Bonny; the newlyweds then left Ireland for the Bahamas. There, James worked as an informant, turning in pirates to the authorities for a tidy sum. While James confronted pirates, Anne befriended them: she became especially close with Jack Rackam, also known as "Calico Jack." Jack was a pirate who had sworn off pirating so as to receive amnesty from the Bahamian governor, who had promised not to prosecute any pirate who gave up his pirating ways. In 1719, however, Anne and Jack ran off together, and Jack promptly returned to pirating—this time with Anne by his side. She donned men's clothing in order to join the crew on his ship, the *Revenge,* and was so good at the work that she was accepted as a crewmate even by those men who discovered she was actually a woman.

When the *Revenge* took another ship during a raid and absorbed its crew, Anne discovered she was no longer the only woman on board: a woman by the name of Mary Read had also disguised herself as a man to be accepted as a pirate. Mary, born in London in the late 1600s, had spent nearly her whole life disguised as a man. Mary's mother had raised her as a boy almost from birth to keep the family out of poverty. (Mary's father died before she was born, and her brother, who would have been the only legal heir, also died. Back then, only men could inherit wealth, so baby Mary became baby Mark.) As a young girl living as a boy, Mary worked as a messenger and eventually enlisted in the infantry, fighting in Flanders and serving with distinction. She fell in love with another soldier (to whom she revealed her true gender), and they soon married, leaving the army to run a tavern called The Three Horseshoes. Sadly, her husband died in 1717, and Mary once again had to disguise herself as a man to earn a living. She put on her dead husband's clothes, enlisted in the army, and went to Holland. She found no adventure there, so she boarded a ship for the West Indies. That was when her ship was captured by the *Revenge,* and her life intersected with those of Calico Jack and his mistress, Anne Bonny.

Anne and Mary became close friends, and once Anne knew the truth about Mary, she swore that she would never reveal Mary's true identity. But Calico Jack, jealous of Anne's attention, grew suspicious of their friendship and demanded an explanation. Soon the secret was out, but, luckily for Mary, Jack was relieved and not angered to discover she was a woman. He allowed her to continue on the crew, and just as Anne had been accepted by her crewmates despite being female, Mary was accepted too. Unfortunately for the crew of the *Revenge,* the Bahamian governor was not so accepting of pirates who flouted amnesty agreements by returning to pirating after promising not to, and he issued a proclamation naming Jack Rackam, Anne Bonny, and Mary Read as "Pirates and Enemies to the Crown of Great Britain."

In 1720, the *Revenge* was attacked by a pirate-hunter eager to capture an enemy of the Crown. Calico Jack, along with nearly the entire crew, was drunk at the time, and the men quickly retreated to hide below deck and wait out the attack. Only Anne and Mary stayed above, fighting for the ship. It is said that Anne shouted to the crew, "If there's a man among ye, ye'll come out and fight like the men ye are thought to be!" Enraged by the crew's cowardice, Anne and Mary shot at them, killing one man and wounding several others, including Calico Jack. Despite the women's efforts, the ship was captured.

The crew was taken to Jamaica and tried for piracy in November of 1720. All of them were hanged, save for Anne and Mary, who were granted stays of execution due to the fact that they were both pregnant. Mary was brave in the face of her punishment, telling the court, "As to hanging, it is no great hardship. For were it not for that, every cowardly fellow would turn pirate and so unfit the sea, that men of courage must starve." But as it turned out, Mary never had to face the gallows: she died in prison of a fever. As for Anne, after the piracy trial, the historical record is silent. Rumors say alternately that she was hanged a year later; that she was given a reprieve; that she reconciled with the father who disowned her, or with her first husband, whom she had left; that she gave up the pirate's life and became instead a nun. We may never know for sure what happened to her.

CHING SHIH

Ching Shih—also known as Shi Xainggu, Cheng I Sao, Ching Yih Saou, or Zheng Yi Sao—ruled the South China Sea in the early 19th century, overseeing about 1,800 ships and 80,000 male and female pirates.

She became the commander of the infamous Red Flag Fleet of pirates after her husband Cheng Yi, the former commander from a long line of pirates, died in 1807; she went on to marry Chang Pao, formerly her husband's right-hand man. To say that Ching Shih ran a tight ship was an understatement: pirates who committed even innocuous offenses were beheaded. Her attitude in battle was even more intense, with hundreds of ships and thousands of pirates used to engage even a small target.

Ching Shih was also a ruthless businesswoman. She handled all business matters herself, and pirates not only needed her approval to embark on a raid, they were also required to surrender the entire haul to her. She diversified her business plan by expanding beyond the raiding of commercial ships, working with shadowy businessmen in the Guangdong salt trade to extort the local salt merchants. Ev-

---

BOOKS ABOUT PIRATES

Granuaile: Ireland's Pirate Queen, 1530–1603
by Anne Chambers
This book was made into a Broadway musical called *The Pirate Queen*. It tells the story of Grace O'Malley, also called Granuaile, a remarkable and notorious Irish pirate.

The Pirate Hunter: The True Story of Captain Kidd
by Richard Zacks
A vivid account of the often brutal nature of pirate life and politics in the seventeenth century.

Under The Black Flag: The Romance and the Reality of Life Among the Pirates
by David Cordingly
A look at the realities of the oft-romanticized pirate life through stories of real and fictitious pirates between 1650 and 1725.

The Pirates Own Book: Authentic Narratives of the Most Celebrated Sea Robbers
by Charles Ellms
Originally published in 1887, this book features pirates reporting in their own words.

Booty: Girl Pirates on the High Seas
by Sara Lorimer
Stories of twelve women pirates from the ninth century to the 1930s.

---

ery ship passing through her waters had to buy protection from her, and Ching Shih's fleet of mercenaries torched any vessel that refused to pay up.

The Red Flag Fleet under Ching Shih's rule could not be defeated—not by Chinese officials, not by the Portuguese navy, not by the British. But in 1810, amnesty was offered to all pirates, and Ching Shih took advantage of it, negotiating pardons for nearly all her troops. She retired with all her ill-gotten gains and ran a gambling house until her death in 1844.

RACHEL WALL

Rachel Schmidt was born in Carlisle, Pennsylvania, in 1760. When she was sixteen, she met George Wall, a former privateer who served in the Revolutionary War; against the wishes of her mother, she married him. The two moved to Boston, where George worked as a fisherman and Rachel worked as a maid in Beacon Hill. George, whom Rachel's mother had considered more than slightly shady to begin with, fell in with a rough crowd and gambled away what money they had. Unable to pay the rent, and lured by the fun of his fast-living fisherman friends, he hit upon pirating as the answer to their financial woes and convinced Rachel to join in.

George and Rachel stole a ship at Essex and began working as pirates off the Isle of Shoals. They would trick the passing ships by having the blue-eyed, brown-haired Rachel pose as a damsel in distress, standing at the ship's mast and screaming for help as the ships came near. Once the rescuing crew came aboard to help, George and his men would kill them, steal their booty, and sink their ship. Rachel and George were successful as pirates, capturing a dozen boats, murdering two dozen sailors, and stealing thousands of dollars in cash and valuables.

Their evil plan was cut short in 1782, when George, along with the rest of his crew, was drowned in a storm. Rachel, who really did need rescuing in that situation, was saved, brought ashore, and taken back to Boston, but it was hard to leave her pirating ways. She spent her days working as a maid, but by night she broke into the cabins of ships docked in Boston Harbor, stealing any goods she could get her hands on. Her luck ran out in 1789, when she was accused of robbery. At her trial, she admitted to being a pirate but refused to confess to being a murderess or a thief. She was convicted and sentenced to death by hanging. She died on October 8, 1789, the first and possibly the only woman pirate in all of New England, and the last woman to be hanged in Massachusetts.

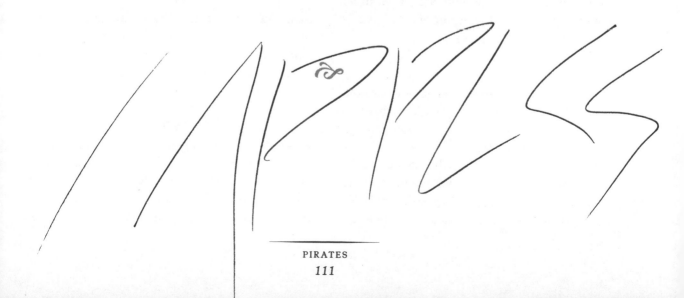

A Short History of
Women Inventors and Scientists

EVEN THOUGH it's said that "necessity is the mother of invention," women's contributions to inventing and science have been, in the past, often overlooked. It's likely women have been using their creativity and intelligence to engineer new ideas and products since the beginning of human experience, but nobody really kept track of such things until a few hundred years ago. Below we've assembled some of our favorite daring women inventors, scientists, and doctors—from Nobel Prize winners to crafters of practical devices, from women who revolutionized the way diapers were changed to women whose revolutionary ideas changed the world.

1715

Sybilla Masters becomes the first American woman inventor in recorded history, though in accordance with the laws of the time, her patent for "Cleansing Curing and Refining of Indian Corn Growing in the Plantations" was issued in her husband Thomas' name by the British courts. Her husband was issued a second patent for another of her inventions, entitled "Working and Weaving in a New Method, Palmetta Chip and Straw for Hats and Bonnets and other Improvements of that Ware."

1809

Mary Dixon Kies of Connecticut becomes the first U.S. woman to be issued a patent in her own name, for her invention of a process for weaving straw with silk or thread.

1870

Martha Knight patents a machine to produce flat-bottomed paper bags. She also becomes the first woman in the United States to fight and win a patent suit, when she defended her patent against a man who had stolen her design and filed for his own patent on it. He claimed a woman couldn't possibly have the mechanical knowledge needed to invent such a complex machine, but Knight was able to back up her claim. After her success, she went on to develop and patent several other machines, including rotary engines and automatic tools.

1875

Susan Taylor Converse of Woburn, Massachusetts, invents a one-piece, nonrestrictive flannel undergarment. It was patented by manufacturers George Frost and George Phelps and marketed to American women (eager to free themselves from traditional tightly bound corsets) as the "Emancipation Suit."

1876

Susan Hibbard patents the feather duster over protestations of her husband, George Hibbard, who claimed the invention was his. The patent court justly awarded ownership of the patent to her.

1876

Emeline Hart, a member of the Shaker community, invents and patents a commercial oven featuring pierced metal shelves for even heating, four separate oven compartments, isinglass (mica) windows, and a temperature gauge.

1885

Sarah E. Goode, born a slave in 1850, obtains the first patent by an African American woman inventor for her folding cabinet bed, a space-saver that when folded up could be used as a desk, complete with compartments for stationery and writing supplies.

1888

Miriam Benjamin, a Washington, DC, school-teacher, becomes the second black woman to receive a patent. Her invention, "The Gong and Signal Chair for Hotels," allowed hotel customers to summon a waiter from the comfort of their chairs and was adapted and used in the United States House of Representatives.

1889

Josephine Garis Cochran, of Shelbyville, Illinois, invents the first working automatic dishwasher. Her invention was first shown at the 1893 World's Fair in Chicago, Illinois, and eventually went on to become associated with the KitchenAid company.

1902

Ida Henrietta Hyde is named the first female member of the American Physiological Society. She was also the first woman to graduate from the University of Heidelberg and the first woman to do research at the Harvard Medical School. She went on to invent the microelectrode in the 1930s, which revolutionized the field of neurophysiology.

1903

Mary Anderson, of Alabama, invents the windshield wiper. Patented in 1905, windshield wipers became standard equipment on cars a decade later.

1903

Scientist **Marie Curie** is awarded the Nobel Prize in Physics for her discovery of the radioactive elements radium and polonium. She is awarded the Nobel Price for Chemistry in 1911, making her the first person to win two Nobel prizes.

PATENT FACTS

The U.S. Patent Act of 1790 allowed anyone to protect his or her invention with a patent. However, because in many states women could not legally own property independent of their husbands, many women inventors didn't apply for patents, or only did so under their husbands' names.

The majority of the U.S. origin patents held by women inventors are in chemical technologies.

About 35 percent of the women granted U.S. patents between 1977 and 1996 were from California, New York, or New Jersey.

With over 125 patents in areas related to organic compounds and textile processing, Dr. Giuliana Tesoro (born in 1921) is one of the most prolific scientists in the world.

1912

Beulah Henry of Memphis, Tennessee, receives her first patent, for an ice-cream freezer. She went on to create over 100 inventions, including the first bobbinless sewing machine, an umbrella with changeable covers, and continuously attached envelopes for mass mailings. She earned a total of forty-nine patents, the last one issued in 1970.

1914

Mary Phelps Jacob invents the modern bra. She was inspired to fashion a comfortable upper-body undergarment after becoming fed up with restrictive corsets. Her brassiere, made from two silk handkerchiefs and a ribbon, became so popular that after she patented the invention, she went on to sell it to the Warner Corset Company.

1930

Ruth Graves Wakefield, proprietor of the Toll House Inn in Whitman, Massachusetts, invents chocolate chips and chocolate chip cookies. Her cookie invention was called the Toll House Cookie and used broken-up bars of semi-sweet chocolate.

1932

Hattie Elizabeth Alexander, an American pediatrician and microbiologist, develops a serum to combat Hemophilus influenzae, which at that time had a fatality rate of 100 percent in infants. In 1964, she is the first woman to be elected president of the American Pediatric Society.

1935

Irene Joliot Curie, the French scientist and daughter of Marie Curie, is awarded the Nobel Prize for Chemistry with her husband, for their discovery of radioactivity, making the Curies the family with most Nobel laureates to date.

1938

Katherine Blodgett, American physicist, invents a micro-thin barium stearate film to make glass completely nonreflective and "invisible." Her invention has been used in eyeglasses, camera lenses, telescopes, microscopes, periscopes, and projector lenses.

1941

The actress **Hedy Lamarr** invents (along with George Anthiel) a "Secret Communications System" to help combat the Nazis in World War II.

1950

Marion Donovan invents the disposable diaper. When established manufacturers show little interest in this invention, she starts her own company, Donovan Enterprises, which she sells along with her diaper patents to Keko Corporation in 1951 for one million dollars.

1951

Bessie Nesmith invents Liquid Paper, a quick-drying white liquid painted onto paper to correct mistakes. She was a secretary in Texas when she hit upon her invention, which became so successful it grew into the Liquid Paper Company. (Fun fact: Her son, Michael Nesmith, grew up to be a member of the 1960s rock group the Monkees.)

1952

Mathematician and U.S. naval officer Rear Admiral **Grace Murray Hopper** invents the computer compiler, which revolutionized computer programming. She and her team also developed the first user-friendly business computer programming language, COBOL (COmmon Business-Oriented Language).

1953

Dr. Virginia Apgar, a professor of anesthesiology at the New York Columbia-Presbyterian Medical Center, devises the Apgar Scale, a test now used all over the world to determine the physical status of a newborn baby.

1956

Patsy Sherman invents Scotchgard. She was inducted into the Minnesota Inventors Hall of Fame in 1983. Patsy Sherman and her colleague Sam Smith jointly hold thirteen patents in fluorochemical polymers and polymerization processes.

1957

Rachel Fuller Brown and **Elizabeth Lee Hazen,** researchers for the New York Department of Health, develop the anti-fungal antibiotic drug nystatin. The scientists donated the royalties from their invention, totaling over $13 million dollars, to the nonprofit Research Corporation for the Advancement of Academic Scientific Study. They were inducted into the National Inventors Hall of Fame in 1994.

1958

Helen Free, a biochemist and expert on urinalysis, invents the home diabetes test. She and her husband were inducted to the National Inventors Hall of Fame in 2000.

1964

Dorothy Crowfoot Hodgkin, a British biochemist and crystallographer, wins the 1964 Nobel Prize in Chemistry for using X-ray techniques to determine the structures of biologically important molecules, including penicillin, vitamin B-12, vitamin D, and insulin.

1964

Chemist **Stephanie Louise Kwolek** invents Kevlar, a polymer fiber that is five times stronger than the same weight of steel and is now used in bulletproof vests, helmets, trampolines, tennis rackets, tires, and many other common objects.

1966

Lillian Gilbreth becomes the first woman to be elected to the National Academy of Engineering. This inventor, author, industrial engineer, industrial psychologist, and mother of twelve children patented many kitchen appliances, including an electric food mixer, shelves inside refrigerator doors, and the foot-pedal, lid-opening trash can. In her work on ergonomics, she interviewed over 4,000 women to design the proper height for stoves, sinks, and other kitchen fixtures.

1975

Physicist **Betsy Ancker-Johnson** becomes the fourth woman elected to the National Academy of Engineering, one of the highest honors an engineer can receive.

1975

Dr. Chien-Shiung Wu is elected the first woman president of the American Physical Society. The nuclear physicist studied beta-decay, worked on the Manhattan Project, and helped develop more sensitive Geiger counters.

1983

Barbara McClintock, an American scientist and cytogeneticist, becomes the first woman to win, unshared, the Nobel Prize in Physiology or Medicine, for her discovery of a genetic mechanism called transposition.

1984

Frances Gabe invents the self-cleaning house. Each room of the house has a 10-inch square "Cleaning / Drying / Heating / Cooling" device on the ceiling. At the push of a button, the cleaning unit sends a powerful spray of soapy water around the room and then rinses and blow-dries everything. Each room has a sloped floor to aid the water drainage, and all valuable objects and other things that should not get wet are stored under glass. The house, in the woods of Oregon, also has self-cleaning sinks, bathtubs, and toilets; a cupboard that doubles as a dishwasher; and closets that can clean and dry the clothes hung inside them.

1988

Gertrude Belle Elion is awarded the Nobel Prize in Physiology or Medicine. The biochemist invented many life-saving drugs, now commonly used to fight leukemia and other diseases.

1991

Chemist **Edith Flanigen** is awarded the Perkin Medal, the nation's most distinguished honor in applied chemistry. She was the first woman ever to have received the award. She retired in 1994, having earned 108 U.S. patents in the fields of petroleum research and product development.

1993

Ellen Ochoa becomes the first Hispanic female astronaut in space. The veteran of three space flights, who has logged over 719 hours in space, is also an electrical engineer with patents on high-tech optical recognition systems and optical systems for spacecraft automation.

1993

Betty Rozier and **Lisa Vallino,** a mother and daughter team, invent the intravenous catheter shield, making the use of IVs in hospitals safer and easier.

1995

Physical chemist **Isabella Helen Lugoski Karle** receives the National Medal of Science for her work on the structure of molecules.

1997

Dr. Rosalyn Sussman Yalow wins the Nobel Prize in Medicine for her 1959 invention of RIA, a revolutionary way to diagnose illness at the molecular level.

1999

Eye surgeon **Dr. Patricia Bath** becomes the first African American woman doctor to receive a patent for a medical invention: a device that removes cataracts with a fiberoptic laser.

Sleep Outs

A QUICK BACKYARD TENT can be made with just a rope, some stakes, and two tarps—big plastic, waterproof sheets essential to camping. First, string a rope between two branches on two different trees. Then stretch one tarp out on the ground and hang the second over the rope. Lastly, stake the four corners of the hanging tarp to the ground, using a hammer or a rock.

Store-bought tents are much larger than ever before, and come with flexible poles that fold into foot-long lengths and stow away in a nylon sack, making tent-pitching relatively simple. They also better protect us from the number one evil scourge of camping: bugs. (The number two evil scourge, should you ask, is poison ivy.) This leads to the prime rule of tents: Keep the zipper shut, because it's nearly impossible to shoo a mosquito out of your tent once it's in.

Before you pitch your tent, you may want to lay down an extra tarp to keep things extra clean and dry. (If you do, tuck the edges under so the tarp is slightly smaller than your tent.) Then set out the tent, and follow directions for inserting the poles. The fly, which protects from rain and dew, goes over the top of the tent and usually clips on, is staked to the ground, or both. Finally, bang the tent pegs into the ground, lest large gusts of wind send your tent soaring toward Kansas.

You've just made your home outdoors. Here are the basic furnishings:

- The sleeping bag. To make things a bit more comfortable, add a sleeping pad underneath and bring along a pillow or just a pillow case you can stuff with clothes. Sleeping pads have gotten softer, longer, and more elaborate, and can even involve air pumps, which your parents will undoubtedly appreciate if you invite them to sleep out with you. If you don't have a sleeping bag, a jellyroll does the trick. (That's when you roll your sheet and blanket together inside your pillowcase, and sling it over your shoulder for the journey to your tent.)

- Flashlight and bug spray. Enough said.

- A cooler. Filled with lots of drinking water and camping food staples like fresh apples, dried fruit, trail mix, and beef jerky. Marshmallows are a necessity, too, if a campfire's involved, as are the other ingredients for s'mores: chocolate bars and graham crackers.

The anti-litter mantra for sleeping and camping outdoors is: take it in, take it out. Since there are no garbage cans in the wilderness, bring a bag for your wrappers and other trash.

Once you've learned to pitch a tent and roll out the sleeping bag in your backyard, you can graduate to the full-out camping experience, where the refrigerator and indoor toilet are not close at hand.

Camping is gear-intensive and takes careful planning, especially if you're hiking, a few miles out. You must carry in several days' food and water in your backpack, not to mention a camping stove and mess kit, soap and a toothbrush, and so much more. When you're ready for a first experience at a wilderness campground, find a friend whose family are pros, and learn from them.

Whether you are in your backyard or the Rocky Mountains, remember the whole point of sleeping out is to breathe in the night air, listen to nature's songs, and drift off to sleep under the stars.

The Sit-Upon

THE SIT-UPON is a homemade waterproof cushion that makes the perfect seat for around the campfire, near a tent, your backyard, a sporting event, or any use you can imagine.

The Very Simple Sit-Upon

Needed:

✻ Plastic bags, the kind from the grocery store, about 12 inches by 12 inches with the handles cut off. Can be larger if you wish; any size bag will work.

✻ Lots of newspaper for the padding. The more, the comfier; try a pile 1½ to 2 inches high.

✻ Duct tape, or other strong and wide packing tape.

Stack the newspapers neatly. Cut or fold them to fit inside the plastic bag. Place them in the bag. Squeeze the air from the bag and fold it tightly around the newspaper. Use a second bag if necessary, to catch the other side of the newspaper stack. Tape all sides of the bag to keep out water and debris.

The Fancier Sit-Upon

Like most everything, a Sit-Upon can be made fancier and more decorative. The newspapers in the plastic bag can be covered with a waterproof cover.

Needed:

- The Very Simple Sit-Upon, as on previous page.
- Pieces of old wallpaper make an excellent cover, as do squares cut from a vinyl tablecloth, oilcloth, or a shower curtain. Be as creative as you'd like; the only guideline is that the material should be as waterproof, or water-resistant, as possible. Cut into 15 by 15 inch squares. If you prefer an even larger sit-upon, choose any measurement, cutting the squares $1\frac{1}{2}$–2 inches larger on each side than the newspaper-and-plastic sit-upon that will fit inside.
- A hole punch.
- Cord, twine, lanyard, or other strong string, measuring six or seven times the length of one side of the cover.

To Construct:

Cut the square covers to size. Punch holes every inch or so around all four edges of the covers, doing both at the same time, so the holes match up. Then place the Very Simple Sit-Upon between the two covers. To sew, string the cord through the holes using an overcast stitch (start on top, enter the hole, pull the cord through and out to the side, take it over to the top, and then sew in from the top of the next hole.) If needed, wrap tape around the end of the string to stiffen it and make it easier to sew. Leave extra cord at start and finish for the square knot at the end.

The Sit-Upon Traveler's Edition

You might be taking your Sit-Upon with you on a hike, or someplace where it would be handy not to have to hold it while you walk.

To make the fanny-pack carrier, procure a belt or rope that is long enough to tie around your waist. Before you sew the edges of the Sit-Upon, lay the rope or belt along one side. Stitch the rope or belt to the Sit-Upon as you sew that side of the cover. When you tie on the belt, the Sit-Upon will lay behind you as you walk.

For the messenger-bag alternative, attach an even longer piece of rope that will go over your head and over one shoulder, messenger-bag style, with the Sit-Upon resting across your back.

Lamp, Lantern, Flashlight

TAKE APART a flashlight and you'll see it's simply a battery-holding tube with an on-off switch at the side. You can build one with a quick trip to the hardware store.

WHAT YOU NEED:

* Some D-cell batteries
* Copper wire (long strands of aluminum foil may be substituted)
* Electrical tape
* Flashlight bulb
* An empty mason jar or any glass jar
* Possibly tape, aluminum foil, paper, empty toilet paper tube, scissors, or wire cutters

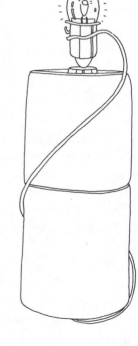

Start with a D-cell battery and a piece of copper wire about 10 inches long or so. With electrical tape, connect one end of the wire firmly to the bottom terminal of the battery. Wrap the other end of the wire tightly around the metal casing of a small flashlight light bulb. Position the light bulb so it touches the top of the battery. It should light up.

You've created a simple circuit that works when energy flows from the battery to the wire to the light bulb and back to the battery. If the bulb doesn't light, fiddle with the wires and connections until it does.

Once it lights, wrap the wire around the battery so the bulb stays put on top. That's the lamp. If the bottom wobbles, look for a holder. The electrical tape roll usually does a good job. If you spy an empty mason jar on the shelf, turn it upside down and place over the lamp and you have yourself a lantern, for indoors or out.

You'll notice that the light bulb isn't that bright, and that regular flashlights use two D-cell batteries. Stack a second battery on top of the first. Use as much electrical tape as necessary to bind the two batteries together. Place the bulb on the top battery and you'll see the difference. The bulb will become slightly hot; don't touch it and burn yourself.

To adapt into a flashlight, fashion a holder, whether it be poster board cut and taped to fit, a toilet-paper tube (lead the wire outside the tube), or lots more electrical wire wrapped around the two batteries (its bright colors provide decorative possibility).

Now for the on-off switch. For simplicity's sake, this can be accomplished by pulling the wire, forcing the bulb to move away from the battery and turn off. You can also cut the wire in half. To make the light go on, connect the wires and attach a sprig of electrical tape to hold them together. Remove the tape to detach the wires, break the circuit, and turn the flashlight off.

Explorers

AMELIA EARHART

Amelia Mary Earhart, born in 1897, was a pilot who received the Distinguished Flying Cross—and worldwide fame—for being the first woman to fly solo across the Atlantic Ocean. During World War I, she trained as a nurse's aide through the Red Cross and worked in a hospital in Ontario, Canada, until after the war ended in 1918. Around that time she saw her first flying exhibition, and she was captivated. She stood her ground when one of the pilots flew low to buzz the crowd, and later said of the experience, "I did not understand it at the time, but I believe that little red airplane said something to me as it swished by." The next year, she visited an airfield and was given a ride; a few hundred feet in the air and she was hooked. She began working odd jobs, including driving a truck and working at a telephone company, to earn money for flying lessons with female aviator Anita "Neta" Snook. After six months of lessons, she bought her own plane, a used yellow biplane that she nicknamed "The Canary," and in October 1922 she flew it to an altitude of 14,000 feet, setting a world record for women pilots. In May 1923, Earhart became the sixteenth woman to be issued a pilot's license by the Fédération Aéronautique Internationale (FAI). She not only broke aviation records, she also formed a women's fly-

> ### TWO OTHER NOTABLE WOMEN AVIATORS
>
> In 1921, Bessie Coleman became the first woman to earn an international pilot's license, and the first black woman to earn an aviator's license. One of thirteen children, Coleman discovered airplanes after graduating from high school, but she couldn't find an aviation school that would teach a black woman to fly. She went to Paris, where she was able to train and earn her license.
>
> Jacqueline Cochran, who in 1953 became the first woman to break the sound barrier, holds more distance and speed records than any pilot, male or female. She was the first woman to take off from and land on an aircraft carrier; to reach Mach 2; to fly a fixed-wing jet aircraft across the Atlantic; to enter the Bendix Trans-continental Race; and to pilot a bomber across the north Atlantic. She was the first pilot to make a blind landing, the first woman in Ohio's Aviation Hall of Fame, and the only woman to ever be president of the Fédération Aéronautique Internationale.

Amelia
Earhart

ing organization (The Nine-ty-Nines) and wrote best-selling books. She was the first woman to fly across the Atlantic, the first woman to fly across the Atlantic alone, and the first person, man or woman, to fly across the At-lantic alone twice. Earhart was also the first woman to fly an autogyro (a kind of flying craft) and the first person to cross the United States in an autogyro; the first person to fly solo across the Pacific between Hono-lulu and Oakland, Califor-nia; the first person to fly solo nonstop from Mexico City to Newark, New Jer-sey; and the first woman to fly nonstop coast-to-coast across the United States. Her final accomplishment was becoming an enduring mystery: at age thirty-nine, in 1937, Amelia Earhart disappeared over the Pacific Ocean during an attempt at making a circumnavigational flight. The official search efforts lasted nine days, but Amelia Earhart was never found.

Alexandra David-Néel

ALEXANDRA DAVID-NÉEL

Alexandra David-Néel, born Louise Eugénie Alexandrine Marie David (1868-1969), was the first European woman to travel to the for-bidden city of Lhasa, Tibet, in 1924, when it was still closed to foreigners. She was a French explorer, spiritualist, Buddhist, and writer, penning over thirty books on Eastern religion, philosophy, and the experiences she had on her travels. By the time she was eighteen, she

had already made solo trips to England, Spain, and Swit-zerland, and when she was twenty-two, she went to In-dia, returning to France only when she ran out of money. She married railroad engi-neer Philippe Néel in 1904, and in 1911 she returned to India to study Buddhism at the royal monastery of Sikkim, where she met the Crown Prince Sidkeon Tulku. In 1912 she met the thirteenth Dalai Lama twice and was able to ask him questions about Buddhism. She deepened her study of spirituality when she spent two years living in a cave in Sikkim, near the Tibetan border. It was there that she met the young Sikkimese monk Aphur Yongden, who became her lifelong traveling companion, and whom she would later adopt. The two trespassed into Ti-betan territory in 1916, meeting the Panchen Lama, but were evicted by British authorities. They left for Japan, traveled through China, and in 1924 arrived in Lhasa, Tibet, disguised as pilgrims. They lived there for two months. In 1928, Alexandra separated from her hus-band and settled in Digne, France, where she spent the next ten years writing books about her adventures. She reconciled with her hus-band and traveled again with her adopted son in 1937, at age sixty-nine, going through the Soviet Union to China, India, and eventually Tachienlu, where she continued her study of Tibetan literature. It was an arduous journey that took nearly ten years to complete. She

WOMEN EXPLORER TIMELINE

1704 Sarah Kemble Knight journeys on horseback, solo, from Boston to New York.

1876 Maria Spelternia is the first woman to cross Niagara Falls on a high wire.

1895 Annie Smith Peck becomes the first woman to climb the Matterhorn.

1901 Annie Taylor is the first person to go over Niagara Falls in a barrel.

1926 Gertrude Ederle is the first woman to swim the English Channel.

1947 Barbara Washburn becomes the first woman to climb Mt. McKinley.

1975 Junko Tabei of Japan is the first woman to climb Mt. Everest.

1976 Krystyna Choynowski-Liskiewicz of Poland is the first woman to sail around the world solo.

1979 Sylvia Earle is the first person in the world to dive to a depth of 1,250 feet.

1983 Sally Ride becomes the first American woman in space.

1984 Cosmonaut Svetlana Savitskaya becomes the first woman to walk in space.

1985 Tania Aebi, at nineteen, becomes the youngest person ever to sail alone around the world.

1985 Libby Riddles is the first woman to win the Iditarod Dog-Sled Race in Alaska.

1986 American Ann Bancroft becomes the first woman in the world to ski to the North Pole.

2001 Ann Bancroft and Norwegian Liv Arnesen are the first women to cross Antarctica on skis.

2005 Ellen MacArthur breaks the world's record for sailing solo around the world.

2007 Eighteen-year-old Samantha Larson becomes the youngest American to climb Mt. Everest and also the youngest person to climb the Seven Summits. (She and her father, Dr. David Larson, are the first father-daughter team to complete the Seven Summits.)

returned to Digne in 1946 to settle the estate of her husband, who had died in 1941, and again wrote books and gave lectures about what she had seen. Her last camping trip, at an Alpine lake in early winter, 2,240 meters above sea level, was at age eighty-two. She lived to be 100, dying just eighteen days before her 101st birthday.

Freya Stark

FREYA STARK

Dame Freya Madeleine Stark (1893–1993) was a British travel writer, explorer, and cartographer. She was one of the first Western women to travel the Arabian deserts, and was fluent in Arabic and several other languages. She traveled to Turkey, the Middle East, Greece, and Italy, but her passion was the Middle East. When she was thirty-five, she explored the forbidden territory of the Syrian Druze, traveling through "The Valley of the Assassins" before being thrown into a military prison. In the 1930s, she went to the outback of southern Arabia, where few Westerners had explored, and discovered the hidden routes of the ancient incense trade. During World War II, she joined the Ministry of Information and helped create propaganda to encourage Arabic support of the Allies. Even in her sixties, she continued her travels, retracing Alexander the Great's journeys into Asia and writing three more books based on

Florence Baker

those trips. By the time of her death, at age 100, she had written two dozen books on her adventures.

FLORENCE BAKER

Lady Florence Baker (1841–1916), was born Barbara Maria Szász. She was orphaned at seven, and at age seventeen she was due to be sold at an Ottoman slave market in Hungary when a thirty-eight-year-old English widower, Sam Baker, paid for her and rescued her from her captors. She was renamed Florence, and years later she became Samuel Baker's wife. They were a perfect match: Sam was an established explorer, and Florence a natural-born adventurer, and so the two of them traveled to Africa, searching for the source of the Nile and shooting big game. They managed to reach the secondary source of the Nile, which they called Lake Albert in honor of Queen Victoria's recently deceased husband, and then in 1865 they made the journey to Britain, where they married (and where she met her stepchildren, Sam's children by his first wife) and where Sam received a knighthood. They returned to Africa in 1870 to report on the slave trade along the Nile. Later they journeyed to India and Japan before returning to Britain. Florence outlived Sam by twenty-three years and was cared for in her old age by her stepchildren.

Building a Campfire

S ITTING AROUND A CAMPFIRE is probably one of the oldest human activities. Nowadays, unless you're on a solo wilderness hike, a campfire is less a tool of survival than a social event—a chance to sing songs and tell stories and be out in the dark in nature with friends.

A fire needs three things: fuel, heat, and air. The most common fuel is wood—main fuel such as logs cut from trees, and smaller fuel like tinder (twigs, strips of paper, or anything small that burns well) and kindling (branches and twigs about the size of a pencil and no thicker than a finger). Heat, which comes in the form of a flame or spark generated from matches, lighters, friction, or even focused sunlight, should be generated from the smaller fuel, which will then ignite the larger fuel. And of course, fire needs oxygen, so make sure that your fuel is packed loosely enough to allow for air circulation. When there's not enough oxygen present, the fire goes out, which is why dousing flames with water or smothering a small fire with sand extinguishes the flames.

What you'll need to build your own campfire

- A fire ring, a fire pit, a fire pan, or other temporary fire site
- Water or sand to extinguish the fire
- Tinder
- Kindling
- Main fuel (thick, dry wood and logs—the thicker the wood, the longer the fire will burn)
- Matches or a lighter

BUILDING THE FIRE

The first item of business when building a fire is deciding where to make it. Find a spot away from tents, trees with low-hanging branches, or other flammable elements. Once you've determined your location, you can begin to assemble your fire. Ideally, you can use an existing fire pit or fire ring. If there isn't one handy, you can create a fire site yourself. One way is to clear away a space on the ground, dig a pit, line it with small rocks, and then cover that area about half an inch deep with sand or aluminum foil. Otherwise you can use a fire pan, either a store-bought metal pan for the purpose of making fires, or any round metal surface, such as a pizza pan or a trash can lid.

Once you have your site established, place your tinder (the small pieces you collected) in a small pile in the middle of the fire site. Around that, place the kindling, taking care not to pack it too tightly, as your fire will need air in order to burn. Arrange the kindling in a kind of "teepee" format, as though you are creating a small tent around your tinder. Leave an opening so that you can light the tinder, and keep some of your kindling in reserve, so you can add more to the fire as it takes hold.

Using a match, lighter, or your preferred method of ignition, light the tinder and gently fan or blow on it until it becomes a strong flame and ignites the kindling around it. Once the kindling is burning, you can add your main fuel—those large, thick logs that will burn long and bright. Add more kindling to the fire to keep the fire burning, but take care to keep the fire manageable. Also make sure to place your wood carefully, and not just throw it onto the fire.

Once the fire is dwindling and it's time to put it out, use water to douse the flames completely. You can also use sand, if that is available, to smother the fire. Water is the most thorough method of putting out a fire, and when it comes to extinguishing fires, you definitely want to be thorough. Check to make sure there's nothing still smoldering, even when it seems like the fire is out. Everything—the fire site, the burned fuel, the area around the fire—should be cool to the touch before you leave. A fire that is carelessly put out, or not put out thoroughly enough, can flare up again.

WHAT TO DO AROUND THE FIRE

If you have some long sticks or branches handy, and a bag full of marshmallows or a pack of hotdogs, you can use them to cook over the open fire. Skewer a marshmallow and hold it over the flames to toast it—if you have some handy, graham crackers and a chocolate bar can turn toasty marshmallows into delicious s'mores. Or break out the hotdogs and buns, spear a dog with your branch, and roast it to perfection. A campfire is also the perfect setting for singing songs and telling ghost stories. Once you've had your fill of s'mores and hotdogs, crack open your copy of this book (which you of course packed with you on your camping trip) and check out the following pages for campfire song lyrics. Also, see our tips on telling spooky ghost stories later in this book.

Precautions and tips

- Check with the local firehouse or Park Ranger to see if campfires are permitted. Often you will need a permit to make any type of open fire outside—even in your own backyard.
- Clear the fire site before you start and after you're done. You don't want to leave a mess behind—or anything that could potentially start another fire.
- Never use flammable liquid or aerosols on a fire.
- Build your campfire far enough from your tent and other trees and low-hanging branches so that stray sparks won't start a fire outside the pit.
- Do not build your fire on peat or grass.
- Don't pick up burning wood.
- Wind can spread fire quickly, so make sure to build your fire in a place shielded from gusts.

Campfire Songs

SINGING SONGS TOGETHER is a fun way to pass the time around a campfire, on the school bus, or in the car ("John Jacob Jingleheimer Schmidt" is especially fantastic for annoying your parents on long trips). Here are some of our favorites from summer camp and family sing-alongs.

In addition to these, other great campfire songs include "Puff the Magic Dragon," "Do A Deer," "I've Been Working on the Railroad," "Take Me Out To The Ballgame," "Goodnight Irene," "Michael Row Your Boat Ashore," "There Is a Hole in the Bucket," "On Top of Spaghetti," "Red River Valley," and "This Land is Your Land."

JOHN JACOB JINGLEHEIMER SCHMIDT

John Jacob Jingleheimer Schmidt,
His name is my name, too.
Whenever we go out,
The people always shout,
There goes John Jacob Jingleheimer
*   Schmidt.*
Dah dah dah dah, dah dah dah!
John Jacob Jingleheimer Schmidt,
His name is my name, too.
Whenever we go out,
The people always shout,
There goes John Jacob Jingleheimer
*   Schmidt.*
Dah dah dah dah, dah dah dah!
(repeat endlessly)

(variations: sing the verse as soft as possible and the "dah dah dah" part as loud as possible;

sing the song in an "opera voice"; sing the song in an impossibly slow tempo, then sing it again incredibly fast; after singing the song over and over, stop as if you're done, then bust out another round when your friends/parents/camp counselors least expect it.)

KUMBAYA

Kumbayah my Lord, kumbayah
(repeat three times)
Oh Lord, kumbayah

Someone's singing Lord, kumbaya
(repeat three times)
Oh Lord, kumbayah

Someone's laughing, Lord, kumbaya
(repeat three times)
Oh Lord, kumbaya

Someone's crying, Lord, kumbaya
(repeat three times)
Oh Lord, kumbaya

Someone's praying, Lord, kumbaya
(repeat three times)
Oh Lord, kumbaya

Someone's sleeping, Lord, kumbaya
(repeat three times)
Oh Lord, kumbaya
Oh Lord, kumbaya

GREEN GRASS GREW ALL AROUND

There was a hole (There was a hole)
in the middle of the ground
    (in the middle of the ground)
The prettiest hole (the prettiest hole)
that you ever did see
    (that you ever did see)
Well the hole in the ground
And the green grass grew all around
    and around
And the green grass grew all around.

And in this hole (repeat)
there was a root (repeat)
The prettiest root (repeat)
that you ever did see (repeat)
Well the root in the hole
And the hole in the ground
And the green grass grew all around
    and around
And the green grass grew all around.

And on this root (repeat)
there was a tree (repeat)
The prettiest tree (repeat)
that you ever did see (repeat)
Well the tree on the root
And the root in the hole
And the hole in the ground
And the green grass grew all around
    and around
And the green grass grew all around.

And on this tree (repeat)
there was a branch (repeat)
The prettiest branch (repeat)
that you ever did see (repeat)
Well the branch on the tree
And the tree on the root
And the root in the hole
And the hole in the ground

And the green grass grew all around
    and around
And the green grass grew all around.

And on this branch (repeat)
there was twig (repeat)
The prettiest twig (repeat)
that you ever did see (repeat)
Well the twig on the branch
And the branch on the tree
And the tree on the root
And the root in the hole
And the hole in the ground
And the green grass grew all around
    and around
And the green grass grew all around.

And on this twig (repeat)
there was a nest (repeat)
The prettiest nest (repeat)
that you ever did see (repeat)
Well the nest on the twig
And the twig on the branch
And the branch on the tree
And the tree on the root
And the root in the hole
And the hole in the ground
And the green grass grew all around
    and around
And the green grass grew all around.

And in this nest (repeat)
there was an egg (repeat)
The prettiest egg (repeat)
that you ever did see (repeat)
Well the egg in the nest
And the nest on the twig
And the twig on the branch
And the branch on the tree
And the tree on the root
And the root in the hole
And the hole in the ground

And the green grass grew all around
    and around
And the green grass grew all around.

And in this egg (repeat)
there was a bird (repeat)
The prettiest bird (repeat)
that you ever did see (repeat)
Well the bird on the egg
And the egg in the nest
And the nest on the twig
And the twig on the branch
And the branch on the tree
And the tree on the root
And the root in the hole
And the hole in the ground
And the green grass grew all around
    and around
And the green grass grew all around.

And on this bird (repeat)
there was a wing (repeat)
The prettiest wing (repeat)
that you ever did see (repeat)
Well the wing on the bird
And the bird on the egg
And the egg in the nest
And the nest on the twig
And the twig on the branch
And the branch on the tree
And the tree on the root
And the root in the hole
And the hole in the ground
And the green grass grew all around
    and around
And the green grass grew all around.

And on this wing (repeat)
there was a feather (repeat)
The prettiest feather (repeat)
that you ever did see (repeat)
Well the feather on the wing

And the wing on the bird
And the bird on the egg
And the egg in the nest
And the nest on the twig
And the twig on the branch
And the branch on the tree
And the tree on the root
And the root in the hole
And the hole in the ground
And the green grass grew all around
    and around
And the green grass grew all around.

DARLING CLEMENTINE

In a cavern, in a canyon,
Excavating for a mine,
Dwelt a miner, forty-niner,
And his daughter Clementine.

Refrain:
    Oh my darling, oh my darling,
    Oh my darling Clementine
    You are lost and gone forever,
    Dreadful sorry, Clementine.

    Light she was, and like a fairy,
    And her shoes were number nine,
    Herring boxes without topses,
    Sandals were for Clementine.

Refrain

    Walking lightly as a fairy,
    Though her shoes were number nine,
    Sometimes tripping, lightly skipping,
    Lovely girl, my Clementine.

Refrain

Drove she ducklings to the water
Ev'ry morning just at nine,
Hit her foot against a splinter,
Fell into the foaming brine.

Refrain

Ruby lips above the water,
Blowing bubbles soft and fine,
But alas, I was no swimmer,
Neither was my Clementine.

Refrain

In a churchyard near the canyon,
Where the myrtle doth entwine,
There grow rosies and some posies,
Fertilized by Clementine.

Refrain

Then, the miner, forty-niner,
Soon began to fret and pine,
Thought he oughter join his daughter,
So he's now with Clementine.

Refrain

I'm so lonely, lost without her,
Wish I'd had a fishing line,
Which I might have cast about her,
Might have saved my Clementine.

Refrain

In my dreams she still doth haunt me,
Robed in garments soaked with brine,
Then she rises from the waters,
And I kiss my Clementine.

Refrain

DOWN BY THE BAY
(call and response)

Down by the bay (Down by the bay)
Where the watermelons grow
        (Where the watermelons grow)
Back to my home (Back to my home)
I dare not go (I dare not go)
For if I do (For if I do)
My mother will say (My mother will say)
"Did you ever see a whale
With a polka dot tail?"
Down by the bay.

Down by the bay (Down by the bay)
Where the watermelons grow
        (Where the watermelons grow)
Back to my home (Back to my home)
I dare not go (I dare not go)
For if I do (For if I do)
My mother will say (My mother will say)
"Did you ever see a bear
Combing his hair?"
Down by the bay.

Down by the bay (Down by the bay)
Where the watermelons grow
        (Where the watermelons grow)
Back to my home (Back to my home)
I dare not go (I dare not go)
For if I do (For if I do)
My mother will say (My mother will say)
"Did you ever see a moose
Kissing a goose?"
Down by the bay.

Down by the bay (Down by the bay)
Where the watermelons grow
        (Where the watermelons grow)
Back to my home (Back to my home)
I dare not go (I dare not go)

For if I do (For if I do)
My mother will say (My mother will say)
"Did you ever see a fly
Wearing a tie?"
Down by the bay.

Down by the bay (Down by the bay)
Where the watermelons grow
    (Where the watermelons grow)
Back to my home (Back to my home)
I dare not go (I dare not go)
For if I do (For if I do)
My mother will say (My mother will say)
"Did you ever see some llamas
Wearing pajamas?"
Down by the bay.

Down by the bay (Down by the bay)
Where the watermelons grow
    (Where the watermelons grow)
Back to my home (Back to my home)
I dare not go (I dare not go)
For if I do (For if I do)
My mother will say (My mother will say)
"Did you ever have a time
When you couldn't make a rhyme?"
Down by the bay.

ERIE CANAL

I've got a mule,
Her name is Sal,
Fifteen years on the Erie Canal.
She's a good old worker
And a good old pal,
Fifteen years on the Erie Canal.
We've hauled some barges in our day
Filled with lumber, coal and hay
And ev'ry inch of the way I know
From Albany to Buffalo.

Low Bridge, ev'rybody down,
For it's Low Bridge,
We're coming to a town!
You can always tell your neighbor,
You can always tell your pal,
If you've ever navigated
On the Erie Canal.
Low Bridge, ev'rybody down,
For it's Low Bridge,
We're coming to a town!
You can always tell your neighbor,
You can always tell your pal,
If you've ever navigated
On the Erie Canal.

We better get along
On our way, old gal,
Fifteen miles on the Erie Canal.
Cause you bet your life
I'd never part with Sal,
Fifteen miles on the Erie Canal.
Git up there, mule, here comes a lock,
We'll make Rome 'bout six o'clock.
One more trip and back we'll go
Right back home to Buffalo.

Low Bridge, ev'rybody down,
For it's Low Bridge,
We're coming to a town!
You can always tell your neighbor,
You can always tell your pal,
If you've ever navigated
On the Erie Canal.
Low Bridge, ev'rybody down,
For it's Low Bridge,
We're coming to a town!
You can always tell your neighbor,
You can always tell your pal,
If you've ever navigated
On the Erie Canal.

Coolest Paper Airplane Ever

ORDINARY PAPER AIRPLANES that look like jumbo jets and fighters are one thing. This airplane is something else altogether. We don't have an official name for it (why not make one up yourself?), but this folded wonder is something special.

HOW TO MAKE IT

A Take a piece of ordinary 8½″ × 11″ paper. Hold the paper so it's tall rather than wide, and fold the page in half lengthwise. Crease the center, using your fingernail. Unfold. That's fold #1.

B Fold the left side in to touch the center crease. You've just made a new left edge. That's fold #2.

C Fold the new left edge to touch the center crease, creating again a new left edge (fold #3). **D** Then fold the edge over the center line, and crease the top with your fingernail (fold #4).

So you can make your airplane into a circle, soften the paper. Wrap it around your hand, or pull it against the edge of a desk or table, as when you curl ribbon **E**. This breaks down the fibers in the paper. Soon the paper will be very pliable, and you can bend it into a cylinder shape, with the folded edge on the inside. Slip one end of the fold under the other, about an inch or so, to hold everything in place **F**. Add tape to secure. It looks like a squat tube, and the folded edge is the front of the plane **G**.

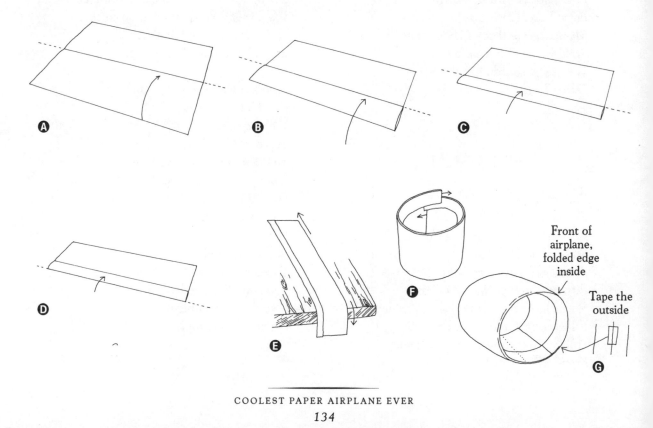

Front of airplane, folded edge inside

Tape the outside

HOW TO FLY IT

To fly, the plane needs power and spin. Hold it fully in your palm, facing forward. As you pull your arm back, ready to throw, flick your wrist and fingers. But, here's the trick: do not let your wrist or hand bend downward. Keep them straight up. This gives the plane spiral spin.

Be ready to use your determination and patience, as it may take some practice to perfect this technique. Once you have it down, though, your unique airplane will fly beautifully. And you'll use this same technique for tossing a football, so here you've learned two skills in one.

WHY IT WORKS

Airplanes—real and paper—stay in the air for two reasons. Understand these reasons, including a few technical terms, and you will possess the mental tools to design many a flying object.

Reason 1: The lift force is greater than the airplane's weight.

Lift is what keeps the plane up in the air. It happens when the air pressure pushing the plane up is more powerful than the pressure of air pushing the plane down. Lift counters the force of gravity, which always pulls objects back down to Earth.

Reason 2: The thrust force is stronger than drag.

Thrust gets the plane moving forward. In paper airplanes, thrust is the power of your toss. In real airplanes, designers keep materials as light as possible and use powerful engines. The heavier a plane is, the more thrust it needs.

Thrust counteracts drag, which is any quality that makes it harder to cut through the air (like sideways gravity). Here's a great way to explain drag: Turn your hand flat, palm down, and wave it back and forth, slicing the air horizontally. Then turn your hand sideways, thumb-up, pinkie-down, and wave it through the air, as if you are clapping or fanning yourself. Feel how much more air is in your way when your hand is sideways? That's drag. For airplanes, drag is the force of the air the plane must push through to get where it wants to go.

Airplanes fly when engines and wing design counter gravity and drag. Paper airplanes fly when you thrust them with gusto that overcomes gravity, and when they have a shape that is low-drag and can gracefully slice through the air. This creative design accomplishes everything you need to soar your new air flyer.

Abigail Adams' Letters with John Adams

L ETTER WRITING, real letter writing, is a storied part of American life. Friends and spouses built relationships, and political thinkers changed the world, by expressing their thoughts and sending them through the mail.

The correspondence between Abigail Adams and John Adams during the American Revolution tops the list of our country's famous letter writing, both for the couple's modern relationship and the important political events they discussed. The relationship was modern because John so valued the opinions of Abigail, who was well educated and believed learned women had much to contribute to society. The events they discussed were so important because they shaped the birth of our nation, and John would later become the second President of the United States.

Abigail Adams, born Abigail Smith, came of age as a member of the wealthy Smiths of Massachusetts Bay Colony, related to the Quincys on her mother's side. Many generations of men in her family had studied at Harvard, but, as the college didn't accept girls, Abigail's mother and grandmother tutored her at home in math, literature, and writing.

John Adams was the son of a shoemaker from Braintree, Massachusetts, and his mother helped run their family's farm. He earned a law degree from Harvard. They met because Abigail's sister Mary courted and then married John's close friend Richard Cranch. Several years later, in 1764, John and Abigail married; Abigail was a few days shy of twenty, and John, several years older, had just turned twenty-nine.

John's passion for reading, like Abigail's, drew them together, and they formed an extraordinary bond. They pored over important books of the time, by such authors as Adam Smith, Mary Wollstonecraft, and Jean-Jacques Rousseau, discussing them at length and, at least on John's part, making voluminous comments in the margins. As John grew more involved in public life, the couple developed relationships with important thinkers, including Abigail's famous friendship with Mercy Otis Warren, who lived in nearby Plymouth and documented the American Revolution.

Between the years 1774 and 1783, John spent long stretches away from Abigail. He worked with the Continental Congress in Philadelphia to draft the Declaration of Independence. He went to France to join Benjamin Franklin in crafting the Treaty of Paris, which ended the War for Independence (also known as the American Revolution). Abigail stayed in Massachusetts to tend their four children and their home.

During this period, Franklin was the Postmaster General, multiplying post offices and introducing the stagecoach as a means of delivering mail reliably between the emerging States. John and Abigail made good use of this new postal system. We know of 284 letters between them from this time, thanks to their grandson, Charles Francis Adams, who kept and edited the letters, releasing them for the nation's centennial in 1876. Throughout their lives, they wrote more than 1,100 letters to each other.

John to Abigail, Philadelphia, 29 March 1776

I give you joy of Boston and Charlestown, once more the Habitations of Americans. Am waiting with great Impatience for Letters from you, which I know will contain many Particulars. We are taking Precautions to defend every Place that is in [Danger]—The Carolinas, Virginia, N. York, Canada. I can think of nothing but fortifying Boston Harbour.

Abigail to John, Braintree, 31 March 1776

I long to hear that you have declared an independency—and, by the way in the new Code of Laws which I suppose it will be necessary for you to make I desire you would Remember the Ladies, and be more generous and favourable to them than your ancestors. Do not put such unlimited power in the hands of the Husbands . . . That your Sex are Naturally Tyrannical is a Truth so thoroughly established as to admit of no dispute, but such of you as wish to be happy willingly give up the harsh title of Master for the more tender and endearing one of Friend.

John to Abigail, Philadelphia, 3 July 1776

Your Favour of June 17 dated at Plymouth, was handed me, by yesterday's Post. I was much pleased to find that you had taken a journey to Plymouth, to see your Friends in the long Absence of one whom you may wish to see. The Excursion will be an Amusement, and will serve your Health. How happy would it have made me to have taken this journey with you?

Yesterday the greatest Question was decided, which ever was debated in America, and a greater perhaps, never was or will be decided among Men. A Resolution was passed without one dissenting Colony "that these united Colonies, are, and of right ought to be free and independent States, and as such, they have, and of Right ought to have full Power to make War, conclude Peace, establish Commerce, and to do all the other Acts and Things, which other States may rightfully do." You will see in a few days a Declaration setting forth the Causes, which have impell'd Us to this mighty Revolution, and the Reasons which will justify it, in the Sight of God and Man. A Plan of Confederation will be taken up in a few days.

Abigail to John, Boston, Sunday, 14 July 1776

By yesterday's post I received two Letters dated 3 and 4 of July and tho your Letters never fail to give me pleasure, be the subject what it will, yet it was greatly heightened by the prospect of the future happiness and glory of our Country; nor am I a little Gratified when I reflect that a person so nearly connected with me has had the Honour of being a principal actor, in laying a foundation for its future Greatness. May the foundation of our new constitution, be justice, Truth and Righteousness. Like the wise Mans house may it be founded upon those Rocks and then neither storms or tempests will overthrow it.

. . . all our Friends desire to be rememberd to you and foremost in that Number stands your Portia.*

---

* The wife of the Roman Republican Senator, Brutus. Abigail often signed her letters with that name.

Clubhouses and Forts

EVERY GIRL SHOULD have a clubhouse or fort of her own, and here are some ideas for making one. Several weekends may be spent sweating over the plans for a long-lasting clubhouse of wood beams and nails and real roofing tile. But there are ways to make quicker work of this endeavor.

QUICK FORT

With 6-foot metal garden stakes, you can construct an outdoor clubhouse or fort almost immediately. Garden stakes haven't the stability of wood beams, but the swiftness with which the walls go up easily makes up for that. Five stakes will do the trick.

The stakes come with footholds. Stand on them and they should push into the ground rather effortlessly. If there's a problem, a rubber mallet or a taller person can help; if it proves intractable, that may mean that there's a rock in the ground and you need to move the stake. Use one stake for each of the four corners. Set the fifth stake along one of the sides to create a space for the door.

Wrap the whole structure, except the doorway, with chicken wire or deer netting, or lighter-weight bird netting. Garden stakes have notches in them and you can attach the materials to the notches to form the basic wall. (Trim the bottom of the netting neatly at ground level, lest chipmunks and other small animals inadvertently get tangled inside; this happened to us.)

To add privacy, use burlap or a white painter's dropcloth as a second layer, or cardboard (you'll figure a way to attach these to the stakes). If you want a ceiling, the burlap or dropcloth will help, although they won't be waterproof, and rainwater will collect on top. You can use a tarp, but the plastic can make the inside very hot. You'll figure it out. A sixth stake, taller than the rest, can be added to the center to create a sloped ceiling. From here, use twine, rope, duct tape, wire, scissors, sticks, cardboard, plywood, and any other wood scraps you can scare up to build walls, create windows, ceilings and floors, and otherwise make it your own. There are no rules; it's your fort.

LEAN-TO

A lean-to is a very primitive form of shelter that's little more than a wall or two and a roof. It's meant to keep you safe from the worst of the rain and wind, and often leans into existing walls or fences, hence the name. Find any tucked-in spot or corner, rig a tarp roof with some ropes knotted to trees, and lean a side of plywood against the house. Build up the front with branches, odd pieces of old fence your neighbors left out on trash day, or even a picnic table turned on its side.

INDOOR FORT

The classic formula of couch cushions, blankets, and the backs of sofas and chairs is a good start for an indoor fort, as is throwing blankets over the top of the dining room table (stacks of books on top help keep them in position).

You can improve upon these traditional forts. To make a hanging wall, screw a line of hooks or eyebolts into the ceiling. Run picture-hanging wire or clothesline rope through them. Attach clips or clothespins, and from these, dangle all sorts of sheets, light blankets, large swaths of cloth, holiday lights, or your mother's oversized scarves to create a different kind of fort.

Daisy Chains and Ivy Crowns

TO MAKE A DAISY CHAIN, pick twenty or so daisies. Near the bottom of the stem, but not too close, slit a slender lengthwise hole with your fingernail. Thread the next daisy through this hole until the flower head rests on the first stem. Take care not to pull too hard; daisy chains are lovely, but fragile. If you want to see lots of stem between the daisies, make the slit farther from the blossom. If you prefer a tightly packed garland, slit closer to the flower itself, and pinch off the rest of the stem. Continue until the daisy chain seems long enough fit around the top of your head. To finish, tangle the last stem around the first daisy, and tie it off with a longish piece of grass. Put the chain of daisies on your head, close your eyes, and make a wish. You can also make them into a necklace, or preserve them by leaving them to dry in the back of a dark closet shelf.

In ancient Greece and Rome, circles of ivy, laurel, and olive branches crowned the victories of athletes and marked as excellent the pursuits of scholars, artists, and soldiers. As the ancient Greek playwright Euripedes wrote in *The Bacchantes*: "Come, let us crown your head with ivy."

Ivy crowns are incredibly simple to make, too. Ivy has large leaves and long, thick stems. Start with a piece of ivy many times the circumference of your head. Mark off the size you want and then start twining the ivy around itself, until the crown is full. Tuck the end under and don your new headpiece.

God's Eyes / Ojos de Dios

OJOS DE DIOS (oh-hoes day DEE-oes), or "God's Eyes," are yarn and stick creations traditionally made by the Huichol Indians. The Huichol, who live in the southern mountains of Mexico's Sierra Madre Occidental Range, call their God's eyes *sikuli,* which means "the power to see and understand things unknown." The design, created by yarn wrapped around the intersection of two sticks at right angles, forms the shape of a cross that is meant to symbolize the four elements: earth, air, fire, and water. When a child is born, a *sikuli* or *ojo de dios* is made by the father; every year on the child's birthday, another one is woven, until the child reaches the age of five. The *ojos de dios* are bound together and are kept throughout the person's life as a means of guaranteeing health and well being.

An *ojo de dios* can be as simple or complex as you like. Create one using different colored yarns; attach feathers or other decorations on the ends; or make two and combine them to form an eight-sided god's eye.

To make a basic four-sided *ojo de dios,* you'll need:

❖ Multi-colored yarn, or different colors of yarn

❖ 2 Popsicle sticks, or other sticks (chopsticks, wooden skewers that aren't sharp—you can even use toothpicks to make tiny ones)

❖ Glue

Take your base sticks and cross them over each other. If glue is handy, a small dab on the sticks helps to secure their intersection.

With your yarn, make a knot and tighten it where the sticks intersect, to hold the cross shape. (Don't cut the yarn from the skein—you can cut it later, when you determine whether or not you'll be switching yarns or weaving until you reach the end of the sticks.) The knot should face the back side of your *ojo de dios*.

Wind the yarn in a figure eight around the intersection, up and down, then from left to right, to stabilize the sticks and cover the middle.

Once you have the intersection of the sticks covered and they are secure, weave the yarn by bringing it over a stick, then looping it around, and continuing the same over-around pattern on the other sticks.

You can continue in this pattern until you reach the end of the sticks. However, you may also mix things up by reversing the direction—if you're weaving in a clockwise pattern, switch to counter-clockwise after a few rows, and vice versa. This provides a varied texture of recessed and raised rows.

If you wish to change yarn colors, make sure to tie the new yarn to the previous yarn so that the knot is on the back side of the god's eye. Clip off any excess yarn only at the end, when you're done.

When you are about a half-inch from the ends of the sticks, cut your yarn, leaving about 8 inches of yarn at the end. Tie a knot in the yarn close to the stick to end the weaving. You can use the "tail" of yarn to hang up the god's eye when you are done.

If you have feathers, bells, charms, or other decorations, you can glue or tie them to the four ends of the sticks.

GOD'S EYES / OJOS DE DIOS

Writing Letters

WRITING GOOD OLD-FASHIONED letters has somewhat fallen out of style, with the advent of technology and the tempting immediacy of email, instant messaging, and texting. But there are still circumstances where a typed or handwritten formal letter is required that calls for something more personal and professional than CU L8R, KTHXBYE!

The Thank-You Letter

When you receive a gift or other form of hospitality, it is polite to send a thank-you note or letter in response—and it is most polite to have the letter be handwritten. Begin by greeting the person and then start the letter right away by saying "Thank you." You don't have to get fancy with an introduction; the whole point of the letter is to say thanks. So start with that: A simple "thank you for your gift" will do. Then, mention how the gift will come in handy for you (or, if writing in response to a favor or gesture of hospitality, how useful their actions were to you: "I really ap-

---

LETTER WRITING TIPS

from *Eight or Nine Wise Words About Letter Writing*, published in 1890 by Charles Dodgson (the pseudonym of *Alice in Wonderland* author Lewis Carroll)

Here is a golden Rule to begin with. Write legibly. The average temper of the human race would be perceptibly sweetened, if everybody obeyed this Rule! A great deal of the bad writing in the world comes simply from writing too quickly.

. . . My second Rule is, don't fill more than a page and a half with apologies for not having written sooner! The best subject, to begin with, is your friend's last letter. Write with the letter open before you. Answer his questions, and make any remarks his letter suggests. Then go on to what you want to say yourself. This arrangement is more courteous, and pleasanter for the reader, than to fill the letter with your own invaluable remarks, and then hastily answer your friend's questions in a postscript. Your friend is much more likely to enjoy your wit, after his own anxiety for information has been satisfied.

A few more Rules may fitly be given here, for correspondence that has unfortunately become controversial. One is, don't repeat yourself. When once you have said your say, fully and clearly, on a certain point, and have failed to convince your friend, drop that subject: to repeat your argu-

---

preciated being able to stay with you when I visited New York last week."). If you can, it's always nice to mention looking forward to seeing them at some future event. Then say thanks again and wrap up the letter by signing off with "love," "with gratitude," "yours truly," or your preferred way of closing. A brief example:

Dear Aunt Jessie,

Thanks so much for the fantastic roller skates! I can't wait to use them at the skating party next month. When you come visit over the summer, maybe we can go skating together. Thanks again!

Love,
Emi

ments, all over again, will simply lead to his doing the same; and so you will go on, like a Circulating Decimal. Did you ever know a Circulating Decimal come to an end?

Another Rule is, when you have written a letter that you feel may possibly irritate your friend, however necessary you may have felt it to so express yourself, put it aside till the next day. Then read it over again, and fancy it addressed to yourself. This will often lead to your writing it all over again, taking out a lot of the vinegar and pepper, and putting in honey instead, and thus making a much more palatable dish of it! . . .

My fifth Rule is, if your friend makes a severe remark, either leave it unnoticed, or make your reply distinctly less severe: and if he makes a friendly remark, tending towards "making up" the little difference that has arisen between you, let your reply be distinctly more friendly. . . .

My sixth Rule (and my last remark about controversial correspondence) is, don't try to have the last word! How many a controversy would be nipped in the bud, if each was anxious to let the other have the last word! . . .

My seventh Rule is, if it should ever occur to you to write, jestingly, in dispraise of your friend, be sure you exaggerate enough to make the jesting obvious: a word spoken in jest, but taken as earnest, may lead to very serious consequences. I have known it to lead to the breaking-off of a friendship. . . .

My eighth Rule. When you say, in your letter, "I enclose cheque for £5," or "I enclose John's letter for you to see," leave off writing for a moment—go and get the document referred to—and put it into the envelope. Otherwise, you are pretty certain to find it lying about, after the Post has gone!

Personal Letters

Longer than a thank-you note, a personal letter (or social note) has five parts and can be handwritten or typed.

The Heading: This consists of your address and the date, each on its own line, indented to the middle of the page. After the heading, skip a line. If you are writing on preaddressed stationery, just write the date.

The Greeting: This can be formal or informal—beginning with "Dear," or just writing the person's name (or even simply, "Hi"). Either way, the greeting ends with a comma, and you skip a line afterwards.

The Body: The main text of your letter. In this kind of letter, the beginning of each paragraph is indented, and no lines are skipped between paragraphs.

The Closing: After the body, skip a line and write your closing line, which is usually just a few words like "All best," "Sincerely," "Looking forward to seeing you," "With love," etc. Whatever you write, this line should end in a comma and should be indented the same amount as your heading.

The Signature Line: This is where you sign your name. If you are typing the letter, skip three lines after the closing and type your name there, then put your handwritten signature just above your printed name. If your letter contains a postscript, skip a line after the signature line, begin the postscript by writing "P.S." and end it with your initials.

An additional postscript should be noted as P.P.S. rather than P.S.S., as it is a post (after) postscript and not a postscript script.

Reading Tide Charts

EVERY BEACH on the planet has a unique cycle of tides, and thus its own tide chart. Look for one in the local newspaper, or at a nearby marine store or surf shop.

Reading tide charts helps you pick the best times to go fishing, crabbing, or surfing. With boats, it helps to know what the water is doing, as paddling a canoe into a creek when the tide is trending low is a great deal harder than, say, swooping in with the rush of a coming high tide.

Tide charts come in different forms. Once you know the basics of high and low tide, water height, and moon phases, you'll be able to read any tide chart.

FISHING: A NEW YORK TIDE CHART

This simple tide chart from Southold, New York, a fishing area, predicts tides for the first nine days of August 2006.

August 2006		
Day	**A.M.**	**P.M.**
1	4:25	5:02
2 ◖	5:19	5:51
3	6:17	6:43
4	7:17	7:36
5	8:15	8:28
6	9:08	9:20
7	9:59	10:11
8	10:47	11:01
9 ○	11:35	11:52

Plum Gut: minus 1 hour, 5 minutes.
Shinnecock Canal: plus 50 minutes.
Sag Harbor: minus 40 minutes.

● new moon
◖ first-quarter moon (waxing moon)
○ full moon
◗ three-quarter moon (waning moon)

This is a high tide chart because it's primarily for fishing. When you fish, you wake up in the morning and before even opening your eyes you wonder, "When's high tide?" High tide is when the fish are out and moving, whether on the incoming flood tide or the outgoing ebb tide. At least that's what you hope. A small-print note at the bottom of this chart mentions that low tide comes about six hours later.

The names and times beneath the chart explain how to calculate the tides for nearby beaches, since every bay and inlet will have slightly different tides.

Notice several things. First, high tide comes 50–60 minutes later each day. The tidal day is slightly longer than our regular 24-hour day, at 24 hours and 50 minutes. (Why? Because our regular days rely on the earth rotating around the sun, and tidal days rely on the moon rotating around the earth, which takes 50 minutes longer.)

Second, the tide chart lists the phases of the moon. During the first few days of August the moon will wax to a first-quarter crescent. The moon will be full by August 9th—and with any luck it will be a bulgingly orange late-summer moon, rising low and pumpkin-like in the sky.

Tide charts show the moon phases because tides are caused by the pull of the moon's gravity—and the sun's gravity—on earth's water. It's an awe-inspiring concept that the moon's pull—even at 239,000 miles away—is so strong that it can control our ocean waters. Next time you are at the seashore, with the waves lapping at your feet, you can observe the power of the moon.

More practically, tide charts list moon phases because it matters when you go fishing. High tides are higher during the new moon and the full moon. These are called spring tides. People who fish don't much like spring tides—the water level is higher, and silt and sand from the bottom churn up and make the water murky. The result: Fish can't see the bait on your line, and that's no good if you're trying to catch them. Some people will plan their fishing trips way in advance using the moon phases of tide charts, knowing to avoid the few days around new and full moon.

The opposite of high water spring tides are neap tides. They happen during the first and third quarters, when the moon waxes and wanes. There's less water at high tide, and slightly less current.

There are two more moon trivia words you'll want to know: a crescent moon is anything less than half, and any phase slightly-more-than-half to just-under-whole is a gibbous moon.

CRABBING: A CAPE COD TIDE CHART

Date	Day	Time	Height	Time	Height	Time	Height	Time	Height
7/10/07	Mon	5:18 AM	0.0 L	11:10 AM	2.1 H	5:09 PM	0.4 L	11:24 PM	3.1 H

The next chart shows low tide, which makes it helpful for crabbing and beachcombing. The initial *Time* column lists the first tide after midnight, no matter whether it's low or high. Set your alarm clock, because that first tide comes in at 5:18 in the morning. The next column, *Height,* tells that the height of the water is 0.0, or average water level, and that the tide is L, or low. If you're not an early riser, look for the second low tide of the day. Reading from left to right, you'll see a high tide at 11:10 A.M., and then another low tide at 5:09 P.M. That's the one you want.

At 4:00, then, head for the beach. The hours just before and after low tide are especially good for beachcombing and crabbing. Low tide is also a good time to see birds along the shore. They'll be there picking at small animals and crabs that were left on the beach after the water receded.

SURFING: A COSTA RICAN TIDE CHART

This chart from Nosara, on the Pacific coast of Costa Rica shows the tides in 24-hour time, which is used throughout the world, especially in non-English-speaking nations. (In the United States, 24-hour time is called Military Time, since that's where it's most often used.)

Hours 13–24 are equivalent to 1 P.M.–12 A.M. on the 12-hour clock, so to convert, just subtract 12. Thus high tide at 16:13 is 4:13 P.M., and low tide at 22:21 is 10:21 P.M.

Date	Day	High Time/Height	Low Time/Height	High Time/Height	Low Time/Height
February 19, 2007	Monday	03:49/ 9.56 ft.	09:55/ -1.01 ft.	16:13/10.05 ft.	22:21/-0.96 ft.

Globe-trotting surfers, even American ones, must get used to 24-hour time so they can easily read the tide charts as they travel across continents, surfboard under arm, seeking the perfect wave. This chart does a great job of showing how high the waves will swell. For surfing, the combination of tide, wind, and swell determine whether any given surf spot, or break, will have rideable waves at any given hour.

For example, a reef break means the waves are created (or break) when incoming water hits a reef that comes up from the ocean floor. At low tide, a reef break may give an excellent ride, on fast, steep waves. At high tide, however, the water may be so deep that it does not make strong impact with the reef, and this results in barely any wave to ride at all.

On the other hand, a beach break means waves form off large sandbars underwater. Often a higher tide is best for these surf spots, because they need the force of a lot of water rushing over the sandbars to make long, rounded waves.

BOATING: A CALIFORNIA TIDE CHART

By now you're an old hand at reading charts. The last chart comes from Half Moon Bay, California. It includes longitude (37.5017° N) and latitude (122.4866° W), which you'll want to know if you're taking a boat out on the Pacific Ocean and using your navigation equipment to find your way back to shore.

The chart also gives times for sunrise and sunset, so you can get out on the water early and you'll know when you'd best return to the marina before nightfall. Notice, too, how the date is notated, as year-month-day; that's standard tide-chart notation.

Tuesday 2007-07-03			
Sunrise	5:53 AM	Sunset	8:34 PM
Moonrise	11:04 PM	Moonset	9:00 AM
High Tide		12:13 AM	5.76 feet
Low Tide		7:22 AM	-1.00 feet
High Tide		2:29 PM	4.59 feet
Low Tide		7:23 PM	2.93 feet

Making a Seine Net

A SEINE NET is just a long fishing net used for dipping into the ocean to collect and study marine life.

WHAT YOU NEED

◆ Seine netting, often sold as minnow seine. Ours is 4 feet deep and 15 feet long, with a ⅛ inch mesh, but these measurements are flexible, depending on how big or small you want your net to be, and what's available. It's nice when the net has a bit of Styrofoam at the top edge to keep it afloat, and some metal weights on the bottom to help it sink. Some seine netting comes this way. It can be bought at marina shops.

◆ Two 4-foot poles or lengths of wood, to control the net, and to wind it up when you're done.

◆ A large bucket, to keep your catch in water and to store the net.

Attach the shorter sides of the net to the poles. Do this by drilling a hole at each end of the pole (they might do this for you at a marine shop, if you ask). Or, use a Swiss Army knife to whittle a channel at each end of the pole, and wrap the rope there. Or forget the whittling and just wrap the rope very tight. If there's not already a thin rope at each corner of your net, find a small length of light rope or twine and use that.

One person stands at the shoreline and holds a pole. The other person holds the second pole and wades into the water until the net is fully extended. Keep the top at water level and let the rest of the net sink. This is where the metal weights come in handy.

After a time, walk back to shore in a sweeping motion, keeping the net fully extended so that when you get to shore, you'll be a net-length away from your friend or parent holding the other end of the net. As you get closer to shore, slowly change the net direction from vertical—where it is catching fish and other creatures—to horizontal, where you can scoop them up and lay out the net on the wet sand to see what you've got.

If you're not catching much of anything, change your position, or your location, or trawl some, walking around with the net stretched, giving more fish more time to end up in your hands. Both of you can walk farther into the river or surf.

Toss back everything within a few minutes so that your spider crabs, starfish, striped bass, tiny snails, and shiny minnows can continue their lives at sea. Many towns have laws that tell you to toss the sea animals back where they belong, or else you will suffer a stiff penalty. (Some beaches ban large-scale commercial seine netting, but these small ones are usually okay.)

If you're going fishing, though, those little minnows are good bait.

HOW TO CLEAN A SHELL

When your beachcombing and seine netting land you choice shells, here are two ways to clean them and turn them into long lasting treasures.

1. Bury the shells 12 inches underground in your backyard and let the earthworms and all those soil bacteria do their work. This can take several months.

2. Boil for five minutes in a large pot, in a solution that is half water and half bleach. You'll see when the shells are clean. Take them out carefully with tongs, or ask someone older to do it, because the water is scalding. Rinse with cool water.

Women Spies

From the Revolutionary War to World War II

UNLIKELY SPIES

Julia Child

Before she became a famous chef, Julia Child was a spy. She worked for the Office of Strategic Services, a precursor of the CIA, and went undercover to Sri Lanka (called Ceylon at the time) with top security clearance. In World War II, she helped the U.S. Navy solve their problem with sharks—who had a habit of setting off underwater explosive devices, foiling U.S. plans to blow up German U-boats—by developing shark repellent. She met diplomat Paul Child when she was working for the OSS, and they married. When Paul was posted to Paris, Julia trained at the famous Cordon Bleu cooking school and began her second life as a chef.

Hedy Lamarr

Hedwig Eva Maria Kiesler is best known as Hedy Lamarr, movie star of the 1930s and '40s. But she was also an inventor who patented an idea that was to become the key to modern wireless communication. During World War II, Hedy, along with George Antheil, invented a way to make military communications secure through frequency-hopping, an early form of a technology called spread spectrum. Hedy's status as a beautiful and successful actress provided her with the perfect cover: she was able to visit a variety of venues on tour and interact with many people, none

Hedy Lamarr

of whom suspected that the stunning starlet might be listening closely and thinking of ways to help the U.S. cause.

Josephine Baker

Josephine Baker was another World War II–era entertainer whose celebrity status helped distract from her mission as a spy. Josephine was an African American dancer and singer

Josephine Baker

from St. Louis, Missouri. She found some success in the United States, but was hindered by racial prejudice. She moved to Paris when she was nineteen and became an international star. When World War II began, she started working as an undercover operative for the French Resistance, transporting orders and maps from the Resistance into countries occupied by Germany. Her fame and renown made it easy for her to pass unsuspected, as foreign officials were thrilled to meet such a famous performer, but she wrote the secret information in disappearing ink on her sheet music just in case.

The Girl Guides

During the First World War, the Girl Guides—the British version of Girl Scouts—were used as couriers for secret messages by MI-5, Britain's counter-intelligence agency. Messengers were needed to work in the War Office at the time, and at first Boy Scouts were used. But they proved to be difficult to manage, so Girl Guides were asked to serve instead. The girls, most of whom were between fourteen and eighteen years old, ran messages and patrolled on the roof; for their efforts they were paid ten shillings a week, plus food. Like all employees of MI-5, they took a pledge of secrecy. But unlike many employees of MI-5, they were among the least likely spies to arouse suspicion.

REVOLUTIONARY WAR SPIES

During the Revolutionary War, many women up and down the East Coast passed important information along to General Washington at Valley Forge. Philadelphian Lydia Barrington Darragh spied on the British for American officers. Two Loyalists (citizens loyal to Britain), "Miss Jenny" and Ann Bates, spied on the Americans for the British. Ann Trotter Bailey carried messages across enemy territory in 1774, as did Sarah Bradlee Fulton, nicknamed the "mother of the Boston Tea Party"; Emily Geiger rode fifty miles through enemy territory to deliver information to General Sumter. The anonymous spy "355"—a numerical code that meant "lady" or "woman"—was a member of the Culper Ring, a New York–based secret spy organization. She was seized by the British in 1780 and died on a prison ship—but not before she named Benedict Arnold as a potential traitor.

CIVIL WAR SPIES

Pauline Cushman was an actress who worked as a Union spy. She was captured with incriminating papers and sentenced to be executed, but was rescued just three days prior to her hanging. President Abraham Lincoln gave her the honorary commission of Major, and she toured the country for years, telling of her exploits spying for the Union.

Mary Elizabeth Bowser was a freed slave who served as a maid in the Confederate White House. Her servile status—and the mistaken assumption that she could neither read nor write—allowed her to be present for key conversations but largely ignored. She smuggled important information and papers to the Union Army.

Sarah Emma Edmonds disguised herself as a man so that she could serve in the Union Army, where she became known for her bravery and chameleonlike ability to blend in, whether she was masquerading as a black slave or "disguised" as a woman. She successfully fought for the Union as Frank Thompson until she became sick with malaria. She checked herself into a private hospital to avoid having to reveal her true identity. But when she learned that "Frank Thompson" was listed as a deserter, she came clean, and worked as a nurse for the Union—under her real name—until the end of the war. She wrote about her experiences in a memoir titled *Nurse and Spy in the Union Army*.

Rose O'Neal Greenhow spied so well for the Confederacy that Jefferson Davis credited her with winning the battle of Manassas. She was imprisoned twice, once in her own home, and the second time with her eight-year-old daughter in Washington, D.C.'s Old Capital Prison. After she was released from prison, she was exiled to the Confederate states, where Jefferson Davis enlisted her as a courier to Europe.

Nancy Hart served as a Confederate spy, carrying messages between the southern armies. When she was twenty, she was captured by the Union; she was able to escape after shooting one of her guards with his own weapon.

Elizabeth Van Lew was a spy for the North. She realized when she visited Union prisoners held by the Confederates in Richmond that they were excellent sources of information, as they had been marched through Confederate lines. Over the next four years, she worked as a spy, bringing food and clothing to Union prisoners and smuggling out information. For her efforts, she was made Postmaster of Richmond by General Grant.

Dr. Mary Edwards Walker was an abolitionist, a prisoner of war, a feminist, and a surgeon who dressed as a man and worked as a physician and spy for the Union. She is the only woman ever to receive the Congressional Medal of Honor.

Harriet Tubman is most famous for her work in freeing slaves, but she also served with the Union Army in South Carolina, organizing a spy network and leading expeditions in addition to fighting as a soldier, working as a cook and laundress, and aiding the wounded as a nurse. Through her experience with the Underground Railroad, leading more than 300 slaves to freedom, she came to know the landscape intimately and was able to recruit former slaves to be her eyes and ears, reporting on movements of the Confederate troops and scouting out the rebel camps. In 1863 she went on a gunboat raid, with Colonel James Montgomery and several black soldiers, that ultimately freed more than 700 slaves, thanks to the inside information from Harriet's scouts.

Ginnie and Lottie Moon were sisters who spied for the Confederates during the Civil War. Lottie began her career as a spy delivering messages for an underground Confederate organization at the behest of her husband. Ginnie too delivered messages over Union lines, on the pretext that she was meeting a beau. Ginnie and the girls' mother risked considerable danger when they accepted a mission to retrieve sensitive papers and supplies from the

Knights of the Golden Circle in Ohio. They were apprehended by Union agents; Ginnie was able to swallow the most important written information they carried, but their cache of medical supplies was discovered and confiscated, and they were put under house arrest. Lottie came in disguise to plead with General Burnside—a former beau—for their release, but instead she was placed under arrest with her sister and mother. Ultimately the charges were dropped. Lottie eventually became a journalist, and in the 1920s Ginnie headed to Hollywood, where she had bit parts in several movies—none of them with plots as exciting as the sisters' real life adventures.

WORLD WAR I SPIES

Two famous and controversial World War I women spies, both of whom were executed, were Mata Hari (born Margaretha Geertruida Zelle McLeod) and Edith Cavell. Mata Hari was a dancer who used her vocation as a cover for her spy work for the Germans. She was shot by the French as a spy in 1917. Edith Cavell was a British nurse who worked in Belgium during the war. She secretly helped British, French, and Belgian soldiers escape from behind the German lines, and she hid refugees in the nursing school she ran. By 1915 she had helped more than 200 British, French, and Belgian soldiers, but the Germans grew suspicious and arrested her. She was executed by firing squad.

WORLD WAR II SPIES

Virginia Hall, an American originally from Baltimore, Maryland, spied for the French during World War II. She was chased by the Nazis over the Pyrenees Mountains into Spain and eluded them, even though she had a wooden leg. After escaping, she trained as a radio operator and transferred to the OSS, America's secret spy agency. In 1943 she returned to France as an undercover spy, gathering intelligence, helping to coordinate air drops in support of D-Day, and working with the French underground to disrupt German communications. After the war, Virginia was awarded America's Distinguished Service Cross, the only American civilian woman to receive such an honor. She continued to work for the OSS, and later the CIA, until her retirement in 1966.

Princess Noor-un-nisa Inayat Khan was an author and a heroine of the French Resistance. The Princess trained as a wireless operator in Great Britain and was sent into occupied France as a spy with the code name "Madeleine." She became the sole communications link between her unit of the French Resistance and home base before she was captured by the Gestapo and executed.

Violette Bushell Szabo was recruited and trained by the British Special Operations Executive after her husband, a member of the French Foreign Legion, was killed in North Africa. She was sent to France, where she was captured during a shoot-out. She refused to give up her information and was sent to the Ravensbruck concentration camp, where she was eventually killed. She was awarded the George Cross and the Croix de Guerre posthumously in 1946.

Amy Elizabeth Thorpe, also known as Betty Pack and "Code Name Cynthia," was an American spy first recruited by the British secret service and later by the American OSS.

She is probably best remembered for her procurement of French naval codes, necessary to the Allies' invasion of North Africa, which she accomplished by tricking a man connected to the Vichy French Embassy into giving them to her. Not only did she steal French naval code books from the safe in his locked room, she also stole his heart: after the war they were married, and they spent the rest of their lives together.

❧

How To Be a Spy

THE WORD "spy" comes to us from ancient words meaning "to look at or watch." And indeed, despite the modern movie emphasis on technology and machines as integral to a spy's bag of tricks, in essence what makes an excellent spy is her ability to watch, pay attention, look, and learn.

TOP-SECRET COMMUNICATION

Girl Scout whistle and hand signals
These secret signals have been used by the Girl Scouts since before World War I. You can use them to alert or direct your spy team when you are out in the field.

Whistle signals
- One long blast means "silence / alert / listen for next signal"
- A succession of long slow blasts means "go out / get farther away" or "advance / extend / scatter"
- A succession of quick short blasts means "rally / close in / come together/ fall in"
- Alternate short and long blasts mean "alarm / look out / be ready / man your alarm posts"

Hand signals
- Advance / forward: Swing the arm from rear to front, below the shoulder
- Retreat: Circle the arm above the head
- Halt: Raise the arm to full extension above the head.

Secret codes
A code is a way to send a message while keeping it a secret from someone who isn't supposed to know about it. Codes can be easy or complicated—the trick is to make sure the person on the receiving end of your secret message has the key to decode it without making it too easy for anyone else to crack. Here are a few simple codes you can use.

- Write each word backwards
- Read every second letter
- Use numbers for letters (A=1, B=2, C=3, etc.)
- Reverse the alphabet (A=Z, B=Y, C=X, etc.)
- Sliding scale alphabet (move the alphabet by one letter: A=B, B=C, C=D, etc.)
- Use invisible ink (write with lemon or lime juice; after it dries hold the paper up to a light source to read the message).
- Pigpen code: Each letter is represented by the part of the "pigpen" that surrounds it. If it's the second letter in the box, then it has a dot in the middle.

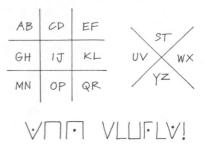

PIGPEN CODE

TOP SECRET!

TOOLS

In movies, spies often use high-tech equipment to accomplish covert tasks, but all spies are grounded in the basics: good, old-fashioned, low-tech observation that can be performed without the aid of any fancy hardware. In World War II, women spies used something called an "escape and evasion" scarf—these were scarves with maps printed on one side, so that any agent who needed to find an escape route or nearby town or road had a map that was easy to get to but not so easily detectable by someone else. You can make your own with an old scarf or other fabric and a permanent marker (providing you get permission to mark up the scarf first).

A few other tools that would be good for a spy to have handy are things like binoculars; a small notepad and pen; walkie-talkie; magnifying glass; Swiss Army knife; hat or wig for quick disguising; sneakers or other quiet shoes for stealth walking; clothes in dark or subdued colors. The best tools of all, though, are your eyes, your ears, and your ingenuity. Pay attention to everything that's going on around you, blend into your surroundings so you can observe without being noticed, look for subtle clues to tell you more about what's happening, and write everything down. With any luck, you'll not only become a great spy, you'll be on your way to becoming a great writer. You know, just in case the espionage career doesn't work out.

YOUR SPY TEAM

The life of a spy can be a lonely one, with so much secrecy and subterfuge and no one to share it with at the risk of blowing your cover. It's much more fun to operate within a spy ring and work as a team to accomplish your undercover goals. On a team, spies can have specific tasks or areas of expertise, and of course code names.

The Agent-in-Charge: This is the head spy. She is responsible for directing, planning, and organizing the mission. All team members report to her.

The Scout: This is the person who scopes out the physical landscape to see if it's safe for the rest of the team to move in. She goes ahead of the team when they are out in the field, and no one moves in without a signal from her. She should have excellent eyesight and hearing and should be an expert on geography and the outdoors.

The Tracker: This person acts as the "trigger," the spy whose job it is to monitor the target of investigation. She tracks and observes the suspect's actions and alerts the rest of the team when the suspect is in range.

The Techie: This is the group's technology maven. She knows about computers, tools, and gadgets, from using them to fixing them to creating new ones. She is the one who draws up any maps, plans, or charts, and also keeps notes about the mission.

The Wheel Artist: This is the person who organizes the get-away, or who can use her wheels to accomplish any stealth maneuver. If she can drive, that's great, but she doesn't have to be commandeering a car. The wheels can be anything that gets your spy team out of the field in a timely manner. She can oversee a fleet of scooters, ride another spy to safety on her bike, or even accomplish a sensitive mission lightning-quick on her skateboard or roller skates.

The Stealth Master: This is a small, quiet person who can sneak into tight places and generally move around unnoticed. It helps if she is also a master of disguise, and an illusionist, able to use card and magic tricks for purposes of distraction.

The Social Engineer: This person is brave, chatty, outgoing, and able to interact with suspects and others to extract information. She can be the public face of the team while other team members gather evidence or perform surveillance, using her considerable social skills to both distract and engage.

Of course, no matter what her specialty, a spy should be able to: appraise a situation, balance, bluff, climb, be diplomatic, escape when necessary, gather information, hide, intuit, be insightful, jump, listen, move silently, read lips and body language, respond quickly, tumble, transform, and, above all, be levelheaded.

After each mission, all members of the spy team should rendezvous at an agreed-upon meeting place or secret hideout, where they will report to the agent-in-charge and exchange information. No matter what her role on the team is, a spy should always note suspicious activity, try not to be seen or heard, cover her tracks, and never reveal her true identity to outsiders.

SPY LINGO

Acorn
Someone who is performing an intelligence function.

Agent
A person officially employed by an intelligence service. (Also undercover agent: *a secret agent;* deep-cover agent: *an agent under permanent cover;* double agent: *an agent simultaneously working for two enemies;* agent-in-charge: *the head agent.)*

Babysitter
Bodyguard.

Blowback
Unexpected negative consequences of spying.

Blown
Detected, as in "your cover is blown."

Bona Fides
Proof of a person's claimed identity.

Brush Contact or Brush Pass
Brief contact between two agents who are passing information, documents, or equipment.

Burn notice
An official statement from an intelligence agency saying that an individual or group is an unreliable source.

Chicken feed
Low-grade information given by a double agent to an adversary to build the credibility of the double agent.

Cobbler
Spy who creates false passports, visas, diplomas, and other documents.

Comm
Small note or other written communication.

Cover
A secret identity.

Dead drop
A secret hiding place somewhere in public where communications, documents, or equipment are placed for another agent to collect.

Doppelganger
A decoy or look-alike.

E&E
Escape and evasion.

Ears only
Material too secret to commit to writing.

Eyes only
Documents too secret to be talked about.

Floater
A person used occasionally or even unknowingly for an intelligence operation.

Friend
An agent or informant providing information.

Front
A legitimate-appearing business created to provide cover for spies and their operations.

Ghoul
Agent who searches obituaries and graveyards for names to be used by agents.

Honey Pot/Honey Trap
Slang for use of men or women to trap a person using affection or romance.

Informant
A person who provides intelligence to the surveillance team.

Joe
A deep-cover agent.

Legend
Background story or documents to support your cover.

Letterbox
A person who acts as a go-between.

Mole
An agent who penetrates enemy organizations.

Naked
A spy operating without cover or backup.

Paroles
Passwords agents use to identify each other.

Peep
Photographer.

Pocket Litter
Items in a spy's pocket (receipts, coins, etc.) that add authenticity to her identity.

Ring
A network of spies or agents.

Safehouse
A secret hideout.

Sanitize
To "clean up" a report or other document to hide sensitive information.

Sleeper agents
Spies who are placed in a target country or organization, not to undertake an immediate mission, but to be activated later.

Spook
Another word for spy.

Target
The person being spied on. (Also hard target: A target who actively maintains secrecy and doesn't let on that she is aware of the surveillance team.)

The Take
Information gathered by spying.

Trigger
An agent who watches for the target and alerts the rest of the surveillance team when the target is spotted.

Unsub
An unknown subject in a surveillance operation.

Undercover
Disguising your identity, or using an assumed identity, in order to learn secret information.

Walk-ins
Agents who offer their services.

Window Dressing
Like pocket litter, this is extra information included in a cover story to help make it seem more real.

Climbing

JO MARCH, the heroine of *Little Women,* declares that no girl can be her friend who refuses to climb trees and leap fences. Louisa May Alcott wrote that book in 1868. British author Charlotte Yonge wrote in the late 1800s that girls showed "a wholesome delight in rushing about at full speed, playing at active games, climbing trees, rowing boats, making dirt-pies and the like." Award-winning actress Beah Richards penned a poem in 1951 called "Keep Climbing, Girls," in which she urged girls to "climb right up to the toppermost bough of the very tallest tree." To keep you in tune with your adventuresome foremothers, here are some tree-climbing tips that Jo March might have suggested to new friends, along with some ideas for shimmying up ropes.

TREES

The key to successful tree climbing is understanding that you are not pulling yourself up vertically; tree-climbing is hard enough without trying to entirely defy gravity. You are sturdily pushing the plane of your body into the tree diagonally while your arms reach around the trunk, and shimmying up, inch by inch. Tree climbing doesn't necessary cause injury, but falling out of one surely does. Climb with caution.

ROPES

Read these directions and trust that when you're standing in front of a rope in gym class, they will make good sense. Here's how to tackle the miraculous feat that is rope climbing:

♦ Grab the rope with your hands, and pull the rope down as you jump up.

♦ This sounds odd, but it works: Right after you grab and jump, grapple the rope with your legs so that one ankle wraps around the rope, then end in a position where your two feet hold tightly against the rope. You are up.

♦ To climb: Hold tight with your legs and stretch your arms, one after the other, as high up as possible on the rope. Now comes the secret trick. Use your stomach muscles, or abdominals, to crunch your legs up toward your arms. You may not move far, but keep shimmying, inch by inch. Reach your arms, crunch with your stomach, and grab the rope with your feet. As your torso gets stronger, and your arms and legs, too, rope climbing will become much easier, and all the more gratifying.

Climbing walls at gyms are a great place to practice. Keep climbing, but remember once you go up, you still have to figure out how to safely get down!

Queens of the Ancient World III

Cleopatra of Egypt: Queen of Kings

CLEOPATRA VII was the last of a long line of ancient Egyptian queens. She ruled Egypt for twenty-one years, from 51 to 30 BC, and was famously linked with the Roman generals Julius Caesar and Marc Antony. It was the Greek historian Plutarch (46–122 AD), however, who turned Cleopatra into a legend. Plutarch reports that although she was not conventionally beautiful, Cleopatra's persona was bewitching and irresistible. The sound of her voice brought pleasure, like an instrument of many strings, and she was intelligent, charming, witty, and outrageous.

Cleopatra's City: Alexandria

Cleopatra was born in 70 BC, one of King Ptolemy XII's six children. She came of age in Alexandria, Egypt's capital city and a bustling port on the Mediterranean Sea. The Pharos Lighthouse, one of the Seven Wonders of the Ancient World, gleamed over Alexandria's harbor and welcomed ships and people to this vibrant and cosmopolitan city. The celebrated mathematician Euclid had lived there and published his thirteen-volume *Elements,* filled with all the known principles of geometry and algebra. Alexandria's marble Library was the largest in the world, and philosophers in the Greek tradition of Aristotle and Plato roamed Alexandria's streets.

Egypt was wealthy, besides. Craftspeople produced glass, metal, papyrus writing sheets, and cloth. The fertile countryside produced grain that was shipped all over the Mediterranean region to make bread.

Queen of a Threatened Nation

Despite this grand history, in the 50s BC, Egypt was struggling. Rome's armies had already conquered most of the nearby nations. Egypt remained independent, but no one knew how long it would be able to survive Rome's expansion. Cleopatra's father, Ptolemy XII, had made an unequal alliance with Rome. He had lost several territories, like the island of Cyprus, and faced political rebellions from his own children.

When her father died in 51 BC, Cleopatra was only eighteen years old. Still, she was named his successor, along with her twelve-year-old brother, Ptolemy XIII. Throughout her long reign, she vowed to protect Egypt's independence. She did so until the bitter end with the help of a strong navy and her romantic alliances with the most powerful men of Rome.

Cleopatra and Julius Caesar

When Cleopatra became queen, Rome was embroiled in its own civil drama. Rome had long been a republic that prided itself in democracy and in measured rule by its Senate. Now, ambitious men were taking over. Three of these power-hungry men—Julius Caesar, Pompey, and Crassus—secretively joined forces as The First Triumvirate in 60 BC to gain more control. Soon though, they began to fight each other.

In 48 BC, Julius Caesar conquered Gaul, just north of Italy. Flush with the thrill of victory, he led his soldiers back to Rome. There was a tradition that no general's soldiers were to cross the Rubicon River into the city, but Caesar ignored that and brought his army across. He waged armed civil war against his now-enemy Pompey and the Senate, on land

and at sea. Pompey fled to Alexandria, with Caesar in pursuit.

Alexandria had fallen into violence. Cleopatra and her brother were quarreling, as each tried to steal power from the other, and there was no law and order. The sibling rulers looked to Roman rivals Pompey and Julius Caesar, knowing they needed to make an alliance, and not knowing which of them they should trust.

As the fighting in Alexandria worsened, Cleopatra fled the city with her younger sister. At the same time, one of her brother's fighters, feeling emboldened, assassinated Pompey. He hoped the act would endear him to Julius Caesar, who would then take the brother's side and install him as sole Pharaoh of Egypt. However, when Caesar saw the remains of Pompey, including his signet ring with an emblem of a lion holding a sword in his paws, he was furious. Roman generals had their own sense of honor, and this was no way for the life of a famed Roman leader to end. Julius Caesar was angry with the brother and banished him from Egypt.

And so in 47 BC, Cleopatra became the sole Queen of Egypt. Julius Caesar named her Pharaoh and Queen of Kings, and Cleopatra styled herself as the incarnation of the Egyptian mother-goddess Isis. She and Julius Caesar also fell in love. The Roman conqueror and the Egyptian queen had a child together. They named him Ptolemy Caesar, thus joining the traditional names of Egypt and Rome. His nickname was Caesarion.

ANTONIUS et CLEOPATRA

Soon after Caesarion's birth, a cabal of Roman senators who feared Caesar's growing power assassinated him on the infamous Ides of March (the 15th of March, 44 BC). Cleopatra and her son had been with Caesar in Rome, and after his death, they returned by ship to Alexandria. Having seen Roman politics up close, Cleopatra knew that Rome would play an important role in her future, but she knew not how.

Cleopatra and Marc Antony

After Caesar's death, Rome was ruled by a Second Triumvirate: Octavian, Lepidus, and Mark Antony. Antony was in charge of Rome's eastern provinces and had his eye set on Egypt. In 42 BC, he summoned Cleopatra to a meeting. Cleopatra finally agreed to meet Mark Antony in the city of Tarsus. She arrived in grandeur, on a golden ship with brilliant purple sails, and demanded that he come aboard and talk with her there. They too fell in love, and nine months later, she gave birth to their twins, named Alexander Helios and Cleopatra Selene II.

Marc Antony was worn out by the political life of Rome. Despite his great popularity with the Roman people, he was losing political ground to his nemesis, the brilliant Octavian. Antony moved to Alexandria to live with Cleopatra, and they had another child.

Cleopatra's fate would now be inseparable from that of Marc Antony and his foe Octavian. Octavian wanted Egypt's wealth, and he general Agrippa captured one of Antony's Greek cities, Methone. On a September morning in 31 BC, Antony and Cleopatra commanded a flotilla of ships to arrive at the Gulf of Actium, on the western coast of Greece, to win the city back.

Egypt's Last Queen

The battle would be a disaster for Cleopatra. Before day's end she would turn her ships back to Alexandria, followed by Marc Antony, who had lost many ships and many men. Their day was over. Soon, Octavian's forces threatened Alexandria. With Antony already dead by his own hand, Cleopatra chose to kill herself rather than be taken prisoner and displayed in Octavian's triumphal march through the streets of Rome.

Still considering Caesarian a threat, Octavian had the twelve-year-old put to death. He brought Cleopatra's three children with Marc Antony to Rome, where they were raised by Octavian's sister Octavia, who had also been Antony's Roman wife and was now his widow.

One era ended, and another began. Cleopatra was independent Egypt's last Queen and reigning Pharaoh. Having defeated Cleopatra, Octavian declared Egypt a Roman province. He commandeered Egypt's immense treasure to pay his soldiers. Having vanquished Marc Antony, Octavian ushered in the Pax Romana, or Roman Peace, and became the first Emperor of Rome.

wanted Marc Antony's power. Julius Caesar had named Octavian his legal heir before he died, but Octavian still feared that Caesarion (Caesar's son with Cleopatra) would one day challenge him for the leadership of Rome.

Octavian and the Roman Senate declared war against Antony and Cleopatra. Octavian's

Lemonade Stand

A LEMONADE STAND is a great way to earn a little spending money and meet your neighbors. What you need:

- Lemonade, in a pitcher or large thermos
- Ice (and a cooler to keep it frozen)
- Snacks
- Cups and napkins
- Change box, or the cash register you played with in kindergarten, if your little sister hasn't broken it
- Folding card table
- Big sign, most definitely, and a price list
- Chairs or a bench, if you'd like
- Optional: Music, or another way to call attention to the stand

Lemonade and brownies are a classic combination. Baking brownies from a box is quick work, and we've included recipes for other treats as well.

Crafts are good, too—perhaps friendship bracelets, which you can work on between customers. You might also devote half the table to a mini yard sale, and sell odds-and-ends you've outgrown. This is where the card table's size comes in handy.

RECIPES FOR YOUR STAND

Lemonade

If you want to squeeze fresh lemons, here's the basic recipe, which yields 4 cups. You can see that making enough fresh lemonade for your stand will entail much lemon-juicing time.

- 4 cups of water
- Juice from 6 lemons
- ¾ cup of sugar, or more, depending on whether you prefer sweet or tart lemonade

Mix together by hand or in a blender, adjust sweetness, and serve over ice.

Alternately, you can make lemonade from frozen lemonade concentrate, available at the grocery, or from dry mix. There's nothing wrong with these not-from-scratch options, especially if the idea is to get out to the street and sell some lemonade, not stand at the kitchen counter all morning juicing lemons. Follow the directions on the can or bag. You can always cut some thin lemon slices, and add one to each cup of lemonade you pour.

Lemon Candy Straw Treats

To make this old-fashioned treat, push a lemon candy stick (these are hollow inside) into the open side of a lemon that's been cut in half. The combo of the tart lemon and the sweet stick is perfect. To make this treat from a whole lemon, use an apple corer, lemon juicer, or a sharp knife to make a hole for the candy straw. You can also use oranges or limes.

BAKED GOODS

Shortbread makes an excellent and unexpected addition to any full-service lemonade stand, as does fudge. Both recipes are incredibly easy, although fudge will take forethought, as it needs two hours or so in the refrigerator to become firm.

Shortbread

- 1 cup of sugar
- 1 cup of butter (equals two sticks, or ½ pound)
- 3 cups of all-purpose flour

Preheat the oven to 275 degrees. Cream the sugar and butter. Measure in 2½ cups of flour, and mix thoroughly. Flour a tabletop, counter, or wooden board with the leftover ½ cup of flour, and knead until you see cracks on the dough's surface. Roll out the dough to ¼ inch thick, and cut into squares, bars, or any shape you wish. With a fork, prick the cookies, and put them on an ungreased cookie sheet. Bake for 45 minutes, until the tops are light brown. You can also add almonds, hazelnuts, or chocolate chips to the dough if you like.

Fudge

- ❦ 2 packages, or 16 squares, of semi-sweet baking chocolate
- ❦ 1 can of sweetened condensed milk, the 14-ounce size
- ❦ 1 teaspoon vanilla

Melt the chocolate with the condensed milk, either in a microwave for 2–3 minutes, or on top of the stove. The chocolate should be almost but not entirely melted. Stir, and the chocolate will melt fully. Add vanilla. Line a square pan (8 inches is a good size) with wax paper, and pour in the chocolate-milk-vanilla mixture. Chill for two hours or more if needed, until firm. Cut into bars or squares.

CALCULATING YOUR PROFIT

If you are working your lemonade stand to save up dollars for a Swiss Army knife or a special book, you must understand how to figure out how much you earned—that is, your profit. Let's say you make the expanded-version lemonade stand. From the sale of lemonade, fudge, and three Beanie Babies, you earned $32.

First figure the profit, using this standard equation:

Revenue (money taken in) minus **Expenses** (food, drink, etc.) equals **Profit**

Revenue: You sold 30 cups of lemonade and 20 pieces of fudge, charged 50 cents for each item and earned $25. Plus, someone paid you $7 for those Beanie Babies your great aunt brought for your second birthday. At the end of the day you took in $32.

Expenses:

3 cans of frozen lemonade	2.50
38 plastic cups	1.50
fudge ingredients	2.00
Total Expenses	6.00

Now plug the numbers into the equation: 32 minus 6 equals 26. You cleared $26 in profit.

How to Paddle a Canoe

THERE ARE LARGER, faster and more complex boats than a canoe, kayak, or raft, but in none of those fancier boats can you feel the water so closely, touch the mussels that cling tight in willow shoals, or slip into creeks and shallow wetlands to drift silently alongside cormorants, osprey, and swan.

Paddling a boat is an art that, like most pursuits, just needs practice to master. Huck Finn may have floated the Mississippi on a raft, and white-water kayaking is a thrill, but short of those, nothing beats a canoe for a water adventure.

Sometimes you need to be alone, and your canoe is there for you. Other times you want to adventure with a friend, and canoeing together is an exhilarating lesson in teamwork.

To learn to canoe, you should know these basic boat words, strokes, and concepts.

The ordinary canoe stroke is the *forward stroke.* To paddle on the right, grab the grip (or top knob of the paddle) with your left hand, and the shaft with your right. Put the paddle into the water, perpendicular to the boat, and pull it back and then out of the water. Keep your arms straight and twist your torso as you paddle. To paddle on the left, hold the grip with your right hand, the shaft with your left, and repeat.

To change course and return from whence you came, turn the boat, and then paddle forward in the new direction. The *back stroke,* then, merely causes the boat to slow, or even stop. Put the paddle in the water slightly back, near the line of your hips, and pull toward the front, and then out.

It's important to remember that a canoe is not a bicycle. If you turn bicycle handlebars to the right, the bike will turn rightward. Not so in a canoe. When you paddle to the right, the boat will shift left. The opposite is true, too: left paddling pushes the boat to the right. Rotate your body as you paddle, since the power comes not from your

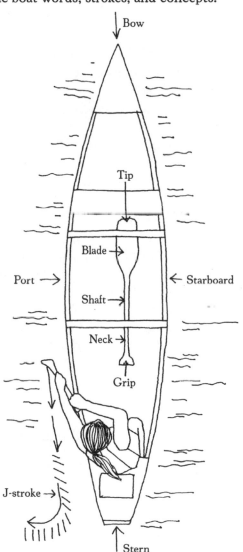

arms, exactly, but from your torso. With practice, you will learn to do this instinctively, using your hips and body weight to control the boat's direction.

Two-person canoeing is a delicate dance whereby the person at stern steers and gives directions while the person at bow paddles, changing sides at will to keep the boat in its line.

When you paddle alone it is essential to know the *J-stroke,* which, by means of a small flip at the end, keeps the boat in a straight line. The J-stroke is just that. As you paddle on the left side, draw the letter J (see the canoe illustration). On the right side, it will look like a mirror-image J, or a fishhook. In other words, put the paddle in the water close to the canoe, and before your forward stroke ends, turn the paddle out and away from the boat; that's the J. Then lift the paddle out of the water, and ready it to start again.

Some beginning canoers constantly move the paddle from right to left sides, but that's a quick way to tire your arms. Using a *C-stroke* to steer will allow you to paddle to one side more of the time. Start as with a forward stroke, but trace a C (on the left, or its mirror image on the right) in the water. When you do this, turn the blade so it's nearly parallel to the water.

This next stroke has many names, *crossback* being one of them. It's a stop. Drag the blade into the water and hold it still. Really, really hold the paddle tight against the water's rush. This stops the boat. It also turns it to that side, but this is not a suggested way to turn, since it slows the boat down too much.

One final stroke is perfect for when you find yourself in a cove with no company other than a family of sea otters and two seals nestling on the nearby rock. The **quietest possible stroke** will break no water and make no sound. Put the paddle in the water and keep it there, making a figure eight, over and again.

Now, in the big scheme of life, all you need is a boat and a paddle. In real life, some additional gear is essential, the first being a lifejacket. It's itchy and annoying and you'll be tempted to leave it on shore. Don't. Please. It will save your life in a storm. In a less dire circumstance, if you tip, it will give you a leg up as you grab your paddle and pull yourself into your boat.

Drinking water is necessary, and, last but not least, bring a rope. Ropes are key to canoe adventures. You might find a stray canoe that needs to be towed to shore, or need to tie the canoe to a tree while you explore a riverbank. Perhaps the tide has gone out in a creek and you need to hop out of the boat and pull your canoe back to deeper waters. Lifejacket, water, rope, and you're set.

Last tips: In general, the closer to the boat you paddle, the straighter it will go. To turn, paddle farther from the boat. Crouch low in the boat when getting in and out. Read the tide charts so you know where the water is.

Breathe deep, paddle smart, and enjoy your voyage.

The Ultimate Scooter

Handlebar Scooter

THIS SCOOTER is not only about racing down the street and zooming around corners, it's a chance to build an impressive wood-and-bolts project. (But once you do get to the racing and zooming around, don't forget to use a helmet!)

Here is a detailed game plan for making a handlebar scooter with three wheels. It's just like the metal scooters, except it doesn't fold, and the platform angles up a bit. So that you won't have to reinvent the wheel, so to speak, know that we found these wood sizes and bolts more easily at smaller lumberyards and hardware stores.

Rest assured that even with perfectly sized materials, problems will arise. Directions will be misread, a hole mismeasured, an incorrect bolt purchased. The secret to woodwork is to experience the problem and unearth the solution. Measure again. Redrill the hole two inches down. Cut a new piece of wood. Professional carpenters solve problems like these and worse all day long. If something goes wrong, don't fret, you're in good company. Take the problem and solve it.

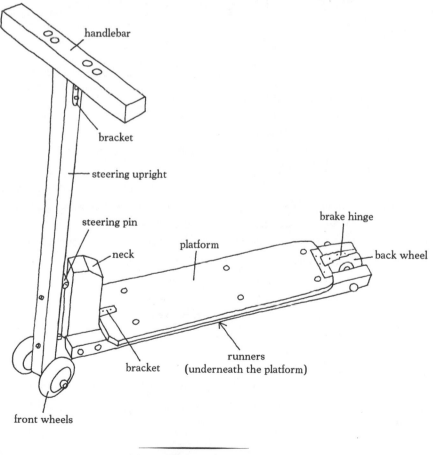

WHAT YOU NEED

◆ Three scooter wheels, 4 inches, or 100 mm, in diameter, with $\frac{1}{4}$ inch holes for the axis. These are available wherever replacement scooter wheels are sold. Or borrow the wheels from two metal scooters.

◆ 2 × 2 wood, 104" long (if sold by the foot, a ten-foot length is ideal). Cut into two pieces 30" long, one piece 32" long, and one piece 12" long. Pine is good, but if you use untreated pine, be sure and store your scooter indoors. High-quality, non-knotty, "clear" pine makes the scooter stronger, and is highly recommended.

◆ 2 × 3, 10" piece of pine or other wood.

◆ $\frac{3}{4}$" plywood, cut to $5\frac{3}{4}$" × $22\frac{1}{2}$".

Ask the lumberyard to cut the wood to size; many will do it for free or a small charge. These are American standard lumber sizes, which measure $\frac{1}{2}$ inch smaller than their size (thus the 2 by 2 actually measures $1\frac{1}{2}$" by $1\frac{1}{2}$" and the 2 by 3 is $1\frac{1}{2}$" by $2\frac{1}{2}$").

HARDWARE

◆ Two $\frac{1}{4}$" eyebolts, 3" long, with a $\frac{5}{8}$" hole.
◆ Two $\frac{1}{4}$" eyebolts, 4" long, with a $\frac{5}{8}$" hole. Note: the $\frac{5}{8}$" hole size is important, because these bolts fit around a $\frac{1}{2}$" carriage bolt.
◆ Four $\frac{1}{4}$" × $1\frac{3}{4}$" long carriage/coach bolts, with four washers and four nuts. Use stop nuts if available.
◆ Six $\frac{1}{4}$" × $2\frac{1}{2}$" carriage/coach bolts with six washers and six nuts. Use stop nuts if available. Note: The preferred size bolt is $\frac{1}{4}$" × $2\frac{3}{4}$", but this is a specialty size and not widely available.
◆ Two $\frac{1}{2}$" × 6" carriage/coach bolts with two washers and two nuts
◆ One $\frac{1}{2}$" × 8" carriage/coach bolt with two nuts
◆ Two $\frac{1}{4}$" × $1\frac{3}{4}$" hex bolts with two nuts. Use stop nuts if available.
◆ Two $\frac{1}{4}$" × 5" hex bolts, with six nuts and ten washers.
◆ Three 2" × 2" angle brackets, and four wood screws.
◆ One 4" hinge

Last, purchase an assortment of extra $\frac{1}{2}$" nuts and $\frac{1}{2}$" washers and nylon spacers, and a few extra $\frac{1}{4}$" nuts, for lock nuts and because they invariably drop and disappear. Plastic screw protectors are nice to protect bare ankles from any bolts that stick out past the nut, but you won't know what you need until you're done.

GENERAL OBSERVATION ABOUT BOLTS

Riding the scooter causes vibrations, and vibrations will loosen the bolts over time. Two nuts tightened together, called lock nuts, will prevent this. Or try stop nuts, which have a coating inside that prevents them from vibrating off. You can only use stop nuts once, so one option is to put the scooter together with regular nuts, and when you know everything fits together, replace them with stop nuts. As you ride it, tighten the nuts from time to time.

Additionally, due to the discrepancies of wood sizing, depending where you live, you may need slightly shorter or longer or wider or thinner bolts, or you may decide to move the holes over a half inch here or there.

TOOLS

Handsaw or jigsaw; drill, with $1/4''$ and $1/2''$ bits; pencil; measuring tape; straightedge or carpenter's square (3-foot is best); adjustable wrench; hammer; work area, and saw horse (or any setup to cut and drill wood).

Step One: Cut the Wood

If the lumberyard wasn't able to cut the wood, then pull out the saw and cut the six pieces. Tip: when cutting the 2 by 2 length, measure and cut the 32-inch steering upright first, from the store-cut end of the wood, and mark this end "top." This may seem picky now, but it will save you immense time later by ensuring that the cleanest, flattest end is where it is most needed. You may cut an angle into the neck, as in the illustration. Mark points at either end of the cut and run the saw between them. Don't overdo it, and leave lots of room for the drill holes. Have an adult help, if needed.

Step Two: Mark the Drill Holes

Measure precisely. Pencil directions on the wood to remind you which panel is front or side, top or back.

Centering is important, so draw the center line first and mark the drill spots on that line. On the four pieces cut from the 2 by 2, the centerline is $3/4$ inch in from either side. Draw that line on all sides, yes *all* sides, even if it feels like overkill. This line will guide the drill holes, help line up parts precisely, and show whether you've drilled a straight hole through the wood.

These directions assume that you have a straight edge or measuring tape lined up, and that you mark spots in a row all at the same time, from the starting side; in other words, do not add the second and third measurements to the first, just keep counting. When in doubt, refer to the illustration.

On the two 30-inch runners, holes will be marked on both the top and the side.

Top: Mark holes from left at 6, 16, and 24 inches.

Side: Mark three holes: from left at $1/2$ inch and 2 inches, and from right at 2 inches.

The 32-inch steering upright fits beneath the handlebars and connects to the rest of the scooter via an ingenious steering column also known as the 8-inch carriage bolt. Look for where you wrote "top" when you cut the wood. Mark holes on both the back/front and the side.

Back/front: Mark holes from the bottom at 5 inches and at $10^{1}/4$ inches.

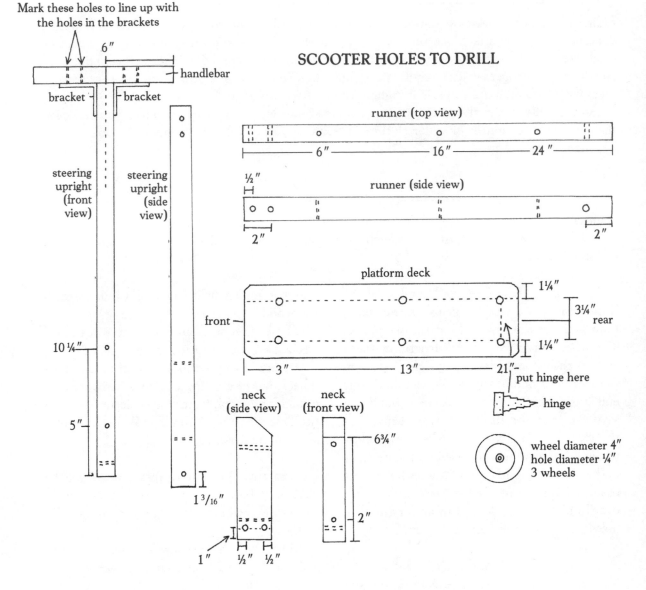

Mark these holes to line up with the holes in the brackets

6"

handlebar

bracket · bracket

steering upright (front view)

steering upright (side view)

10¼"

5"

SCOOTER HOLES TO DRILL

runner (top view)

6" — 16" — 24"

½"

runner (side view)

2" 2"

platform deck

1¼"

3¼" rear

front

1¼"

3" — 13" — 21"–

put hinge here

hinge

neck (side view)

neck (front view)

6¾"

wheel diameter 4"
hole diameter ¼"
3 wheels

1³/₁₆"

2"

1" ½" ½"

Side: Mark one hole from bottom at 1³/₁₆ inches. At the top, line up the two-inch angle bracket against the wood, and mark the bracket holes. In some brackets, the two holes are a bit off-center, so don't think yours was mis-manufactured if that's the case.

The 12-inch handlebar is connected to the steering upright.

Side: Draw a vertical line at the center—6 inches—from top to bottom. Line up this 6-inch mark with the ¾-inch center line on the steering upright when you're ready to mark and drill the holes for the brackets.

Bottom: Hold each angle bracket in place and mark the drill spots. Do this on the left and right side of where the upright and the handlebar meet, four holes in total.

The neck is the chunkier piece of wood.

Front: This is the narrower side. On the side that will face the steering upright, from the bottom, mark at 2 inches, then at 6¾ inches. These eyebolts will line up with two others on the steering upright, and the 8-inch carriage bolt will drop into them to form the steering mechanism, but don't do that just yet.

Side: This is the longer plane. Draw a horizontal line 1 inch up from the bottom. On that line, mark ½ inch in from either side. What goes here are the large bolts that bind the neck to the runners.

The platform deck is where you'll stand to race down the sidewalk. Draw two lines, 1¼ inches in from either side, across the length of the deck (the space between these should measure 3¼ inches). In case your wood has been mismeasured, the most important thing to realize at this juncture is that the holes should be 3¼ inches apart. Along each line, measure drill spots from the front/left at 3 inches, 13 inches, and 21 inches.

Step Three: Drill

Before powering up the drill, double-check all measurements, even though it's a bore and your finger is ready for the trigger. Line up the wood pieces to make sure things fit, and then drill.

Use a ¼" bit on all holes except the two front holes on the side of both runners, and the matching holes at the bottom of the neck—these will be drilled with a ½" bit. The ½" bit can be tough to manage, especially on soft pine and drilling so close to the edge of the wood. To prevent the wood from splintering, start a hole with a ¼" bit, then widen it to a ⁵⁄₁₆" bit and then to ⅜". Using each of these bits before bringing out the monster of a ½" drill bit should do it.

The brackets that connect the handlebar and the steering upright can be tough to work with. If so, hold the brackets in place, and drill the holes right through them, not bothering with preliminary marks. Drill and bolt the brackets to the steering upright first, and then place the handlebar on top and do the rest.

Step Four: Assembly

Lay the wood pieces and bolts on the floor and keep these directions and the illustrations nearby.

Use the two ¼" × 1¾" hex bolts to attach the two brackets to the steering upright, and then join the handlebar to the top of the brackets with the four ¼" × 1¾" carriage/coach bolts. Tip: don't fully tighten the bolts in the brackets until all are in place. Marvel that you had the foresight to set aside the flattest edge.

Fasten the platform deck atop the two runners with the six ¼" × 2½" carriage bolts. If on your scooter these are too short, and you can't find the special 2¾" length, try 3" bolts. Stop nuts are recommended.

Bolt the runners to the neck using two ½" × 6" carriage bolts, with a washer and nut on each. If there's any wobbly space in between, use nuts, washers, and spacers on the inside to fill it up.

Attach the two 3" eyebolts to the steering upright, with the eyes facing the body of the scooter, and then attach the 4" eyebolts to the front side of the neck.

Line up the two pairs of eyebolts and drop the ½" × 8" carriage bolt through all four. That's the steering column. Make sure it can turn freely. Then tighten two nuts together at the bottom of the bolt.

Now for the wheels

The front axle fits into the hole at the bottom of the steering upright. Find the ¼" × 5" long

THREE TRICKY THINGS TO LOOK FOR

☞ The scooter wheel may have a spacer inside—you'll see and hear it rattling around. It needs to be threaded onto the axle separately. Pry off one of the plates covering the hole, and you'll find it. Slip the spacer onto the axle separately (as in wheel-spacer-hole cover), and it should work.

☞ Depending on the exact proportions of your wood, you may need a longer 6″ bolt (alas, 5½″ is not a standard size). Similarly, if the openings on the wheels you find are ½″, or ⅜″, just use a larger width hex bolt for the axle and drill a larger hole to match. By now the bolt bins at the hardware store are as familiar as the back of your hand, and you can pull the right bin in your sleep.

☞ Fiddle with the extra ½″ nuts, washers, and spacers to keep the back wheel centered on the axle and the front wheels set apart from the steering upright so they don't rub. Our back wheel has three big ½″ washers on either side, and can use even more. Our front wheel looks like this: washer-wheel-washer-½″ bolt-washer-steering upright-washer-½″ nut-washer-wheel-washer and finally, a ¼″ nut and a ¼″ stop nut to hold it together. Yours might use a similar combination to keep everything in place. Just remember to place washers on both sides of each wheel, and then toy with it till the combination is tight enough to hold everything in place, but still loose enough for the wheels to turn freely.

hex bolt. Place a washer on both sides of both wheels, and push the axle through one wheel, through the upright, and through the other. Make sure everything can turn, and top it off with a pair of nuts, or a stop nut.

The rear wheel sits between the runners, which makes it a bit harder to assemble. Use the other ¼″ × 5″ hex bolt, with washers on either side of the wheel, so it can turn smoothly and won't get caught on the wood.

Once the wheel spacing is fixed, top the axle off with two nuts or a stop nut.

Step Five: Final Touches

If you're the kind who stops her scooter by dragging a sneakered foot alongside, forget this next step, but otherwise, a 4-inch triangle hinge makes a good brake. Attach with screws at the rear of the platform so the hinge leans over the back wheel. The neck and platform can be extra-secured, if you wish, with an angle bracket and wood screws, though we skipped this step on ours.

Adjust and tighten all the nuts, fit plastic safety covers over bolt bottoms, erase the pencil lines and clean up the tools. You're off!

Flat Scooter

WHAT YOU NEED

◆ ¾″ plywood, cut to a 12″ by 12″ square.

◆ Four rubber swivel caster wheels, available at the hardware store. Find the type attached to a plate, with four screw holes.

◆ Sixteen small bolts with nuts (³/₁₆″ and 1″ long).
The caster wheel package will suggest screws, but this option assumes the respectable path of attaching the wheels to a chair or desk, not using them to roll high speed and rough-and-tumble across the floor on a scooter. We suggest small bolts, which are stronger than screws because they are held in place by a nut. If in doubt, ask at the hardware store. See below, you might need sixteen washers, too.

Tools

◆ Drill with a ³/₁₆″ bit

◆ Saw or jigsaw

◆ Adjustable wrench or ³/₁₆″ wrench

◆ Sandpaper. Wrap the sandpaper around a small block of wood secured with some nails or tacks.

Cut the wood to size and sand the edges and top smooth. While you have the saw out, round the four edges to remove the points.

The caster wheels are set at each of the four corners, a half inch away from each side. It helps to draw lines a half inch in on all sides and place the wheels where the lines meet. Put each wheel in position, and mark the holes for screws or bolts through the plate. Use a ³/₁₆″ bit to drill the holes.

Insert the bolts and tighten. Depending on the wheels, there may be some adjustments to make. There are two considerations. The first is that the nuts need to be tight. The second is that space between the plate and the wheel might be limited, and tightening the nuts may slightly get in the way of the wheels turning. We tried several solutions; the best added a washer under the head of the bolt, on top of the scooter.

Bird Watching

BIRD WATCHING might seem difficult (or even boring), but we can assure you, it is not. Birds are everywhere—easy to spot and fun to observe. Most birders keep a life-list journal, a kind of bird diary, by writing down the birds they see. As you begin to bird, you can use a small spiral notebook to make a life-list journal for yourself, writing down the names of the birds you find, or sketching their distinguishing features so you can look them up in a bird identification book once you're back home. All you need to go bird watching is a pair of binoculars, a good bird guidebook, comfortable clothes, your life-list journal—and some patience. Bird watching demands a certain kind of presence on the part of the birder: You must become a part of nature rather than stand outside of it. Here are eight common birds to start you off on a lifetime pursuit of bird watching.

American Robin

The American Robin is one of the most popular species of birds, a regular visitor to front porches and in backyards. The Robin can be seen throughout North America and is recognizable by its gray head, orange underbelly (usually brighter in the male), and distinctive crescents around the eyes. During breeding season, adult males grow eye-catching black feathers on their heads; after the season is over, the plumes fall out (just like their middle-aged male human counterparts). The Robin's song sounds like a whistled musical phrase, sometimes described as "cheerily, cheer up, cheer up."

Cool facts:
The American Robin is the state bird of Connecticut, Michigan, and Wisconsin. And there is a Crayola crayon color named after the color of the eggs: Robin's Egg Blue.

Blue Jay

The Blue Jay, a large crested songbird, is immediately recognizable by its characteristic bold blue coloring. Blue Jays are intelligent, resourceful, and adaptable. They can imitate the sounds of hawks, driving off competitors for their food, and have a reputation for stealing the eggs and nests of smaller birds during breeding season.

Male and female Blue Jays look the same. Blue Jays living in captivity have shown themselves to be capable of using tools, grabbing strips of newspaper to rake in food pellets just outside their cages.

Chickadee

There are five species of Chickadee in North America: the most common, the Black-Capped Chickadee, is found all over North America; the Car-olina Chickadee is found in the southeast; the Mountain Chickadee is found in the Rockies; the Chestnut-Backed Chickadee is found along the Pacific coast; and the Mexican Chickadee is found in Arizona, New Mexico, and west and central Mexico. Chickadees are smaller than sparrows and very acrobatic. The Chickadee has two characteristic calls: one that sounds like "cheeeeeese bur-gers" and one that gives them their name: "chick-a-dee-dee-dee-dee."

Cool facts:
The Black-Capped Chickadee hides seeds for later, and can remember thousands of hiding places. The bird's seemingly simple calls are actually used to communicate sometimes complex information, such as identity or predator alerts, to other Chickadees.

Ruby-Throated Hummingbird

These tiny birds are the only species of hummingbird that breeds in eastern North America and are present as far north as New Bruns-

wick, Canada. The birds hover at flowers, and their name derives from the humming sound emanating from their wings.

In the winter, the Ruby-Throated Hummingbird flies nonstop across the Gulf of Mexico to Central America. To fuel themselves for the journey, they eat so much that they double their body mass in the days before they leave. The Ruby-Throated Hummingbird has an iridescent green back; the males have a bright red throat and the females have a white throat. The female is also larger than the male.

Cool facts:
The Ruby-Throated Hummingbird beats its wings 53 times per second. Also, its legs are so short that is cannot walk or hop, only shuffle. But it manages to scratch its head by lifting its foot up and over its wing.

Red-Tailed Hawk

The Red-tailed Hawk is roughly the size of a small cat (22 inches long and 2 to 4 pounds). Categorized as raptors—birds of prey—they are meat eaters, or carnivores. They have hooked beaks; their feet have three toes pointed forward and one turned back; and their claws,

BIRDING TIPS FROM PETER CASHWELL
(author of *The Verb 'To Bird'*)

1. Get up early. It's good to get outside before sunrise if you want to see and hear birds with the fewest possible distractions (traffic, factory noise, etc.). You can keep birding all day, of course, but the early morning is the best time.

2. Learn a few common birds' appearances well. They give you something to compare to the bird you saw. If you know the Robin cold, you can tell whether this bird was smaller than a Robin, or had a whiter belly, or had a thicker bill.

3. Set up a feeder or a birdbath. This brings birds into your yard where you can watch them up close and over a long time. You'll probably also attract several different kinds of birds, which will help you with #2.

4. Bird with others. More experienced birders can show you all kinds of things you'd probably miss on your own, and most birders like to show less experienced birders the ropes. Even if it's just you and a friend who doesn't know much about birds, two sets of eyes will see more than one (and two sets of field marks will help you figure out what you saw).

5. Bird everywhere. You don't have to be in a National Park to see unusual or interesting birds. Some will be at the beach, others in the city park, still others in your yard, and some in that empty lot across the road. Keep looking and you'll see things everywhere.

or talons, are long, curved and very sharp. They can live as long as twenty-one years, though the more typical lifespan is about ten years. This variety of hawk is found throughout North America, from central Alaska and northern Canada to the mountains of Panama. It has a rasping scream that is most commonly voiced while soaring.

Cool facts:
A Red-Tailed Hawk's eyesight is eight times as powerful as a human's. A hawk kills its prey using its long talons; if the prey is too large to swallow whole, the hawk rips it into smaller pieces with its beak.

Mallard
The Mallard duck is found throughout North America and all across Eurasia, most noticeably in urban park ponds. It is the ancestor of almost all domestic duck breeds. Male Mallards have iridescent green heads, reddish chests, and gray bodies; the female is a mottled brown.

Cool facts:
Mallards are monogamous and pair up long before the spring breeding season. The males are loyal, but only the female incubates the eggs and takes care of the ducklings.

Red-Breasted Sapsucker
The Red-Breasted Sapsucker is common in the forests of the west coast, but rarely seen

in the east. They are recognizable by their markings: red heads and breasts, and a prominent white stripe across black wings. Male and female Red-Breasted Sapsuckers look alike; younger birds are mottled brown but have white wing-stripes, just like the adults. These birds get their name from the way they eat: foraging for food by drilling horizontal rows of holes in tree trunks and later feeding on the sap and the insects drawn to it.

Cool facts:
Hummingbirds often make use of sapsucker feeding holes, nesting near them and following the sapsucker around during the day to feed at the sap wells it keeps active.

American Tree Sparrow
The American Tree Sparrow is actually not closely associated with trees, as it forages and nests on the ground. It is a common "backyard bird" found throughout southern Canada and the northern United States. The American Tree Sparrow is a small songbird, only 6 inches long, with a brown crown and eye-stripe against a grey head, and a dark spot in the center of its breast.

Cool Facts:
In the summer months, the American Tree Sparrow eats only insects. In the winter it only eats seeds and other plant foods.

And now, a birding poem to inspire you:

A BIRD CAME DOWN THE WALK
By Emily Dickinson

A Bird came down the Walk—
He did not know I saw—
He bit an angle-worm in halves
And ate the fellow, raw.

And then he drank a Dew
From a convenient Grass
And then hopped sidewise to the Wall
To let a Beetle pass—

He glanced with rapid eyes
That hurried all abroad—
They looked like frightened Beads,
    I thought—
He stirred his velvet head

Like one in danger, Cautious,
I offered him a Crumb,
And he unrolled his feathers
And rowed him softer home—

Than Oars divide the Ocean
Too silver for a seam—
Or Butterflies, off Banks of Noon,
Leap, plashless as they swim.

Modern Women Leaders

WHILE THE UNITED STATES has yet to elect a woman president, many other countries in the past 100 years have had women leaders.

Country	Name	Years in Office
Argentina	President Isabel Martinez de Peron	1974–1976
Bangladesh	Prime Minister Sheik Hasina	1996–2001
Bangladesh	Prime Minister Khalida Zia	1991–1996
		2001–2006
Bosnia-Herzogovina	President Borjana Krišto	Elected 2007
Botswana	Paramount Chief Muriel Mosadi Seboko	Elected 2003
Burundi	Prime Minister Sylvie Kinigi	1993–1994
Canada	Prime Minister Kim Campbell	1993
Central African Republic	Prime Minister Elisabeth Domitien	1975–1976
Cherokee Nation	Chief Wilma Mankiller	1985–1995
Chile	President Michelle Bachelet Jeria	Elected 2006
Dominica	Prime Minister Mary Eugenia Charles	1980–1995
Finland	President Tarja Halonen	Elected 2000
France	Prime Minister Edith Cresson	1991–1992
German Democratic Republic	Chairman Sabine Bergmann-Pohl	1990
Germany	Chancellor Angela Merkel	Elected 2005
Guyana	President Janet Jagan	1997–1999
Haiti	Prime Minister Claudette Werleigh	1995–1996
Iceland	President Vigdís Finnbogadóttir	1980–1996
India	Prime Minister Indira Gandhi	1966–1977
		1980–1984
Indonesia	President Megawati Sukarnoputri	2001–2004
Ireland	President Mary McAleese	Elected 1997
Ireland	President Mary Robinson	1990–1997
Israel	Prime Minister Golda Meir	1969–1974
Jamaica	Prime Minister Portia Simpson-Miller	Elected 2006
Latvia	President Vaira Vike Freiberga	Elected 1999
Liberia	Chairman Ruth Perry	1996–1997
Liberia	President Ellen Johnson-Sirleaf	Elected 2005
Lithuania	Prime Minister Kazimiera Danutė Prunskienė	1990–1991
Malta	President Agatha Barbara	1982–1987

Country	Name	Years in Office
Mozambique	Prime Minister Luísa Dias Diogo	Elected 2004
New Zealand	Prime Minister Jenny Shipley	1997-1999
New Zealand	Prime Minister Helen Clark	1999-2007
Nicaragua	President Violeta Barrios de Chamorro	1990-1997
Norway	Prime Minister Gro Harlem Brundtland	1981, 1986-1989 1990-1996
Pakistan	Prime Minister Benazir Bhutto	1988-1990 1993-1996
Panama	President Mireya Moscoso	1999-2004
Peru	Prime Minister Beatriz Merino	2003
The Philippines	President Corazon Aquino	1986-1992
The Philippines	President Gloria Macapagal-Arroyo	Elected 2001
Poland	Prime Minister Hanna Suchocka	1992-1993
Portugal	Prime Minister Maria de Lourdes Pintasilgo	1979-1980
Rwanda	Prime Minister Agathe Uwilingiyimana	1993-1994
Sao Tome and Principe	Prime Minister Maria do Carmo Silveira	2005-2006
Sao Tome and Principe	Prime Minister Maria das Neves Ceita Baptista de Sousa	2002-2003
Seminole Nation	Chief Betty Mae Jumper	1967-1971
Senegal	Prime Minister Mame Madior Boye	2001-2002
South Africa	Rain Queen Mokope Modjadji V	1981-2001
South Korea	Prime Minister Han Myung-sook	2006-2007
Sri Lanka	President Chandrika Kumaratunga	1994-2005
Sri Lanka	Prime Minister Sirimavo Bandaranaike	1960-1965, 1970-1977, 1994-2000
Switzerland	President Micheline Calmy-Rey	2007-2008
Switzerland	President Ruth Dreifuss	1999-2000
Turkey	Prime Minister Tansu Çiller	1993-1996
United Kingdom	Prime Minister Margaret Thatcher	1979-1990
Yugoslavia	Prime Minister Milka Planinc	1982-1986

Rules of the Game: Darts

DARTS is another game with a long history. The game is thought to have been invented by soldiers throwing arrows at the bottom of tree trunks or wooden casks. Modern dart boards are most commonly made of boar bristles or sisal fibers (or, in the case of Velcro dart games, felt). Playing darts takes some practice, and some math skills, but mostly it's just fun to throw something across the room. Make sure you give annoying siblings and small animals a wide berth.

Setting up the board

A regulation board has a diameter of 18 inches and is divided by thin metal wire into 22 sections. Make sure to mount your dart board so that the center of the double bull (the bull's-eye) is 5 feet 8 inches from the floor. Mark the toeline, called the oche (pronounced to rhyme with "hockey"), 7 feet, $9\frac{1}{4}$ inches from the face of the board.

Basic rules

To determine shooting order, each player shoots for the bull's-eye. The one who comes closest gets to go first. Each turn consists of three darts, which must be thrown from behind the oche. For a throw to count, the point of the dart must touch the board. If a dart bounces off the board or misses it completely, it does not get a score (and also can't be rethrown).

Scoring

The dart board is divided into wedges, with point values marked along the outer edge of the circle. Two rings overlap the playing area; landing outside these rings scores a player face-value points for that area of the board. Landing between the first inner ring and the second inner ring scores a player double the points for that section. Landing between the second inner ring and the bull's-eye earns triple points. Hitting outside the outer wire scores nothing.

How to throw

First, aim. Look at the target you want to hit. Lift your arm up, bent at the elbow so that the sharp end of the dart faces the dartboard. The dart should be tipped slightly up. Check your aim and line up the dart with your sight line. Move the hand holding the dart back toward your body, then pitch the dart forward, releasing the dart and making sure to follow through with your arm. The optimal follow-through will end with your hand pointing at the target (not having your hand fall to your side). When throwing, try not to move your body—the throwing action should come from your shoulder.

PLAYING THE GAME: THE 301

The object of this game, which is most commonly played by two people, is to start with a score of 301 and count down to exactly zero. Each player has a three-throw turn, and the point value of their hits is subtracted from 301. A player can only start subtracting once they "double"—that is, hit one of the doubles on the board. Once that is accomplished, the scores will begin to count. If the total score of the three throws exceeds the remaining score for that player, the score returns to what it was at the start of the turn. A double must be hit to end the game.

PLAYING THE GAME: ROUND THE CLOCK

In this game, players take turns trying to hit each number, from 1 to 20. Each player has a three-throw turn; players advance to the next number on the board by hitting each number in order. The first person to get to 20 wins.

PLAYING THE GAME: CRICKET

This strategy game is typically played with two players, or two teams of two players each. To win at Cricket, a player must "close" the numbers 15 to 20 and the bull's-eye before any other player, and must also have the highest point count. "Closing" a number means hitting it three times in one or more turns (hitting a single closes a number in three throws; hitting a double and then a single closes a number in two throws; and hitting a triple closes a number in a single throw). You don't have to close numbers in any particular order—but you do want to close them before the other players.

To keep track of the score, you'll need a scoreboard (a blackboard on the wall or a pen and pad of paper will work). Write out the numbers vertically for each player, from 20 down to 15, then "B" for bull's-eye. Each player's turn consists of three throws, and only darts that land in the numbers 15–20 or in the bull's-eye count. (You don't get points for hitting numbers 1–14.) Points start to accumulate once a number is closed, and are tallied as follows: the center of the bull's-eye is worth 50 points and the outer ring of the bull's-eye gets 25; numbers 15–20 are worth their face value, but landing in the doubles ring doubles the number's value, and landing in the triple ring (the inner ring between the doubles ring and the bull's-eye) triples it.

When a player hits a number once, you put a slash (/) by the number. When that number is hit a second time by a player, you turn the slash into an X. When that number is "closed," or hit a third time, you draw a circle around the X. Once a number has been closed, if any player hits it, the points for that number go to the player who originally closed it. Once a number has been closed by all the players, no points are awarded for that number for the rest of the game. Total up the points after one player closes all her numbers plus the bull's-eye, and the person or team with the highest number of points is the winner.

DART LINGO

Arrows: Darts

Bust: Hitting a number higher than you need to go out

Chucker: Indifferent thrower

Clock: Dartboard

Double In: Starting a game with a double

Double Out: Winning a game on a double

Hat Trick: Three bull's-eyes

Leg: One game of a match

Slop: Hitting a number other than the intended

Trombones: A total turn score of 76 points

Wet Feet: Standing with your feet over the line

Math Tricks

E ARLY IN THE LAST CENTURY, sometime between 1911 and 1918, a Hindu scholar and mathematician discovered ancient Indian scriptures outlining a series of mathematical formulas. This hitherto unexplored section of the ancient Indian Vedas, the sacred text written around 1500-900 BC, had been dismissed by scholars who had been unable to decipher any of the mathematics. But Sri Bharati Krishna Tirthaji dedicated himself to translating and examining the texts, and after years of study, he was able to reconstruct what turned out to be a unique system of aphorisms, or easily remembered rules, used to solve a range of mathematical problems from simple arithmetic to trigonometry and calculus. He called this "Vedic Mathematics," playing on both meanings of the word *veda,* which essentially means "knowledge" but also refers to the ancient sacred literature of Hinduism, which dates back over 4,000 years. There are sixteen total *sutras,* or sayings, in Vedic math. The three discussed below will help in many of your everyday math problems: "By one more than the one before" (*Ekadhikina Purvena*); "All from 9 and the last from 10" (*Nikhilam Navatashcaramam Dashatah*); and "vertically and crosswise" (*Urdhva-Tiryagbyham*).

"By one more than the one before"

Remembering this sutra when squaring numbers ending in 5 can help you come up with the answer quickly, and without having to write anything down.

For instance: let's take the number 35^2. To find the answer the usual way, we'd multiply 35 by 35 by writing down the numbers, doing the multiplication and addition, and finally arriving at 1225. Using this first sutra, "By one more than the one before," we can do this problem in our heads. The answer has two parts to it: since the number we're squaring ends in 5, the last two numbers will always be 25, because 5×5 is 25. To arrive at the first two numbers, we use the sutra multiplying "by one more than the one before." In "35," the number "before" the last number is 3. "One more" than 3 is 4. So we multiply 3 by 4 to get 12. We know the last two digits of our answer will be 25. So 1225 is our answer.

Let's try another example: 15^2
We know the last part of our answer will be 25. Following the "by one more than the one before" rule, we need to multiply the first numeral in "15" by one more than itself. So that's 1 (our first numeral) multiplied by 2 (one more than our first numeral, 1), which equals 2. So our answer is 225.

Another example: 105^2
We know the last part of our answer will be 25. Following the "by one more than the one before" rule, we need to multiply 10 by 11 (one more than 10), which equals 110. So our answer is 11025.

"All from 9 and the last from 10"

This is an easy rule for subtracting numbers from 100, 1000, 10000, etc.

In the equation "10,000 - 6347," you can figure the answer by using "all from the 9 and the last from 10": subtracting each of the digits in 6347 from 9, except the last digit, which you subtract from 10. So that's 9 minus 6 (which is 3), 9 minus 3 (which is 6), 9 minus 4 (which is 5), and 10 minus 7 (which is 3), which gives you the answer 3653. This rule works when you have one zero for each digit you're subtracting—no more, no less. Here are some examples in action:

"Vertically and crosswise"

This can be used for multiplying numbers, and also adding and subtracting fractions. Let's tackle fractions first, adding $6/7$ and $5/3$. The way we have traditionally been taught to compute this can get a bit complicated. But using "vertically and crosswise," we can do this in our heads.

$$\frac{6}{7} \diagtimes \frac{5}{3} = \frac{18 + 35}{21} = \frac{53}{21}$$

To get the "top" part of our answer, we multiply 6 by 3 and 7 by 5. That gives us 18 and 35. Add those together to get our final top number, 53. For the bottom number we multiply the two bottom numbers of our equation, 7 and 3. That gives 21, and so our answer is $53/21$.

Let's try another example: $3/2 + 5/6$

$$\frac{3}{2} \diagtimes \frac{5}{6} = \frac{18 + 10}{12} = \frac{28}{12}$$

To get the top number of our answer, multiply 3×6 (that gives us 18) and 2×5 (that gives us 10), then add those together (28). To get the bottom number, multiply the two bottom numbers of the equation, 2 and 6. That gives us 12. So our answer is $28/12$.

This works the same with subtracting fractions. Let's use our second example, subtracting instead of adding this time: $3/2 - 5/6$

$$\frac{3}{2} \diagtimes \frac{5}{6} = \frac{18 - 10}{12} = \frac{8}{12}$$

To get the top number of our answer, multiply 3×6 (that makes 18) and 2×5 (that's 10), then subtract instead of add: $18 - 10 = 8$. That's our top number. Multiply the bottom two numbers of the equation, 2×6, and that gives us our bottom number, 12. Our answer is $8/12$ (which can be further reduced to $2/3$).

"Vertically and crosswise" also works with multiplying numbers. If you've memorized your times-tables, you might know some basic multiplication by rote. But Vedic math offers a creative way to arrive at answers to long multiplication problems that makes multiplying even more fun.

Multiplying 21 × 23 the usual way will get us an answer of 483, but using Vedic math will help us get there faster. Imagine 23 sitting just below 21 and multiply vertically and crosswise, using the following three steps, to arrive at the answer:

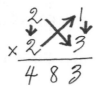

1. Multiply vertically on the right to get the final digit of the answer:
   In this case, that's 1 × 3, which equals 3.

2. Multiply crosswise and then add to get the middle digit of the answer:
   In this case, that's 2 × 3 added to 1 × 2, which gives us 8. (If multiplying crosswise and adding gives you 10 or over, you'll have to carry over the first digit of the number and add that to the answer in step 3.)

3. Multiply vertically on the left (and then add any carried-over number, if necessary) to get the first digit of the answer: In this case, that's 2 × 2, which equals 4.

Here's another example: 61 × 31

Multiply vertically on the right (1 x 1) to get the final digit of the answer (1); multiply crosswise (6 × 1 and 1 × 3) and then add to get the middle digit (9); and multiply vertically on the left (6 x 3) to get the first digit of your answer (18). The result is 1891.

With two-digit numbers that are close to 100, you can use "vertically and crosswise" as follows. Let's try 88 x 97. Write out the equation, and then subtract both 88 and 97 from 100, writing the results to the right, as shown on the next page. (100 – 88 is 12, and 100 – 97 is 3, so write 12 to the right of 88 and 3 to the right of 97.)

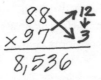

Now use "vertically and crosswise": Multiply the two numbers on the right to get the last two digits of your answer—in this case 36 (12 x 3 = 36). Subtract crosswise, either 88 - 3 or 97 - 12 (it doesn't matter which one you use, as they will both result in the same answer!), to arrive at the first two digits of your answer: 85. So your final answer is 8536.

In some instances, you may have to carry over. For example, let's try 90 x 76. Write this out as before, with 90 above 76. You can use the "all from 9 and the last from 10" rule to subtract both 90 and 76 from 100: write the corresponding answers to the right, as shown below.

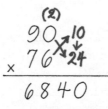

Multiply the numbers on the right to get the last two digits of the answer. But in this case, 10 x 24 gives us 240—a three-digit number. The 2 in 240 is our extra digit, and it must be carried over. Write down 40 beneath the 10 and 24, and carry the 2 over, writing it on top of the 90 so you don't forget to add it later. Now subtract crosswise, 76 - 10 or 90 - 24. Either way will give you the answer of 66. To that, add the 2 you carried over. That gives you 68, the first two digits of your answer. Your final answer is 6840.

Words to Impress

S TRUNK AND WHITE, in *The Elements of Style*, tell us about sesquepedalian words: "Do not be tempted by a twenty-dollar word when there is a ten-center handy, ready and able." But daring girls are never afraid to drop a spectacular multisyllabic bombshell when necessary. Here are some you can use when quotidian vocabulary fails.

aleatoric
(EY-lee-uh-tohr-ik)
dependent on luck or a random outcome, like a roll of the dice
Aurora just laughed when doubters attributed her triumph over the pirate rogues to aleatoric influences.

brobdingnagian
(brob-ding-NAG-ee-uhn)
gigantic, enormous, tremendous
Lydia made constant use of her brobdingnagian vocabulary.

callipygian
(kal-uh-PIJ-ee-uhn)
having shapely buttocks
Jen's callipygian beauty was matched only by her strong right hook.

crepuscular
(kri-PUHS-kyuh-ler)
dim; resembling or having to do with twilight
Janet's habit of planning all her best pranks to occur immediately after dinner led her mother to declare her utterly crepuscular in nature.

diaphanous
(dahy-AF-uh-nuhs)
almost entirely transparent or translucent
Halloween had been a success, thought Belinda, even though little kids kept bumping into her costume's diaphanous fairy wings.

echolalia
(ek-oh-LEY-lee-uh)
repeating or echoing a person's speech, often in a pathological way
The baby's curious echolalia almost sounded like real conversation.

frangible
(FRAN-juh-bull)
fragile; easily broken; brittle
After seeing what happened to his brothers, the third little pig resolved to build his house from a less frangible material.

frustraneous
(fruhs-TREY-nee-uhs)
vain; useless; frustrating
After several frustraneous attempts, Katie gave up on trying to get her sister's attention.

gustatory
(GUHS-tuh-tohr-ee)
of or pertaining to taste or tasting
Rachael dug into her dinner with gustatory glee.

hagiology
(hag-ee-OL-uh-jee)
literature dealing with the lives of saints; a list of saints
Julie's notebook was practically a hagiology of current boy bands.

ineluctable
(in-ih-LUCK-tuh-bull)
inevitable, inescapable
(From the Latin word *luctari*, "to wrestle.")
Sarah was unable to escape the ineluctable gaze of her mother.

jejune
(ji-JOON)
immature, uninteresting, dull; lacking nutrition
Molly resolved to use an interesting vocabulary, the better to avoid appearing jejune.

knurl
(nûrl)
a knob, knot, or other small
protuberance; one of a series
of small ridges or grooves on
the surface or edge of a metal
object, such as a thumbscrew,
to aid in gripping
*Samira learned to rock climb
by grabbing onto the knurls
all the way up the wall.*

languorous
(LANG-ger-uhs)
lacking spirit or liveliness;
dreamy; lazy
*Amelia spent a languorous
day by the pool.*

luculent
(LOO-kyoo-luhnt)
easily understood; clear or
lucid
*Sometimes Brianna's
homework needed to be a little
more luculent.*

mellifluous
(muh-LIF-loo-uhs)
flowing with sweetness or
honey; smooth and sweet
*Anna always enjoyed chorus;
she knew her voice was
mellifluous.*

miasma
(mahy-AZ-muh)
foul vapors emitted from
rotting matter; unwholesome
air or atmosphere
*Emi held her nose as she
passed the miasma of what
her little brother referred to as
"the stinky parking garage."*

natalitious
(nay-tuh-LIH-shis)
pertaining to one's birthday
*Mary designed elaborate
invitations to announce her
natalitious festivities.*

nemesis
(NEM-uh-sis)
a source of harm; an
opponent that cannot be
beaten; mythological Greek
goddess of vengeance
*On a good day, Christina's
brother was her ally; on a bad
day, he was her nemesis.*

obsequious
(uhb-SEE-kwee-uhs)
fawning; attentive in an
ingratiating manner
*Eager to win her parents'
approval, Vanessa was
polite to the point of being
obsequious.*

persiflage
(PURR-suh-flahzh)
light banter; frivolous
discussion
*"We must be careful to keep
our persiflage to a minimum,"
Nola whispered to Margot
during class.*

quiescence
(kwee-ES-uhns)
stillness, quietness, inactivity
*Esme reveled in the
extraordinary quiescence of
early morning when she awoke
before anyone else.*

quotidian
(kwoh-TIHD-ee-uhn)
everyday, commonplace,
ordinary; recurring daily
*Dana sighed, bored by the
quotidian sameness of it all.*

rapprochement
(rap-rohsh-MAHN)
reconciliation; the
reestablishing of cordial
relations
*After holding a grudge against
him for so long, Eleanor felt
it was almost a relief to have
reached a rapprochement with
her brother.*

risible
(RIZ-uh-buhl)
laughable, causing laughter
*The girls knew they could
always count on Jasmine for
a risible remark.*

sesquipedalian
(SESS-kwih-puh-DAY-
lee-un)
characteristic of a long word;
given to using long words
*Daring girls are not shy about
their sesquipedalian abilities.*

sprezzatura
(SPRETTS-ah-TOO-ruh)
nonchalance, effortlessness
After reading The Daring
Book For Girls, *Erin was able
to cartwheel with sprezzatura
and verve.*

Truculent
(TRUCK-yuh-lunt)
pugnacious, belligerent,
scathing
*When Nancy was pushed too
far, she became truculent.*

ultracrepidarian
(ull-truh-krep-ih-DAIR-
ee-uhn)
giving opinions or criticizing
beyond one's own range of
expertise
*"I'd tell you what I think
about your outfit, but
I don't want to be all
ultracrepidarian," said Karen.*

vitiate
(VISH-ee-ayt)
to weaken, impair,
or render invalid
*Penelope's debate in class
vitiated Rob's argument.*

winsome
(WIN-suhm)
sweetly or innocently
charming
*Surya was too busy building
her tree fort to act winsome.*

xenophobe
(ZEE-nuh-fohb)
a person who fears or hates
foreigners
*It was a nerve-racking
moment at the potluck picnic,
when the neighborhood
xenophobe showed up with
potato salad.*

yawl
(Yawl)
a ship's small boat;
a yowl or howl
*Lanie let out a loud yawl as
the boat tipped over.*

zaftig
(ZAHF-tik)
having a shapely figure (From
the Yiddish word *zaftik*,
"juicy.")
*Beyonce was proud of her
strong, zaftig figure.*

zeitgeist
(TSIYT-giyst)
the spirit of the time;
the outlook of a particular
generation
*Shonda was convinced the
latest pop star embodied the
zeitgeist of middle school.*

Tree Swing

WHAT YOU NEED

◆ Wood, 2 x 8, 2 ″ long
◆ Rope
◆ Two eyebolts, 8″ long, with a ³⁄₈″ thread,
  two nuts and four washers
◆ A tennis ball, a sock, and some twine
◆ Drill with ³⁄₈″ bit

THE HARDEST PART of building a tree swing is finding a well-suited branch. We can tell you that a tree-swing branch should be at least 8 inches in diameter, but on a tree tall enough for a swing, that can be difficult to measure precisely. You'll also need a strong rope long enough to get around the branch and down to the ground and back up again.

Your swing should not be on a white birch, because those rubbery branches readily bend. Look for a hardy oak or maple. The spot on the branch where you hang your swing should be far enough from the trunk so no one is hurt when they swing, but close enough so the branch is still strong.

The second hardest part is getting the rope up and over the branch. To forestall several hours of standing with a rope and squinting into the sun, we have a strategy to suggest:

☞ Put a tennis ball in an old sock. Wrap twine around the sock and make a knot so the tennis ball stays put, and make sure you have enough twine on the skein so it can unfurl the length up to the tree branch, and back down again.

☞ Stand under the tree and aim the tennis-ball-in-the-sock over the branch. It may take a few tries, but it is much easier than just flinging the rope up to the branch.

☞ Once up-and-over, the tennis ball sock will land near your feet, trailed by a long strand of twine. Knot the twine to the rope to be used in the tree swing. (Try a sheetbend knot, it's designed to join different sized-ropes.) Pull the twine until the rope is over the branch. You might want to toss the ball/rope combo over again, to double-loop the rope over the branch. When all is in place, detach the twine. The rope is set.

The easiest part is making the seat and procuring a long length of knot. Find or cut a 2-foot long piece of 2-by-8 wood. Draw a line down the center, lengthwise, and measure 2 inches in from

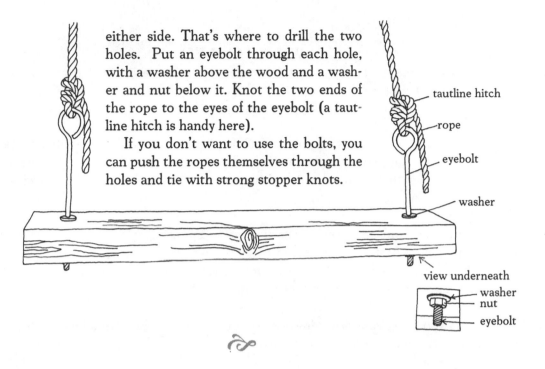

either side. That's where to drill the two holes. Put an eyebolt through each hole, with a washer above the wood and a washer and nut below it. Knot the two ends of the rope to the eyes of the eyebolt (a tautline hitch is handy here).

If you don't want to use the bolts, you can push the ropes themselves through the holes and tie with strong stopper knots.

tautline hitch
rope
eyebolt
washer
view underneath
washer
nut
eyebolt

Yoga: Sun Salutation
(surya namaskara)

THE WORD *yoga* comes from the Sanskrit root *yuj*, "to yoke," or "to unite" and dates roughly from 5000 BC according to Vedic texts. In the Sun Salutation, as with all flowing or dynamic yoga postures, what is joined is your movement and your breathing. The Sun Salutation—*surya namaskara* in Sanskrit—is done differently depending on which style of yoga you choose to follow, but in its most basic form, it is a series of 12 or so postures (*asanas*) linking movement with inhalation and exhalation. Here is the Ashtanga yoga version of the most basic sun salutation.

The most important thing to keep in mind when doing any kind of yoga is your breathing: inhaling with each extension or stretch, and exhaling as you fold or contract. The best way to breathe during this exercise is to first suck in your stomach so that it feels like your belly button is pulled back toward your spine. Now keep it there and breathe—through your nose, with your mouth closed—deeply into your chest. Your chest should rise and fall with your breath as your stomach stays tight, and you should breathe this way through the entire series.

Traditionally, the sun salutation is performed at sunrise—if you're really hard-core, it's done just before dawn, facing the east, with mantras and libations in honor of the sun god, but you don't have to go that far. First thing in the morning, on an empty stomach, is ideal enough. In fact, the sun salutation can be done any time you feel like taking a moment to breathe, move, and become energized. It can be a foundation for your yoga practice, or it can be a practice in and of itself. Either way, the sun salutation is something you can do for the rest of your life.

WHAT YOU NEED

If you have a yoga mat or yoga rug, use that—otherwise, take a large beach towel and lay it on the ground outside, or on the floor inside. (If you're doing the sun salutation inside and are using a towel, make sure to do it on a non-slippery surface.)

❶ Stand in *tadasana*, "mountain pose." Your feet and toes should be firmly on the ground, your arms at your sides, your shoulders back and your neck long. Take a few breaths to prepare yourself (remember to breathe through your nose, with your belly button pulled in towards your spine).

❷ Inhale and raise your arms out to the side, palms up, bringing them up overhead until your palms touch. This is *hasta uttanasana*, raised arm pose. Raise your gaze so that you look up at your thumbs. Try not to tilt your head back or scrunch up your eyebrows when you look up, and also try to keep your shoulders from creeping up around your ears.

❸ Exhale as you bring your arms down in front of you and move into a forward bend (*uttanasana*). If you can place your hands on the ground next to your feet, great. If not, place your hands on your ankles or knees. Try to keep your back extended rather than rounded; if it feels like too much on your lower back, you can bend your knees slightly.

❹ Inhale as you look up, your shoulders back and your fingertips still touching the ground (or your ankles/knees). Your back should be flat, and you should feel like a diver just about to dive into the pool.

❺ Place your palms on the mat, fingers spread, and exhale as you jump or walk back into *chaturanga dandasana*, a low push-up position. Unlike a regular push-up, in this posture your elbows need to stay very close to your body, and your upper arms should be squeezing against your ribcage.

❶ *tadasana* (mountain)

❷ *hasta uttanasana* (raised arm pose) inhale

❸ *uttanasana A* (standing forward bend) exhale

❹ *uttanasana B* (forward bend with flat back) inhale

❺ *chaturanga dandasana* (four limb staff pose) exhale

❻ *urdhva muhka svanasana* (upward-facing dog) inhale

YOGA: SUN SALUTATION

The weight of your body is on your hands and your toes. Take care not to sag your hips down; your body should be a straight line. If this is too much, keep your hands and toes where they are and lower the knees to the ground to help support yourself.

❻ From here, inhale as you push yourself forward into *urdhva muhka svanasana* (upward-facing dog). Push from your toes as you roll through from a flexed foot position to a pointed-toe position. Your hands and the tops of your toes should be the only parts of your body touching the ground. Look up as you arch your back, and try to keep those shoulders down (and those eyebrows from rising).

❼ Exhale as you lift yourself back into *adho mukha svanasana* (downward-facing dog), rolling back over your toes to the soles of your feet and keeping your palms on the floor. Stay here for five deep breaths. When you look at your feet as you breathe in this posture, you should not be able to see your heels. Move your heels so they are in line with your ankles, and try to think about the soles of your feet moving toward the floor. Looking upward toward your stomach will help keep you from hyperextending around your back and rib cage. Think about moving your chest toward your feet and your head toward the floor.

❽ Look toward your hands as you bend your knees, and either jump or walk your feet to your hands.

❾ Inhale as you look up with a flat back, your fingertips on the floor (*uttanasana* B)

❿ Exhale as you bend forward into a full forward bend (*uttanasana* A). Think about having your stomach and chest on your thighs rather than curving over with a rounded back.

⓫ Inhale as you lift all the way up into *hasta uttanasana*, looking up toward your thumbs as your palms touch.

⓬ Exhale as you return to *tadasana*, mountain pose.

❼
adho mukha svanasana
(downward-facing dog)
exhale,
hold for five breaths

❽
Jump forward to

❾
uttanasana B
inhale

❿
uttanasana A
(standing forward
bend)
exhale

⓫
hasta uttanasana
(raised arm pose)
inhale

⓬
tadasana
exhale

Three Silly Pranks

THINK BOYS are the only ones good at pranking? Think again! Here are three classic pranks for any daring girl.

STINK BOMBS
The old-fashioned kind,
from the herb valerian.

Head outdoors with the following:
- a small jar with a screw-on lid
- measuring spoons
- any kind of vinegar you can snag from the kitchen
- valerian root powder—this is the key ingredient for a stink bomb. You can find this at any grocery store that stocks vitamins and herbal remedies. It comes in capsules that can be opened and emptied. If you can only find valerian tea, mash it into a powder.

Mix one or more teaspoons of the powder with 2 teaspoons of vinegar, close the jar very, very quickly and shake. When you're ready to set off the stink bomb, open the jar (don't throw it), yell "Skunk!" and run.

SHORT-SHEETING BEDS
For this prank you'll need to know the old-fashioned skill of making a bed, the fancy way, with tucked-in sheets.

Here's a refresher: Fit the bottom sheet over the mattress. Tuck the top sheet under the foot of the bed and along at least part of the sides. Lay the blanket on top, tuck that in too, and then neatly fold the top edge of the sheet over the blanket, about six inches or so. There. Stand back and observe your handiwork, because you will want the short-sheeted bed to look the same way.

To short-sheet a bed, you merely reposition the top sheet. Instead of tucking it in at the foot of the bed, tuck it in at the head of the bed. Lay out the sheet and halfway down the bed, stop and fold the sheet back toward the pillows. Place the blanket on top and fold a few inches of sheet on top for that neat, just-made look. This bed looks normal, but just try and stretch your legs out!

Important: Don't do this to anyone whose feelings will be hurt, only to those you know will laugh hard or at least giggle when they figure it out.

FAUX BLOOD
Fool your friends with this
easily prepared hoax.

Needed:
- corn syrup
- cornstarch
- red food coloring from the pantry
- a jar with a tight lid
- a spoon
- an eyedropper

Red food coloring can stain, so wear old clothes, although washing with very warm water and strong soap should clean it up. It is best to keep this all outdoors.

Mix 4 small drops of food coloring, 2 teaspoons of water, and 1 to 2 teaspoons of cornstarch in the jar, cover, and shake. Pour in 2 tablespoons of corn syrup. Cover and shake again.

Use an eyedropper or a spoon to drip the fake blood where you want it. Make up a good story.

What is the Bill of Rights?

I N THE DAYS AFTER the United States won its independence from Britain in the 1780s, people vigorously debated how much power a government needed to rule, and how best to protect people's rights from being overly stifled by the government. The now-famous Federalist and Anti-Federalist papers were originally published as letters in newspapers, and instead of using their given names, the letter writers often took names like "Brutus," "Agrippa," and "Cato"— well-known figures from the era of the Roman Republic. In their struggle to create a free society, after having only known life under a king, the early Americans looked to ancient Roman society for inspiration.

The first ten amendments to the Constitution, called the Bill of Rights, were the answer to the power of government versus personal freedom debate. The amendments form our basic sense of what it means to be American. These are the laws that now protect our freedom of religion and speech, our independent press, and our right to assemble peacefully in protest. Among other things, the Bill of Rights establishes our right to bear arms (not arm bears) and to be granted fair and speedy trials, and protects us from cruel and unusual punishment.

The Preamble to the Bill of Rights

Congress of the United States begun and held at the City of New-York, on Wednesday the fourth of March, one thousand seven hundred and eighty nine.

The Conventions of a number of the States having, at the time of adopting the Constitution, expressed a desire, in order to prevent misconstruction or abuse of its powers, that further declaratory and restrictive clauses should be added, and as extending the ground of public confidence in the Government will best insure the beneficent ends of its institution;

Resolved, by the Senate and House of Representatives of the United States of America, in Congress assembled, two-thirds of both Houses concurring, that the following articles be proposed to the Legislatures of the several States, as amendments to the Constitution of the United States; all or any of which articles, when ratified by three-fourths of the said Legislatures, to be valid to all intents and purposes as part of the said Constitution, namely:

Ratified December 15, 1791

AMENDMENT I

Congress shall make no law respecting an establishment of religion, or prohibiting the free exercise thereof; or abridging the freedom of speech, or of the press; or the right of the people peaceably to assemble, and to petition the government for a redress of grievances.

AMENDMENT II

A well regulated militia, being necessary to the security of a free state, the right of the people to keep and bear arms, shall not be infringed.

AMENDMENT III

No soldier shall, in time of peace be quartered i any house, without the consent of the owner, nor in time of war, but in a manner to be prescribed by law.

AMENDMENT IV

The right of the people to be secure in their persons, houses, papers, and effects, against unreasonable searches and seizures, shall not be violated, and no warrants shall issue, but upon probable cause, supported by oath or affirmation, and particularly describing the place to be searched, and the persons or things to be seized.

AMENDMENT V

No person shall be held to answer for a capital, or otherwise infamous crime, unless on a presentment or indictment of a grand jury, except in cases arising in the land or naval forces, or in the militia, when in actual service in time of war or public danger; nor shall any person be subject for the same offense to be twice put in jeopardy of life or limb; nor shall be compelled in any criminal case to be a witness against himself, nor be deprived of life, liberty, or property, without due process of law; nor shall private property be taken for public use, without just compensation.

AMENDMENT VI

In all criminal prosecutions, the accused shall enjoy the right to a speedy and public trial, by an impartial jury of the state and district wherein the crime shall have been committed, which district shall have been previously ascertained by law, and to be informed of the nature and cause of the accusation; to be confronted with the witnesses against him; to have compulsory process for obtaining witnesses in his favor, and to have the assistance of counsel for his defense.

AMENDMENT VII

In suits at common law, where the value in controversy shall exceed twenty dollars, the right of trial by jury shall be preserved, and no fact tried by a jury, shall be otherwise re-examined in any court of the United States, than according to the rules of the common law.

AMENDMENT VIII

Excessive bail shall not be required, nor excessive fines imposed, nor cruel and unusual punishments inflicted.

AMENDMENT IX

The enumeration in the Constitution, of certain rights, shall not be construed to deny or disparage others retained by the people.

AMENDMENT X

The powers not delegated to the United States by the Constitution, nor prohibited by it to the states, are reserved to the states respectively, or to the people.

Seventeen amendments follow these. The last, ratified in 1992, made it harder for our Senators and Representatives to raise their own salaries. This amendment has a long and intriguing history; it was first submitted in 1779 as part of a heated debate about states rights! Amendments are first passed by a two-thirds majority of the full Congress—the Senate and the House of Representatives. Then they must be approved, or ratified, by the legislatures of seventy-five percent of the states. This often means years of spirited discussion for each attempt to pass a new amendment.

The history of the amendments highlights our nation's most impassioned debates. In 1868, the thirteenth amendment abolished slavery. Two years later, the fifteenth guaranteed that our right to vote could not be denied on account of our race, color, or having previously been a slave. The eighteenth amendment made it illegal to manufacture alcohol—and ushered in the prohibition years (which ended two years later, when the amendment was repealed).

In 1920, the nineteenth amendment marked a significant event for girls and women in America when, after 141 years of male-only elections, women were granted the right to vote. Just afterward, Alice Paul, one of the suffragettes, or activists on behalf of women's voting, or suffrage, presented to Congress an amendment to supply equal rights to women. It wasn't until the 1970s, however, that both houses of Congress sent this amendment to the states to ratify. Although the Equal Rights Amendment came close to approval by thirty-eight of our fifty states, the necessary three-quarters, it was defeated.

The Three Sisters

THE THREE SISTERS aren't actually real girls, but they support one another, as sisters should. So named by the innovative Iroquois (the Native American tribe also called the Haudenosaunee), the Three Sisters are corn, beans, and squash.

The Iroquois discovered that, when grown together, these three plants make each other stronger. The sturdy corn stalks double as poles and support the beans. The squash's floppy, oversized leaves perfectly mulch the ground and keep the weeds at bay. This vegetable garden combination has been a North American tradition for centuries. You can try it in your backyard.

GETTING PREPARED

Before planting your seeds of corn, bean and squash (and for the last, feel free to substitute pumpkin), there are three basic strategies you need to know.

1. Nurture Healthy Soil.

As the old saying goes, dirt's beneath your fingernails, soil's under your feet. The truth about gardening is that it's all about preparing good soil, with fertile proportions of water, air, and compost. Humus and manure also add nutrients to your soil, as will the mulch you place on top. Pile on leaves and other garden debris; they will decay in the soil and nourish it from within.

How do you know if soil is healthy? Good soil is something you can feel. It crumbles airily between your fingers and has worms in it.

2. Experiment with Compost.

Gardeners wax eloquent about compost. And you should hear them talk about compost tea, which is when you mix compost and water and sprinkle it over your plants as fertilizer. You can purchase bags of prepared compost at your local nursery.

Compost is also a backyard project, called "a simple heap of green and brown." Green is kitchen scraps—but never meat! Brown is fallen leaves, pine tree needles, and even newspapers, cut into strips. Toss it all together, add water every few days, and turn over with a pitchfork once in a while.

In a few months, the natural process of decay turns this heap to compost, full of vitamins for your plants. Add some to your garden soil. (It must be admitted that despite gardeners' eloquence, sometimes mulch piles don't work. If this happens to you, it's okay.)

3. Know the Date of Last Frost.

Many seeds should not be planted outdoors until after the date of the last frost, and this includes corn, beans, and squash (others, like lettuce and peas, are cold-weather crops and can be planted in mid-spring). The best way to find this magic date is to ask any seasoned gardener in your neighborhood. This is called "talking over the fence," and is without a doubt the best way to learn how to garden.

PLANTING YOUR SISTERS

Now: you are ready, your soil is dark and crumbly and filled with compost, and the last frost is a distant memory. To plant the Three Sisters, prepare a garden spot three to five feet in diameter, and mound the soil up about one foot.

In the center of the mound make five holes, each an inch deep, and plant two corn seeds in each hole.

In two weeks: The corn seedlings will emerge. Prune the smaller, weaker one from each hole; five corn stalks will remain in the mound. (This two-seed planting trick can be used every time you plant; it's the best way to find the seeds most likely to succeed.) Then plant the bean seeds in seven holes in a circle around the corn, planting two seeds in each hole, knowing you'll prune the weaker ones later.

Two weeks after that: The beans will sprout. Once again, prune the smaller ones.

One week later: The beans should be tall enough to start winding through the growing corn stalks; help them find their way. Then plant the seeds for squash or pumpkin in eleven holes around the corn, repeating the two-seed method you now know well.

All summer long: Water very well each day.

In the fall: You'll have a feast of corn, beans, and squash (or pumpkins) that would make the Iroquois—and your sisters—proud.

Peach Pit Rings

FUNNY THE THINGS girls used to do. This piece of girl lore, rubbing a peach pit into a ring, is really a pretext for hanging out with your friends on a late summer afternoon. Here's how to do it.

1. Eat a peach.

2. Scrape the peach pit on the sidewalk or asphalt, back and forth on one side, then back and forth on the other. You will think nothing is happening, but in fact, microscopic peach pit fibers are being rubbed off.

3. Eventually the sides will begin to flatten and the inner pith will peek through.

4. Once the sides are flat the ring is close at hand. Just smooth the top and bottom, and rub the inside smooth with a stick.

If you don't want to make the pit into a ring, you can plant it. Clean the pit and place it in a plastic bag in the back of the refrigerator. In late September, plant it five inches down in healthy soil. In Spring, if you are very lucky—and in the right temperate zone—the peach tree will grow, slowly. Water and fertilize, and in two or three years, the tree might bear fruit.

First Aid

F|IRST AID is basic care in the event of illness, accident, or injury that can be performed by anyone until professional medical treatment is given. It was a concept first put into practice by the Knights Hospitaller, who came up with the term "first aid" and founded the Order of St. John in the 11th century to train knights in the treatment of common battlefield injuries. In a life of adventure, accidents are bound to happen, and a daring girl needs to know about first aid—even if she never plans to be injured in battle.

The information below is not intended to be a substitute for professional medical advice or treatment. Taking a first aid class will provide even more in-depth instruction. But there are definitely actions you can take to help in the event of injury, and below are some tips and techniques to keep in mind.

REMEMBER YOUR ABCs

When accidents happen, sometimes the first casualty is plain old common sense. It's easy to panic and forget about what's important, but these mnemonics can help you remember what to do. Mnemonic devices are formulas, usually in the form of rhymes, phrases, or acronyms, to help you remember things. Some of the most familiar mnemonics in first aid are: the three Ps and the three Bs; the ABCs and CPR; and RICE.

The Three Ps
(Preserve life; Prevent further injury; Promote recovery)

Remembering the Three Ps helps you keep in mind what your goal is in responding to an accident or injury: making sure the person stays alive, ensuring that nothing is done to further injure the person, and taking action to help the person get better.

The Three Bs
(Breathing; Bleeding; Bones)

The Three Bs remind a first-aid responder of what is most important to check when a person is injured, and the order of importance in treating: Is the person breathing? Is the person bleeding? Are there any broken bones?

ABCs

The ABCs stand for Airway, Breathing, and Circulation, and remembering this helps remind you to check that an injured person has a clear airway passage (isn't choking), is able to breathe, and has a pulse. Open the airway by lifting the person's chin with your fingers, gently titling their head back. Listen for breathing sounds, look for a rise and fall of the chest, and feel for breathing movement. Check for a pulse by placing two fingers on the person's neck between the voicebox and the muscle on the side of the neck. If a person is not breathing and does not have a pulse, call 911 and begin CPR.

CPR

CPR stands for cardiopulmonary resuscitation, a procedure performed on people whose heart or breathing has stopped. Once you have checked the ABCs, if a person is unresponsive, call 911. Begin CPR on an adult by pinching the person's nose as you give two breaths into their mouth. Using two fingers, check the person's pulse at the carotid artery (the neck, just under the jaw, between the voice box and the muscle on the side of the neck) for 5-10 seconds. If there is no pulse, make sure the person is on their back, then place your hands one on top of the other on the lower half of the chest. Press down to give 15 compressions, about one every second. Give two more breaths, pinching the nose and breathing directly into the person's mouth. Continue 15 compressions with 2 breaths for 4 cycles. After one minute, recheck pulse and breathing. If the person has regained a pulse, discontinue compressions. If the person is still not breathing, continue giving a breath every 5 seconds until help arrives.

When performing CPR on an infant, use two fingers instead of your whole hand, and compress on the breastbone, just below the nipple line. For children, use two hands for chest compression. For infants and children, alternate five compressions and one slow breath, for a total of twelve cycles.

RICE

Use RICE (Rest, Ice, Compression, and Elevation) for acute injuries like a sprained ankle or injuries due to overuse, like muscle strain.

✔ R: REST
Rest the injured area until pain and swelling go away (usually 1-3 days)

✔ I: ICE
Within 15 minutes of an injury, apply ice by placing a damp towel over the injured area and putting a cold pack, bag of ice, or a bag of frozen vegetables on top of that. Leave the ice on for 10-30 minutes, then take it off for 30-45 minutes. Repeat this ice on/ice off alteration as often as possible for the next one to three days.

✔ C: COMPRESSION
Use a bandage to apply gentle but firm pressure until the swelling goes down. Beginning a few inches below the injured area, wrap the bandage in an upward spiral; if using compression in addition to ice, wrap the bandage over the ice pack.

✔ E: ELEVATION
Try to keep the injured area above heart level to drain excess fluid for at least one to three days.

FOR BURNS, CUTS AND SCRAPES

Burns are classified by degree. First-degree burns are a reddening of the skin, as in a mild sunburn. Second-degree burns are when the skin blisters. Third-degree burns are when the skin is charred. Treatment for first- and second-degree burns is to immerse in cold water for 15 minutes, then apply sterile dressing. For a third-degree burn, cover the burn with a sterile dressing and treat for shock (calm and reassure the injured person, help her maintain a comfortable body temperature with a blanket or remove her from wind or sun, or have her lay down and elevate her legs 8 to 10 inches). NEVER apply ice, butter, oil or any other substance to a burn.

For cuts and scrapes, rinse the area with cool water. Apply firm but gentle pressure, using gauze, to stop any bleeding. If blood soaks through, add more gauze, keeping the first layer in place. Continue to apply pressure.

FOR CHOKING

The universal choking symbol is made by putting your hands around your throat. If you are choking and cannot talk, make this symbol to alert the people around you. If someone who is choking can still talk or is coughing, encourage her to cough more to expel the object. If she cannot talk, or if the cough is weak or ineffective, perform the Heimlich maneuver.

Heimlich Maneuver

Stand slightly behind the choking person and place your arms around her waist, below her ribcage. Make a fist with one hand, placing your thumb just above her belly button, and grab that fist with your other hand. Give five strong upward-thrusting squeezes to try to lift the diaphragm, forcing air from the lungs and provoking a cough. The cough should move and expel whatever is blocking the airway. If it doesn't, perform the maneuver again to dislodge the object. If choking persists, call 911.

EMERGENCIES

Any practiced explorer can tell you that in an emergency, what helps most is being prepared. Make a list of important phone numbers and put them on the wall next to your kitchen phone, or on a notepad stuck to the refrigerator. That way, in the event of an accident, you'll easily find the numbers to call your family doctor, poison control, the fire department, or the police.

The most important emergency number to know, of course, is 911. Calling 911 is free from any phone, even a pay phone. It can be scary to call 911, especially if you're not sure whether or not what you're dealing with is a real emergency, but it's the right thing to do when someone is dangerously hurt, not breathing, or unresponsive. A good rule to remember is: when in doubt, make the call.

What to do when you call 911

✔ Try to speak as calmly as you can.

✔ Give the address you are calling from.

✔ State the nature of the emergency (fire, accident, injury, etc.).

✔ Listen to the 911 operator and follow any instructions you are given.

✔ Do not hang up until the 911 operator tells you it's okay to hang up.

FIRST AID KIT

It's always a good idea to keep a First Aid kit at home, and making one for your family can be a fun project. For the kit itself, you can use a tote bag, backpack, or other container that is clean, roomy, easy to carry, and easy to open. The American College of Emergency Physicians recommends including the following in your First Aid kit:

✚ Band-aids of assorted sizes

✚ Ace bandages

✚ Bandage closures and safety pins

✚ Gauze and adhesive tape

✚ Sharp scissors with rounded tips

✚ Antiseptic wipes

✚ Antibiotic ointment

✚ Hydrogen peroxide

✚ Instant-activating cold packs

✚ Tweezers

✚ Oral medicine syringe (for children)

✚ Prescription medication

✚ Medicines including aspirin, ibuprofen, acetaminophen, cough suppressants, antihistamine, decongestants

✚ A page listing the contents of your kit for easy reference, your list of emergency phone numbers, and a list of family members' allergies and medications.

First Aid on the go: You can make a mini-kit (with Band-Aids, antibiotic ointment, tweezers, and Ace bandages) to take with you on a hike, or when you babysit.

∂

Important Women in First Aid

FLORENCE NIGHTINGALE

Born in 1820 to a well-off family, Florence Nightingale was not expected to work in the not-then respectable profession of nursing. She grew up studying Greek, Latin, French, German, Italian, history, grammar, philosophy, and—over parental objection—mathematics. But in 1837, Florence heard what she called the voice of God telling her that she had a mission in life. Four years later, she discovered that mission—nursing—and abandoned the life of a socialite and mother that was expected of her.

She trained in Germany and Paris, and by 1853 was the superintendent of London's Institution for the Care of Sick Gentlewomen. After the Crimean War broke out and she heard about the awful conditions for wounded soldiers, she volunteered to go to the war front in Turkey and took 38 women with her as nurses. During her time in the English military hospitals in Turkey, she established new standards for sanitary conditions and supplies; six months after her arrival, the mortality rate had fallen from 60 percent to 2 percent. Her status as the only woman in the wards at night led to her being called "The Lady With the Lamp."

She eventually became general superintendent of the Female Nursing Establishment of the Military Hospitals of the Army, helped establish the Royal Commission on the Health of the Army, and in 1860 founded the Nightingale School and Home for Nurses.

But in addition to being a nursing pioneer and health care reformer, Florence Nightingale was also a remarkable mathematician. Her innovations in statistical analysis led to her invention of the "polar-area diagram"—better known to us as the pie chart—and revolutionized the use of statistics to analyze disease and mortality.

In 1858 she was elected the first female member of the Royal Statistical Society and she later became an honorary member of the American Statistical Association. In 1907 she became the first woman to be awarded the Order of Merit. Although bedridden for years before her death, she continued her work in the field of hospital planning. She died in 1910.

CLARA BARTON

Clara Barton, who was born in 1821 and lived until 1912, was the first president of the American Red Cross. She grew up the youngest of five children and began teaching school at age 15; she later clerked in the U.S. Patent Office. After the Civil War broke out and she learned the wounded were suffering from a lack of medical care, she established a service of supplies for soldiers and worked in army camps and on the front lines, earning her the nickname "Angel of the Battlefield." For three years she cared for casualties of war in Virginia and South Carolina, and in 1865 President Lincoln appointed her to organize a program to locate men missing in action. She traveled to Europe in 1870 at the outbreak of the Franco-Prussian War and worked behind the German lines for the International Red Cross. After returning to the United States, she organized the American National Red Cross, which she headed until 1904.

Queens of the Ancient World IV

Boudica's Rebellion against Rome

BOUDICA WAS A WARRIOR QUEEN, with a fierce way about her and brilliant red hair that flowed to her waist. As Queen of the Celtic tribe of the Iceni in the first century AD, Boudica organized a revolt against the Romans, hoping to regain and protect her people's independence.

In the year 43 AD, Roman soldiers marched to the French edge of the European continent, crossed the British Channel, and began their invasion of Britain. The Emperor Claudius, whose reign had begun in 41 and would last until 54, dreamed of conquering the mysterious British island. Rome was at the height of its power. Its huge army helped expand the boundaries of Rome in all directions. Britain was a special challenge. It sat beyond a choppy channel of water and was

the farthest spot to the northwest that the Romans could imagine, with a cold, unfathomable, and terrifyingly large sea beyond.

Britain was the home of Celtic tribes and Druids, with their mystical traditions and religious groves of trees. In Rome, the lives of women and girls were as controlled as the tightly wound hair braids and coils that were the fashion of the day. There, men dominated public life, and women, especially those in wealthy and powerful families, lived more private lives. By contrast, Celtic women had many more rights. They could govern and make laws, marry more freely, own property, and, alongside men, they could work and take part in their community's marketplace. Their hair, too, showed their freedom: the fashion was to grow it long and leave it down, ready to fly with the wind.

Boudica was of the Iceni tribe, which inhabited the eastern part of Britain, and she had married Prasutagus, the tribe's King. As Roman legions invaded and took over the land of the Celts, Boudica watched, unbelievingly. The Romans declared much of Britain to be the Roman province of Britannia. They founded the cities of Londinium—now called London—and Camulodunum, which they made into their capital. There they built a massive Roman-style Temple to the Emperor Claudius and a towering statue of a woman representing Victory.

Facing troops with greater weapons, the Iceni and nearby Celtic tribes followed the path of many local tribes. They feared that active resistance would mean death for many and slavery for the rest, and so they submitted. When the Romans came to the Iceni kingdom, they decided that Prasutagus should continue to rule his people. The Iceni could remain semi-independent so long as they stayed loyal to Rome. The Romans often made arrangements like this, charging local rulers to keep the peace and to collect taxes for the Empire. Prasutagus' small kingdom lasted this way for nearly twenty years, until he died in the year 60, leaving behind Boudica and their two daughters.

Most of what we know about Boudica's life comes to us from the Roman historian Tacitus, who in 109 AD wrote the *Annals*, detailing Rome's first century exploits. Tacitus reports that under Roman rule, Prasutagus and Boudica remained prosperous. After Prasutagus' death, however, it was learned that he had been wheeling and dealing with the Romans, and this included borrowing a great deal of money from the Roman governor. Prasutagus' will directed that half the kingdom be turned over to the Romans to pay his debt. The other half he gave to his two daughters, for them to rule as queens.

Prasutagus had hoped his deathbed directions would protect his family, but this didn't happen. The Roman governor Suetonius had already decided that when Prasutagus died, he would disarm the Iceni people, confiscate their arrows and spears and darts, and annex their land fully into the Roman province of Britannia.

Roman soldiers soon arrived at Boudica's palace to plunder Prasutagus's wealth and claim his entire kingdom as their own. They captured Boudica and made a show of torturing her and her two daughters in front of the Iceni tribesmen and women. Their cousins, aunts, and uncles were made into slaves.

Later that year, the Roman governor Suetonius decided to conquer Wales, on Britain's western shore. As the soldiers of his fearsome Legion marched westward, they left the cities of Camulodunum and Londinium largely undefended.

Boudica sensed her chance. She claimed the mantle of leadership and stirred her people to reclaim their freedom and liberty. She reminded them of the horror and cruelty of Roman rule, and rallied them to win back their lands.

Boudica outlined her plan. Suetonius was in Wales, routing Druids on the Isle of Mona. Leading the way in her horse-drawn chariot, with 100,000 British fighters behind her, she would attack Camulodunum first. All around, miraculous omens pointed to Boudica's success; ancient reports tell us that the city's Victory statue fell from its tall base to the ground below with no cause, as if Rome were already yielding.

Boudica's troops stormed the city's gates. By day's end the city was in flames. A small group of Roman soldiers and leaders locked themselves inside the Temple of Claudius, holding out for two days until Boudica burned the Temple to the ground.

After hearing of Boudica's victory at Camulodunum, the Roman governor Suetonius left Wales and headed straight back to London to protect it from Boudica's rampaging soldiers.

Seeing Boudica's willingness to burn cities to the ground, he decided, however, to abandon London to her fires. Boudica's soldiers left 25,000 people dead in London before advancing to Verulamium, Britain's third-largest city, where they killed everyone who had cooperated with the Romans, and then destroyed the city.

Boudica's army began to falter. As Suetonius' men approached, they burnt the crops in the fields, sending ripened corn and beans into smoke, and leaving nothing to feed Boudica's troops and keep them strong. Boudica had successfully destroyed unarmed cities, but Suetonius and his professional legions were too strong for the relatively untrained British Celts, whose luck now turned. Boudica fought one final battle, the place of which is unknown. Her troops had to start from the bottom of a tall hill and face off against the Romans, who were strategically encamped at the top. Roman arrows and pikes rained down on the Celts. Boudica's fighters were overpowered, and many were lost to battle.

The rebellion was over. As night fell, Boudica abandoned the glorious bronze chariot that had served her well. She grabbed her two teenage daughters by the hand and together the three of them ran through the darkness, returning home to their palace along hidden paths and back roads. Once home, they knew they would be captured and brought to Rome to be displayed in chains to the jeering crowds at the Coliseum. Instead, Boudica decided to end her own life by drinking a cup of poison, and her princess-daughters took the same route. It is said that when her closest relatives entered the palace, they found Boudica wearing her legendary tunic of brilliant colors, covered with a deep auburn cloak, her flaming red hair still untamed.

Roller Skating

THE FIRST ROLLER SKATES, created in the 1700s, resembled today's in-line skates: a single line of metal wheels. Even in the next century, the first patented roller skate design followed the alignment of three wheels in a row. It wasn't until 1863 that a man named James Plimpton revolutionized the design by inventing a skate with two pairs of wheels set side by side, also known as a quad skate. The new skate quickly became the standard, due to its greater control and ease in turning, and even more refinements were made: ball and cone bearings helped improve the skate's maneuverability, and the toe stop was patented in 1876. Roller skating increased in popularity and reached its heyday in the US during the 1970s and 80s; in the 90s a modern inline skate design, the Rollerblade, took the lead as roller rinks gave way to outdoor skating. But roller skates are still made, and the fun to be had on skates is everything it used to be.

If you've never skated before—and even if you have—it's a good idea to get used to your new skates. Find yourself a smooth, flat, safe, traffic-free place to skate, and before you do anything else, practice the skills of starting, turning, and stopping. And even if you're not a beginner, wear protective gear, including knee pads, wrist guards, elbow pads, and a helmet.

STARTING OUT

Before you skate, find your balance and get comfortable in your skates by walking on a flat, grassy, or carpeted surface. First, just stand, feeling the sensation of your weight distributed evenly over the middle of your skates rather than in your toes or heels. Do not lock your knees. Then, stand with your feet in a "V" position, your heels together and your toes apart. Bend your knees slightly, put your arms out at your sides, and then march slowly, right, left, right, left, to get a feel for your skates. When you feel comfortable with this, move to a paved surface and try to balance on your skates. Bend only at the knees, never at the waist.

FALLING

It sounds funny, because a fall should seem like something to avoid, but falling is one of the most important things to practice. When you fall forward on skates, your skate stops but your upper body keeps going. Practicing falling forward on your bed or another cushioned surface can prepare you for how it feels to fall, so that if a fall occurs your reaction can be reflexive and you can minimize injury. When falling forward, drop to your knees (which should always be protected with kneepads) and sit on your backside and thighs—avoid putting your arms down or falling forward onto your hands. When falling backward, try to regain your balance by leaning forward and resist the urge to flail your arms or put your arms out to break your fall.

SKATING FORWARD

Begin with your feet in a "V" position, your heels together and your toes apart. With slightly bent knees and your arms held out to steady you, lean onto your right foot and coast forward, pushing off lightly with your left. Bring your left foot to meet your right foot, again in a "V" with your heels together, and as you place your left foot down, lean to the left, gliding on your left foot and pushing off lightly with your right. Repeat, alternating feet. Remember to relax, keep your knees bent, and lean your body in the direction of the foot carrying your weight.

STOPPING

It's possible to use the toe-stop to stop yourself by pointing your toe and dragging the rubber stop on the ground, but that can be a little tricky. A surer way is the four-wheel "T" stop: Gliding on your forward skate, lift your back skate and bring it behind your front skate at a 45-degree angle, creating a "T." Gradually let the rear skate touch the ground and create a drag to slow you to a stop. Another method of stopping is to simply lean into a turn. If you keep leaning in the same direction, you will gradually spin to a stop.

STROKING

Begin with your feet close together, shift your weight to the right foot and push off to the side with your left. Glide forward on your right foot with your left foot off the floor. Be careful not to bend at the waist, turn or twist your shoulders, or swing your arms. Bring your left skate alongside your right one and place it on the floor. Now shift your weight to your left foot and glide forward the same way. Keep repeating these glides, swaying right and then left, and remember to look ahead of you in the distance, not down at your feet. Gradually make each glide or stroke longer as you build up speed.

STEERING/TURNING

To steer yourself into a curve, lean in the direction of the curve. For a left turn, lean left; for a right turn, lean right.

CROSS-FRONT

After you are comfortable with stroking, you can practice the cross-front. Glide forward, your weight on your left foot, with knees bent and close together. Swinging from the hip, cross your right leg over your left and step your right foot as close to your left as you can. Continually crossing over in front is one way to navigate a turn.

SKATING BACKWARD

Start with your feet in an inverted "V," with your toes together and your heels apart. Press down on the inside of the left foot while lifting your right foot off the floor. Point your right toe down and shift your weight to the right. Lean slightly forward, bend your knees, and look back over your shoulder while you push off with your right foot and glide backward on your left. Bring your right foot backward and alongside the left. Push off your left foot and glide backward on your right. Your balance foot is in front of you. Bring your left foot alongside the right and start over. Another technique for skating backward is to move your skates in an hourglass shape without lifting your feet off the ground. Start with a wide stance, your skates far apart, and then apply pressure on the inside edges of your skates to roll them close together. Once they're close, apply pressure to the outside edges, making your skates roll away from each other. Try this going forward, too!

SKATING A FIGURE EIGHT

Build up speed by stroking, then skate on your right foot only and lean in to the circle; when you complete the circle, switch from your right foot to your left foot and lean in to finish.

Boys

WITHOUT A DOUBT you have already received many confusing messages about what, if anything, you should be doing with boys. Some girls are led to believe that being liked by boys is important above all else. Some girls are told that boys are different, and that girls should adapt themselves to be like the boys they like or take care not to be too threatening—learn about sports if a boy likes sports, or pretend to be stupid about subjects a boy likes to excel in. Some girls are encouraged to think of boys as protectors, or, alternately, as creatures that need protecting. It may seem to some girls that suddenly boys matter a whole lot more than they should; still others wonder what all the fuss is about.

∞

Many things are said of boys: Boys like sports, boys are messy, boys don't have any feelings, boys like trucks, boys don't like girly things, boys like to run around and eat gross food. Whatever the specific generalization, the point of these notions about boys is to set them apart from girls as being entirely different.

Similar statements are made about girls: Girls like pink, girls like flowers, girls are neat and clean, girls are frivolous, girls are emotional. Are any of these things true about all girls? Of course not. But it's easier to think about boys and girls as being entirely different than it is to think about boys and girls as having lots of common ground.

∞

As concerns boys themselves, you have several options. The first, of course, is to ignore them until you (and they) are 19. Or 21. Or 25.

Alternately, you could make a boy your best friend. Boys can be excellent friends. In general, they like to do things, and that makes them rather fun.

Of course a third option is romance. Some girls might be interested in this kind of thing (you will recognize them by their doodles of their name and a boy's name in a heart on their science homework); other girls might think that would be too icky to even imagine. If you are in the latter group, don't worry, you have plenty of company.

If you are in the former group, there are two main things to keep in mind. One, if a boy doesn't like you the way you are, the problem is him, not you. And two, don't try to make a boy change for you—it's important to appreciate people for who they are.

Wherever you fall on the spectrum of how you feel about boys, do treat all your friends, boys and girls, with kindness. This has gone out of fashion, and that's a sad mistake.

Overall, the truth is that there's no great big mystery about boys. Boys are people, and like all people, they are complicated. And that's what makes being friends with other people interesting: you get to learn about how other people think and act, and, in the process, learn a little bit more about yourself.

Robert's Rules

IN 1863, Henry M. Robert had been an engineer in the Civil War, shoring up the defenses of ports in Washington, Philadelphia, and throughout New England. He had improved rivers in Oregon, developed the harbors of Green Bay and Oswego, and constructed dams and locks on the Tennessee and Cumberland rivers. But his greatest challenge came when he was asked to preside over a church meeting. With no knowledge of how a meeting should be run, he bravely attempted to take charge, only to end up embarrassed and thoroughly humbled by the proceedings. He resolved never to attend another meeting until he knew something about parliamentary procedure—the set of rules of conduct at meetings that allows for decisions to be made fairly and without confusion. His *Pocket Manual of Rules of Order for Deliberative Assemblies,* first published in 1876 and known today as *Robert's Rules of Order,* is the result. You and your friends can use these rules to run your own clubs and meetings.

THE BASIC RULES OF PARLIAMENTARY PROCEDURE:

- The rights of the organization supersede the rights of individual members
- All members are equal and their rights (to attend meetings, make motions, speak in debate, nominate, vote, hold office) are equal
- A quorum must be present to do business
- The majority rules
- Silence is consent
- One question at a time and one speaker at a time
- Debatable motions must receive full debate
- Once a question is decided, it is not in order to bring up the same motion or one essentially like it at the same meeting
- Slurs, comments, and personal remarks in debate are always out of order

≈ RUNNING A MEETING ≈

BEING THE CHAIRPERSON

The chairperson is in charge of the meeting and has a gavel, like a judge. She should prepare an agenda, an outline of a meeting that lists the items to be discussed or acted upon. Here is a typical example, with a basic script to follow:

1. Roll call of members present
This is done to determine a quorum—making sure there are enough members present to run the meeting. The secretary reads member's names from a list and members respond.

THE VOCABULARY OF ROBERT'S RULES

Agenda: *A list of items to be discussed at a meeting*

Appeal: *A motion to object to a ruling*

Ballot Vote: *A secret vote, written on a piece of paper*

Bylaws: *Written rules for governing an organization*

Carried: *To adopt a motion*

Debate: *The formal discussion of a motion*

Dilatory Tactic: *The misuse of a parliamentary procedure (such as repeatedly using division or appealing previous decisions)*

Division: *To call for a recount of a vote*

Floor: *To be given permission to speak at a meeting (As in "to have the floor")*

Minutes: *The official written record of a meeting*

Motion: *A proposal that some action be taken or an opinion expressed by the group*

New Business: *New matters brought for consideration*

Nominate: *Formally name a person as a candidate for election or office*

Order of Business: *The schedule of business to be considered*

Out of Order: *Not correct from a parliamentary standpoint*

Pending: *Questions that are under consideration*

Point of Order: *An objection made for improper procedure*

Preamble: *The introduction to a resolution that begins with "whereas"*

Putting the Question: *Placing the motion before the group for a vote*

Quorum: *The number of members that must be present for business to take place*

Recess: *To take a short break during a meeting*

Resolution: *A formal written motion*

Unfinished Business: *Matters from a previous meeting that were postponed or brought over to the next meeting*

Yield: *To give way when you have been assigned the floor*

2. Call to order
"Welcome. A quorum being present, the meeting will come to order." (Bang your gavel once, for good effect.)

3. Read the minutes of last meeting
"The first business in order is the approval of the minutes of the previous meeting. Will [the secretary who keeps the minutes] please read the minutes of the last meeting? Are there any corrections to the minutes? There being no corrections, the minutes are approved as read." (If there are corrections, they should be noted and recorded by the secretary.)

4. Officers' reports
"The next business in order will be the reports of the officers." (Call on those officers you know to have reports.)

5. Treasurer's report
"The treasurer, [call by name], will give her report." After the report is read: "Are there any questions? There being no questions, the report will be filed for audit."

6. Committee reports
"The next business in order will be the reports of committees." After reports have been made: "Thank you. The report will be filed with the minutes of this meeting."

7. Special orders
This is any business previously designated for consideration at this meeting.

8. Unfinished business
Only announce this if there is business that has been postponed from the last meeting to the current meeting. "The next business in order will be the [whatever the unfinished business is] that was postponed to this meeting."

9. New business
"The next business in order will be new business. Is there any new business to come before the group?"

10. Announcements or program
If there are announcements to be made but no program at the meeting: "If there is no further new business to come before the group, the secretary will read the announcements."

If there is a program at the meeting: "If there is no further business to come before the group, [the program chair] will introduce today's speaker."

11. Adjournment
"If there is no further business and there is no objection, the meeting will be adjourned. There being no objection, the meeting is adjourned."

BEING THE SECRETARY

The secretary of your group is responsible for several things: sending out notices of upcoming meetings; maintaining the organization's records, including the membership list, lists of all committees and their members, and an up-to-date version of the group's bylaws; and, most importantly, writing the minutes of the organization. The minutes should be written as concisely and precisely as possible, as they constitute the official record of everything that takes place within your group.

The format for writing the minutes is as follows:

✎ FIRST PARAGRAPH
Include the kind of meeting (whether it's regular or a special meeting), the name of your organization, date and place of meeting, presence of the president and secretary or the names of substitutes, presence of a quorum, time the meeting was called to order, and whether the minutes of the previous meeting were approved or corrected.

✎ BODY
List the reports given, including the name of the reporter and any action taken; all motions; all points of order or appeal; important announcements; if there is a program, the name of the speaker and the topic of the program.

✎ FINAL PARAGRAPH
Record the adjournment and the time of adjournment, and sign and date the document.

When writing minutes, be sure to record all adopted and defeated motions, the name of the person who makes any motion, names of all members who report, names of anyone elected or appointed, and the number of votes on each side in a ballot or counted vote. Do not write down your personal opinion of any discussion, motions that are withdrawn, or entire reports that are given at a meeting. (Instead of transcribing the report, write: "[Person's name and title] reported on [topic]. The report is attached to the original of these minutes.")

After writing the minutes (which you should do as promptly as possible), sign and date them and send a copy to the president of your organization, making sure to alert her to any items of unfinished business. When making corrections, do not erase or obliterate the original. Instead, make any corrections in red ink and note the date of the correction.

BEING THE TREASURER

The treasurer is the person responsible for the money of an organization. Her job is to receive and disburse monies according to the organization's rules, and to bill for and collect any annual dues. She maintains a permanent record of all money received and paid out; any corrections made are clearly indicated in red, just as in the secretary's minutes. The treasurer gives a brief report at each meeting summarizing any collections or expenditures and bringing up any unusual items. Once a year, the treasurer's books are audited, meaning that they are verified and all the numbers checked, and an audit report is dated and signed by the auditing committee.

A treasurer's report should list:

- ✍ The date of meeting
- ✍ Balance on hand at the date of last meeting
- ✍ Receipts (money received)
- ✍ Disbursements (money paid out)
- ✍ Reserve funds (if any)
- ✍ Balance on hand at the date of report (the original balance on hand, plus receipts, minus disbursements, plus reserve fund)

The treasurer should sign the report at the bottom.

BEING A MEMBER

The point of parliamentary procedure is that everyone has a chance for her voice to be heard—even members who aren't officers or chairpeople. A member makes herself and her ideas known through something called a motion. A motion is a method of introducing business in a meeting, and there are two kinds of motions: main motions and secondary motions.

A main motion is a proposal that action be taken (or an opinion expressed) by the group. This kind of motion cannot be made when any other motion is on the floor (that is, being discussed), and always yields to secondary motions. Main motions require a "second" (a second person who supports the motion) unless they are made by a committee. Main motions can be debated and amended, and they always require a majority vote.

A secondary motion is one that can be made while a main motion is on the floor, even before it has been decided. There are three kinds of secondary motions: subsidiary motions, privileged motions, and incidental motions. Subsidiary motions pertain to the main motion on the floor, and their purpose is to change or affect how a main motion is handled. They are voted on before a main motion. Privileged motions are urgent motions, such as recess or adjournment, that do not relate to pending business. Incidental motions deal with process and procedure—correcting errors, verifying votes—and must be considered before the other motion.

Making a motion

First, request the floor by standing and addressing the chairperson: "Madam President." Once you are recognized by the chairperson, introduce your motion by saying, "I move that . . ." and then stating your proposal. Another member (who does not need to stand or be recognized by the chairperson) supports your motion by saying, "I second the motion." If your motion is not seconded, the chairperson can dismiss it, saying "Since there is no second, the motion is not before this meeting." If your motion is seconded, the chairperson announces and restates your motion, saying "It has been moved and seconded that [your proposal here]." Now the motion is "pending," that is, awaiting debate before it can be voted on and finalized. The chairperson asks, "Is there any discussion?" The chairperson recognizes members who wish to debate the motion. After the discussion is over, she puts the question to a vote, saying, "The question is on the motion that [your proposal here]. All in favor of the motion say 'aye'; all opposed say 'no'." The chair then announces the results of the vote.

You can modify or withdraw your motion before it has been stated by the chairperson. After it has been stated by the chairperson, if you wish to change the motion, you may offer an amendment; if you wish to withdraw it, you must ask permission of the group to do so. Keep in mind that your motion may be ruled "out of order" (inappropriate or incorrect) if it: goes against your group's bylaws, repeats a question asked or motion made on the same day, conflicts with another already adopted motion, or is frivolous or rude.

Voting on a Motion

How your group votes depends on the policy of your organization, but in general there are five voting methods most often used: voting by voice, by roll call, by general consent, by division, and by ballot voting. The chairperson counts the vote.

In a voice vote, the chairperson asks those in favor to say "aye," those opposed to say "no." In a roll call, each member answers "yes" or "no" as her name is called. In a vote by general consent, when a motion is likely to be agreeable, the chairperson says, "if there is no objection . . ." and the members demonstrate agreement by remaining silent (but if even one member says "I object," the item must be put to a vote). In a vote by division, a voice vote is clarified by members raising their hands or standing to indicate their vote. And in a vote by ballot, members write their vote on a piece of paper.

Your group can also make a motion instead of voting: you can make a motion to "table," which means to set aside the motion under consideration until a later date. (A "tabled" motion can always be put back on the table.) Or you can make a motion to "postpone indefinitely."

WRITING THE BYLAWS

Bylaws are the fundamental principles and rules governing an organization. They should be clear and concise, as their goal is to help a group by defining and protecting its purpose. A group doesn't officially exist until its bylaws are written. Here is a typical format for constructing your group's bylaws.

ARTICLE I: Your group's name
ARTICLE II: Purpose of your group
ARTICLE III: Members
  1. Classes of membership (active, honorary, etc.)
2. Eligibility or qualifications for membership
3. Membership fees or dues
4. Rights of membership
5. Resignations and disciplinary action

ARTICLE IV: Officers
1. List in order of rank (president, vice president, etc.)
2. Duties (what each officer does)
3. Term of office (how long they get to be an officer)
4. Nominations and elections (how new officers are nominated and elected)

ARTICLE V: Meetings
1. Regular meetings
2. Annual meetings
3. Special meetings
4. Quorum (how many members need to be present for a meeting to take place)

ARTICLE VI: Board of Directors
1. Composition (who is on the board)
2. Powers (what can the board do)
3. Meetings (how often does it meet)
4. Quorum

ARTICLE VII: Executive Committee
A board within the board of directors

ARTICLE VIII: Committees
List all committees, including the committee name, number of members, manner of selection, and duties. Then list "special committees," permitting the establishment "of such special committees as necessary to carry on the work of the organization."

ARTICLE IX: Parliamentary Authority

ARTICLE X: Amendment of the Bylaws
Outlines the procedure for amending the bylaws (usually a two-thirds vote is required)

ARTICLE XI: Dissolution
States what will happen to the assets if the organization should be dissolved

Further Reading on Robert's Rules
Robert's Rules in Plain English (second edition), by Doris P. Zimmerman

༚

Watercolor Painting On the Go

ONE OF THE MOST ENJOYABLE ways to begin watercolor painting is to work outdoors, when the weather is nice and the light is good. Working outdoors is also great because nature is a fabulous subject for beginners to paint. Unlike trying to paint, say, a family portrait, or a picture of your friend, a landscape is a forgiving subject: even if you aren't able to capture the rolling hills and colorful flowers perfectly, your painting can still resemble an outdoors scene. (And you can always call it "impressionistic" if it doesn't!) Here is what you'll need in your traveling watercolor kit.

❦ Brushes
Bring an assortment of round and flat watercolor brushes in a variety of sizes (0, 2, 4, 8, 12). Best brands: Winsor Newton Sceptre Gold, Robert Simmons, Grumbacher. Synthetic sable is an economical, long-lasting alternative to the more expensive pure sable bristles.

Brush holder
A flat bamboo mat that can be
rolled up and tied with a ribbon
or string. Weave a piece of
white elastic band through the
lower third of the mat and insert
brushes. Roll up and tie!

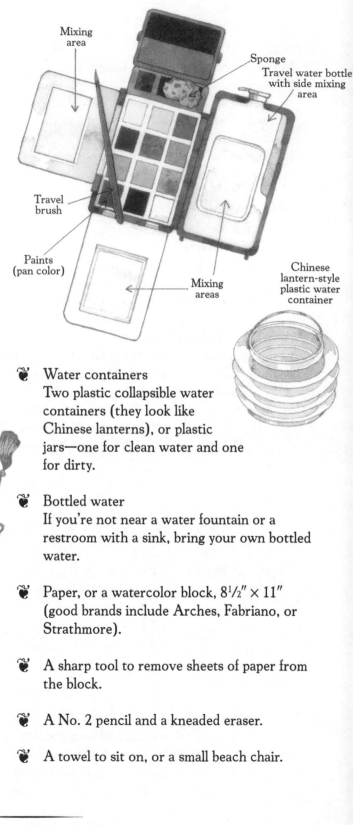

Mixing
area

Sponge
Travel water bottle
with side mixing
area

Travel
brush

Paints
(pan color)

Mixing
areas

Chinese
lantern-style
plastic water
container

Travel-sized palette
Make sure the mixing area is
large enough, and that there's
a good range of colors (red,
orange, yellow, green, blue,
violet, yellow ochre, burnt
sienna).

½″
flat

Round
#12

Round
#8

Round
#4

Round
#2

Water containers
Two plastic collapsible water
containers (they look like
Chinese lanterns), or plastic
jars—one for clean water and one
for dirty.

Bottled water
If you're not near a water fountain or a
restroom with a sink, bring your own bottled
water.

Paper, or a watercolor block, $8\frac{1}{2}'' \times 11''$
(good brands include Arches, Fabriano, or
Strathmore).

A sharp tool to remove sheets of paper from
the block.

A No. 2 pencil and a kneaded eraser.

A towel to sit on, or a small beach chair.

TIPS

Never leave your watercolor brush standing in water—it will ruin the bristles. Instead, keep the brushes on your bamboo mat. Let them dry in the air.

Clean your brushes before adding a new color (especially when changing from dark to light hues).

If you wish to work on a separate sheet of paper rather than a block, use watercolor masking tape to secure all sides and edges of the paper on a board. Not doing so will allow air to get underneath and buckle the paper.

Do not overwork your painting! Wait for an area to completely dry before adding more water or pigment. Too much water can break down the fibers in the paper and make it look too "scrubbed." As with so many things in life, less is more.

Less water will give you a more opaque, darker color. More water will yield a more transparent, lighter color.

Lightly sketch your landscape or seascape in pencil before starting—you can always erase pencils marks, once the paper is completely dry, with a kneaded eraser. Darker, heavier lines are more difficult to remove.

GREAT WATERCOLOR ARTISTS TO CHECK OUT

Beatrix Potter (19th-mid 20th century British watercolorist)
Sara Midda (contemporary British watercolorist and designer)
Winslow Homer (American, 19th-20th centuries)
Andrew Wyeth (American, 20th century)
John Singer Sargent (American, 19th-early 20th century)
Charles Demuth (American, early 20th century)
Carl Larsson (Swedish illustrator, late 19th-early 20th centuries)
Charles Reid (contemporary American watercolorist)
J.M.W. Turner (British, 19th century)
Albrecht Durer (German, Northern Renaissance)
Phansakdi Chakkaphak (contemporary Thai botanical watercolorist)
Charles Rennie MacIntosh (Scottish, late 19th century)

Making a Peg Board Game

PERFECT FOR CAR TRIPS or rainy days, this ancient logic game is surprisingly easy to make but difficult to master. Traditionally, it is a triangular board with fourteen pegs and fifteen holes. The goal is to jump one peg over another until only one remains.

Needed:

- 1 flat board of wood, 6″ × 6″ (at least one inch thick is a good size).
  Any shape is fine; it doesn't have to be triangular.
- 14 fluted dowel pins, ⁵/₁₆″ × 1¹/₂″. Available at any hardware store.
- Ruler
- Power drill, with a ⁵/₁₆″ bit.

Make a dot at the top of the board for your starting point. Lightly draw one diagonal line and then another, marking your triangle on the wood. In addition to the top dot, mark four dots down one side of the triangle, four along the other side, and three dots along the bottom. Draw dots for the middle holes, too. Use your ruler so everything lines up.

You will need adult help with the next power drilling step.

Drill a ¹/₂″ hole right where you have drawn each dot. Some people measure ¹/₂ inch up the drill bit and put some masking tape on that spot so they can easily gauge the hole, although once you do enough of these, you'll get the feel of it. Test each hole with a dowel, making sure the dowel easily moves in and out. When all fifteen holes are done, shake out the sawdust, and you're ready to play.

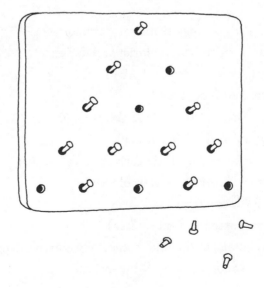

Handclap Games

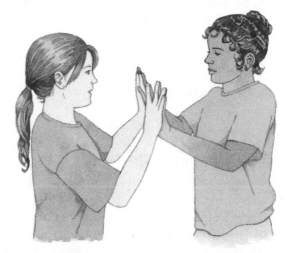

HANDCLAP GAMES, or sidewalk songs, are not only fun to play, they are a fantastic oral storytelling tradition. Many of the rhyming, clapping games flirt with grown-up ideas like "bad words," courtship, and power, and they do so with inventive language, simple songs, and entertaining, sometimes tricky, choreography.

The lyrics and movements to handclap games can vary depending on where a girl lives. Different regions often have different clap sequences or alternate lyrics that become popular with the girls who practice them. Below we've included the most standardized lyrics and verses for the most popular handclap songs, but you and your friends may know other variations.

BASIC

The basic handclapping pattern involves two people standing facing one another. The clapping begins with each person bringing up her right hand, palm facing out, and clapping hands with the other person, then clapping her own hands together, then bringing up the left hand and clapping the other person's left hand, then clapping her own hands together. Repeat this pattern until the rhyme is done. (You can also begin with clapping your own hands, then clapping right hands together, etc.)

CROSS-ARMS

Begin with arms crossed against the chest, uncross your arms and clap your hands on your upper thighs, clap your hands together, clap right hands with your partner, clap your hands together, clap left hands with your partner, clap your hands together, clap right hands with your partner—then back to arms crossed and repeat from the beginning. Repeat until the rhyme is done.

UP-DOWN

Begin facing each other, both players with right hands up, palms facing down, and left hands down, palms facing up. Bring your right hands down and left hands up, clapping together; then switch so your left hands are up, palms facing down, and your right hands are down, palms facing up. Bring your left hands down and right hands up, clapping together. Then clap palms together straight on, then clap your own hands together. Repeat from the beginning until the rhyme is done. (Another variation is to clap as instructed, then after clapping your own hands, clap right hands together, clap your own hands, clap left hands together, clap your own hands, then start from the very beginning.)

BACK-FRONT DOUBLE CLAP

Begin by clapping right hands with your partner, clap your hands together, clap left hands together, clap your hands together TWICE, clap backs of hands with your partner, then palms of hands with your partner, then clap your hands together—then back to the beginning. Repeat until the rhyme is done.

Here are five favorites.

DOWN BY THE BANKS

(This rhyme uses the **basic** handclap pattern, beginning with partners clapping right hands together. This game can also be played as an elimination-style game in a group. Everyone stands in a circle with each girl's right hand on top of the left hand of the girl on her right. Going clockwise, each girl slaps the hand of the girl to her left. At the end of the rhyme, if it is your turn and you manage to hit the next girl's hand before she pulls it away, she is out—but if you miss, you are out. When there are only two people left, the game reverts to the two-person basic pattern.)

> Down by the banks of hanky panky
> where the bullfrogs jump from bank
>   to banky
> with a hip hop, shimmy-shimmy pop
> the bank was too far and they went
>   ker-plop!

THREE SAILORS

(This rhyme uses the **basic** handclap pattern, beginning with a clap, then partners clapping right hands together.)

> Three sailors went to sea, sea, sea
> [point to your eye for each "see" or "sea"]
> To see what they could see, see, see,
> But all that they could see, see, see,
> Was the bottom of the deep blue sea,
>   sea, sea

Other versions, in four verses:

The "I love you" version:
1. *Three sailors went to I, I, I, to see what they could I, I, I . . . etc.*
[point to yourself for each "I, I, I"]
2. *Three sailors went to love, love, love to see what they could love, love, love . . . etc.*
[cross your arms against your chest for each "love, love, love"]
3. *Three sailors went to you, you, you to see what they could you, you, you . . . etc.*
[point to your partner for each "you, you, you"]
4. *Three sailors went to I LOVE YOU*
   To see what they could I LOVE YOU
   But all that they could I LOVE YOU
   Was the bottom of the deep blue I LOVE YOU
[perform all three signs for each "I LOVE YOU"]

The "Disneyland" version:
1. *Three sailors went to diz, diz, diz to see what they could diz, diz, diz . . . etc.*
[twirl your finger around your ear for each "diz, diz, diz"]
2. *Three sailors went to knee, knee, knee to see what they could knee, knee, knee . . . etc.*
[touch your knee for each "knee, knee, knee"]
3. *Three sailors went to land, land, land to see what they could land, land, land . . . etc.*
[put your arms one on top of the other out in front of you for each "land, land, land"]

4. *Three sailors went to DIZ-KNEE-LAND*
   To see what they could DIZ-KNEE-LAND
   But all that they could DIZ-KNEE-LAND
   Was the bottom of the deep blue
       DIZ-KNEE-LAND
   [perform all three signs for each
      "DIZ-KNEE-LAND"]

MISS MARY MACK
(This rhyme uses the "Cross-Arms" pattern.)

Miss Mary Mack, Mack, Mack
All dressed in black, black, black
With silver buttons, buttons, buttons
All down her back, back, back
She asked her mother, mother, mother
For fifty cents, cents, cents
To see the elephant, elephant, elephant
Jump over the fence, fence, fence
He jumped so high, high, high
He reached the sky, sky, sky
And he never came back, back, back
Till the 4th of July, ly, ly.

(Alternate ending: girls point and shout "You
lie!" after the last line about July.)

MISS SUSIE HAD A STEAMBOAT
(this rhyme uses the "Up-Down" pattern)

Miss Susie had a steamboat,
the steamboat had a bell
Miss Susie went to heaven,
the steamboat went to—
HELLO, operator,
please give me number nine
and if you disconnect me,
I'll kick you from—
BEHIND the 'frigerator
there was a piece of glass,

Miss Susie fell upon it
and broke her little—
ASK me no more questions,
I'll tell you no more lies,
Miss Susie's in the kitchen,
Making her mud pies.

SAY, SAY, OH PLAYMATE
(This rhyme uses the "Back-Front Double
Clap," with a small "intro" and a small "ending." Intro: on the words "say, say, oh" you
grab hands and swing them toward each other
for the first "say," back out for the next "say,"
and then clap your hands together on "oh,"
then begin the Back-Front pattern. Ending: at
the words "forever more," on the first and second "more"s you clap hands with your partner
then clap hands yourself, then on the words
"shut the door!" you clap hands with your
partner three times.)

Say, say, oh playmate,
Come out and play with me
And bring your dollies three,
Climb up my apple tree.
Slide down my rainbow,
Into my cellar door,
And we'll be jolly friends
Forever more, more, shut the door!

(sometimes this verse is followed with:
   I'm sorry playmate,
   I can not play with you.
   My dolly has the flu,
   Boo-hoo hoo hoo hoo hoo.
   Ain't got no rainbow,
   Ain't got no cellar door,
   But we'll still be jolly friends
   Forever more more, ever more!)

Finance: Interest, Stocks, and Bonds

WE'VE ALL HEARD THE SAYINGS: "Time is money" and "Put your money where your mouth is." Despite its reputation as being "the root of all evil," money is, most basically, anything that is used as a means of payment. Today we use paper, coins, and plastic cards; in the past, people used rocks, tobacco leaves, cigarettes, and gold and silver. Money buys us everything from food to fun, and it's important to think about money now because pretty soon you'll be in charge of your own money, and the more you understand about it, the more you will be able to make good use of it. Part of learning about money includes knowing where to put your savings, which is the money you keep instead of spending. The value of your savings increases differently, depending on what you do with it.

INTEREST

When you put money in a bank account, you are actually lending your money to the bank. For the privilege of doing this, the bank pays you a tiny bit each year to "rent" your money. This is called interest. You can take your money out of the bank if you need to, but while it's in there, the bank pays you interest—usually a set percent of every dollar that you keep in your account, called an interest rate. So if the annual interest rate is 5% and you put $100 in your bank account, at the end of one year you'll have $105.

COMPOUNDING

Thanks to something called compounding, your money can turn into even more money. If you keep that $105 in the bank for another year, now you're earning 5% interest on $105. So in other words, after two years, the $100 you started with will turn into $110.25. And all you had to do was not spend it. If you saved that $100 for twenty years, with the interest compounding every year you'd end up with $265.33. Without compounding interest, that $100 would only turn into $200 after twenty years.

Compounding interest is why saving even little bits of money can add up to much more later. However, compounding works against you when you are the one borrowing the money—which is what you are doing when you use a credit card. (It might feel like free money, but it's not!) When you buy things with a credit card, you're the one borrowing money, so you're the one being charged interest—interest that compounds. So if you spend money using a credit card and you don't pay off your debt every month when the bill comes due, the $100 you spent turns out to cost you much more.

INVESTING: STOCKS, BONDS, AND MUTUAL FUNDS

Putting your money in a savings account is just one way to invest it, or make your money earn money. There are other ways to invest money, but they are riskier, which means while you might earn more, you can also lose some (or all) of your money. Dealing with money means figuring out how much risk you want to take for different kinds of possible rewards.

Stocks

Stock is ownership of a company. When you buy stock (one piece of which is called a share) in a company, that makes you a stockholder (also called a shareholder), and the more stock you own, the bigger your stake in the company. Owning stock means that you own a small piece of the company—so when a company does well and makes money, you make money too. And if it does badly, well, you can lose money instead.

The price of stock can vary from pennies to thousands of dollars, depending on the company. You get to decide when to buy a stock and when to sell a stock. You do this through a stock broker or directly through the company. The idea is to buy low and sell high to make a profit: buying shares of a stock when it's priced low and then selling that stock at a higher price is one way you make money on your investment with stocks. Stocks are bought and sold—traded—in stock markets, like the New York Stock Exchange, American Stock Exchange, or NASDAQ. You can follow the progress of your stock in the newspaper, on television, or on the Internet.

The other way to make money with stocks is when companies pay out dividends—money paid to all the stockholders every year, the amount of which varies depending on how much a company earns.

Bonds

A bond is basically an "IOU." When you buy a bond, you are lending your money to a company or government, which they will pay you back later. Bonds give you an interest rate that is generally higher than what you're going to get in a savings account. The interest is worked into the bond price, and you get both the interest and your money back on the "maturity date."

Mutual Funds

Mutual funds are another way to invest your money. With mutual funds, a money manager—a person whose job it is to know about investments—decides what stocks and bonds to buy and sell. When you buy into a mutual fund, you buy shares in the fund the same way you buy a share of a single company, but instead you're putting your money into a big collection (a "fund") that the money manager uses to buy and sell investments to make money for you. Of course, she keeps a little piece for herself in the end.

Mutual funds are one way to balance out risk, as they involve diversification. When you diversify your investments, you make an effort to not put all your money in one risky thing, or all your money in one safe thing. Instead, you put a little into something more risky, a little into something safe, and a little into something in between.

Marco Polo and Water Polo

ACCESS TO A POOL, lake, pond, creek, river, stream, ocean, or garden hose is critical on a hot summer day. Contests are always fun: swimming stroke races (on your mark, get set, go!), diving, and seeing who can make up the funniest jumps. Cannonballs are great fun, as you run off the diving board, hurl into the air, grab onto your legs, and make a huge splash. Underwater tricks like handstands and multiple back flips are also a nice way to cool off, as are attempts to mimic the intricacies of synchronized swimming. On a rainy day, you can watch old movies by water-ballet star Esther Williams for inspiration.

With water games, the main challenge is usually not the game itself, at least once you're on your way to mastering swimming—it's your nose, and how to keep water from rushing into it. You have three choices:

1. Breathe out sharply through your nose as you jump or duck underwater. The air coming out of your nose will keep water out.

2. Use one hand to hold your nose.

3. Find yourself an old-fashioned nose plug, the kind attached to the front of a rubber necklace. Clip your nose shut.

Thus prepared, below are a couple of aquatic games for those who can get to a pool or other slow-moving body of water.

MARCO POLO

The famed explorer Marco Polo was seventeen when he left Venice, Italy, to join his dad and uncle on a horseback journey to China. He did not return home for twenty-four years. While traveling, he befriended the Emperor Kublai Khan and was one of the first Western travelers of the Silk Road. He was fascinated by China's use of paper money and its intricate postal delivery system, innovations that far outstripped Europe's development at the time.

How Marco Polo's name got attached the internationally known pool game, no one knows, but here are the rules.

You need at least three kids, and everyone starts in the water. One person is It, and her goal is to tag the other kids. She closes her eyes, thus blinded (or you can use your handy bandana for a blindfold). Then she counts to five, or whatever number you all agree on. To try to find the other kids without seeing them, It must listen and sense where they are. Whenever she wants, she yells "Marco." Everyone in the game must immediately respond "Polo." The girl who is It uses the sounds of the other kids' movements and voices to find and tag someone. Whomever she tags becomes the new It.

VARIATIONS

Now, there are some alterations you can employ to make Marco Polo even more amusing and challenging. If you choose to, you can allow "fish out of water." This means the non-It kids can get out of the pool. However, at any time, It can yell "fish out of water" and if someone is out of the pool, that person automatically becomes the new It. If no one is out of the water, the other players often yell "no." (Hint: This can help It reorient and find them, too.)

You can also allow "mermaid on the rocks," which is similar to "fish out of water." If someone is a mermaid on the rocks, she is sitting on the ledge of the pool or the lakeshore with only her feet in the water. Again, if It yells "mermaid on the rocks," any mermaid becomes the new It. For either of these out-of-the-water variations, if It calls for fish or mermaids and there are none, she must do the start-of-game countdown again.

Another fun addition is "alligator eyes," which allows It to call out "alligator eyes" (or "submarine," if you prefer) and then swim underwater with eyes open for one breath. Usually It is allowed to use this only once. We've heard of some places where It is allowed to go underwater and look around any time, but cannot move until she is above water with eyes closed or blindfold on again. We haven't played this one, but you may want to try it.

Other Marco Polo variations are popular in different places throughout the globe. In Argentina, kids play a version where It has to say the name of whoever she tags. If she is right, the tagged person becomes It, but if she is wrong, she remains It and starts her countdown again. In California, they play "Sharks and Minnows" (called "Silent Witness" other places), which means there is no call and respond, just the sounds of kids moving in the water.

WATER POLO

While Marco Polo can thank the real Marco Polo for its name. water polo's comes from the game's rubber ball, which came from India, where the word for ball is *pulu,* hence polo.

Water polo was invented in England in the 1870s, though a similar kind of game may have been played in rivers in Africa, and in flooded rice paddies in China, many centuries before. While water polo claimed to resemble rugby, in practice it was more akin to underwater wrestling, with players hitting and ducking each other underwater with great regularity. Players would protect the ball by sticking it in their swimsuit and swimming underwater toward the goal. A much-loved but extremely dangerous water polo feat had one player jumping off the backs of teammates, and flying through the air, ball in hand, toward the opposing goal.

Good thing the more civilized "Scottish" rules replaced the former free-for-all. The new rules instituted fouls for pushing and hitting, declared that the ball had to stay above water (no more bathing-suit tricks!), and stated that only a player holding the ball can be tackled (thus lowering the number of players who ended the game in the emergency room).

A water polo team has six field swimmers and a goalie. Teammates pass the ball and keep it from the other side, until one of them can lob it into the goal and score. To move forward in water polo you swim with your head out of water, since you'll need to see where the ball is. To backstroke, you sit in the water, use your arms to make small short strokes, and use the eggbeater kick to stay up and moving: as you sit in the water, bend your knees, and circle each leg toward the other, like an eggbeater.

Rules:

♦ You can touch the ball with your hands—though with only one hand at a time, which means you'll catch the ball and pass it quickly.

♦ Don't touch the bottom of the pool. This sport is about constant motion, no rest, and never touching bottom.

♦ No pushing, pulling, hitting, or holding on to the other players—that's a foul. Fouls also are called if you hold the ball under water, touch it with two hands, or hold onto it longer than 35 seconds; or if you touch bottom, push off the side of the pool, or use bad language.

While Marco Polo will never be an Olympic sport, water polo is. Male Olympians have played water polo since 1900. Ever since the 2000 Summer Olympics in Sydney, women's water polo has been on the roster, too, and there's a terrific story behind its entry. After a decade or two of polite behind-the-scenes negotiation with the International Olympic Committee, the Australian women's national water polo team pushed the issue. The upcoming Olympics were on their turf, after all, and they wanted to compete. In 1998, members of the Olympic leadership were set to arrive at the Sydney airport, in town for a planning visit. Led by their goalkeeper Liz Weekes—she's called the team's "glamour girl" because she's also a model—the Aussie women water polo players put on their swimsuits and caps and strode through the Sydney airport to meet them, and, very much in the public eye, they asked again to be included, and met with success.

Better yet, after fighting so hard to be included, the Australian women's team won the gold medal, with player Yvette Higgins scoring the winning goal during the last second of the championship game, to the applause of fans who filled the stadium.

A Short History of Women Olympic Firsts

1000 BC

Ancient Greece

Women, barred from competing in the all-male Olympics, instead have their own athletic games of Hera every four years from about 1000 BC. Prizes are pomegranates, olive wreaths, and a slice of a sacrificial cow. (By contrast, the prizes for the men's Ancient Olympic chariot races are women.)

440 BC

Ancient Greece

Kallipateria is the first female Olympic boxing coach.

392 BC

Ancient Greece

Kynisca, a Spartan princess, becomes the first female Olympic champion when her horses and chariot compete and win in the Ancient Olympic Games. She will go on to become the first woman champion horse trainer.

1896

Summer Games: Athens, Greece

The first modern Olympics. Women are not allowed to compete, but a Greek woman, Stamati Revithi, unofficially runs the marathon; refused entry to the stadium, she finishes her final lap outside. Athletics officials referred to her as "Melpomene," the Greek muse of Tragedy.

1900

Summer Games: Paris, France

The first modern Games to include female competitors. Helen de Pourtales of Switzerland (Yachting), Elvira Guerra of France (Equestrianism), Mme Ohnier and Madame Depres of France (Croquet), Charlotte Cooper of Great Britain (Tennis), Margaret Abbott of the United States (Golf), and Madame Maison of France (Ballooning) are the first women to compete in the modern Olympics. Golfer Margaret Abbott is the first American woman to win an Olympic gold medal.

1904

Summer Games: St. Louis, Missouri, United States

Lydia Scott Howell wins the first gold medal in archery, an unofficial Olympic sport at these games. Women's boxing is included for the first time as an exhibition sport.

1906

Summer Games: Athens, Greece

Danish women take part in a gymnastics demonstration; it won't be until 1928 that women's gymnastics becomes an official Olympic sport.

1908

Summer Games: London, England

Figure skater Madge Syers of Britain becomes the first woman to win an Olympic gold medal for skating. (In 1902, she entered the men's world championships, since there was no world competition for women. She took second place.)

1912

Summer Games: Stockholm, Sweden

Australian Fanny Durak wins the first Olympic swimming gold medal awarded to women in the 100-meter freestyle. Highboard diving for women is also included for the first time. A fifteen-year-old British schoolgirl enters the modern pentathlon, but her entry is rejected: the event is men only. (It won't be until 2000 that women are allowed to compete in the event.)

1924

Summer Games: Paris, France; Winter Games: Chamonix, France

During the summer games, fourteen-year-old Aileen Riggin becomes the first woman in Olympic history to win medals in both diving and swimming in the same Olympic Games. Tennis player Helen Willis becomes the first woman to win a gold medal for singles and doubles. Women's fencing is contested for the first time, with one event: the individual foil. Figure skating is the only Winter sport open to women. This Olympics marks the first time more than 100 women competed in the games.

1928

Summer Games: Amsterdam, Netherlands; Winter Games: St. Moritz, Switzerland

Women are allowed to compete in track and field events for the first time, and American Elizabeth Robinson becomes the first female gold medalist in a track and field event in Olympic history, winning the 100-meter dash. Women also compete in gymnastics for the first time, and the Netherlands team wins the gold.

1932

Summer Games: Los Angeles, California, United States; Winter Games: Lake Placid, New York, United States

Track stars Louise Stokes and Tydia Pickett become the first black female competitors in the Olympics Games.

1936

Summer Games: Berlin, Germany; Winter Games: Garmisch-Partenkirchen, Germany

Dorothy Poynton becomes the first woman to win the high dive event in successive Olympic Games, winning the gold medal in 1932 and 1936. Thirteen-year-old diver Marjorie Gestering becomes the youngest Olympic gold medalist ever when she wins the springboard event.

1948

Summer Games: London, England; Winter Games: St. Moritz, Switzerland

Vicki Draves is the first Asian American to win an Olympic gold medal, and also the first woman to win both the springboard and high-dive in the same Olympic Games. Alice Coachman wins the high-jump, becoming the first African American woman to win an Olympic gold medal. Her teammate Audrey (Mickey) Patterson becomes the first black woman to win a medal, finishing third in the 200-meter run; she was awarded her bronze medal just before her teammate Coachman won the gold. In the Winter Games, Gretchen Fraser wins the slalom and becomes the first U.S. skier to win an Olympic gold medal.

1952

Summer Games: Helsinki, Finland; Winter Games: Oslo, Norway

Women and men compete together for the first time in Olympic equestrian events. Women gymnasts compete in individual apparatus events for the first time, and Soviet Maria Gorokhovskaya wins the first all-around gold for the USSR in its first Olympics ever. She also is the first woman to win seven medals in a single Olympics.

1960

Summer Games: Rome, Italy; Winter Games: Squaw Valley, California, United States

Ingrid Kramer becomes the first non-American in Olympic history to win all the women's diving events. Wilma Rudolph is the first American woman to win three gold medals at one Olympiad, winning the 100- and 200-meter dashes and the 400-meter relay.

1964

Summer Games: Tokyo, Japan; Winter Games: Innsbruck, Austria

Swimmer Dawn Fraser wins her third consecutive 100-meter Olympic gold medal. Soviet gymnast Larissa Latynina completes her Olympic career with a total of eighteen medals—more than any other athlete in Olympic history at the time.

1968

Summer Games: Mexico City, Mexico; Winter Games: Grenoble, France

Wyomia Tyus wins the gold for the 100-meter and becomes the first winner of back-to-back Olympic gold medals in the event, which she also won in 1964. Deborah Meyer is the first swimmer to win three individual gold medals at one Olympic Games.

1972

Summer Games: Munich, West Germany; Winter Games: Sapporo, Japan

Dianne Holum is the first American woman to earn an Olympic gold medal in speed skating.

1976

Summer Games: Montreal, Quebec, Canada; Winter Games: Innsbruck, Austria

Swimmer Kornelia Ender is the first woman to win four gold medals at one Olympics, all in world-record time. Basketball is an Olympic event for women for the first time. Nadia Comaneci becomes the first gymnast ever—male or female—to score a perfect 10 in an Olympic event; she is also the first Romanian gymnast to win the all-around title at the Olympics and the youngest Olympic gymnastics all-around champion ever.

1984
Summer Games: Los Angeles, California, US; Winter Games: Sarajevo, Yugoslavia
Candy Costie and Tracie Ruiz win the first gold medal awarded for duet synchronized swimming. Ruiz also wins gold in solo. Mary Lou Retton becomes the first American woman gymnast to win the all-around title for the Olympic gold medal, and the first American to earn a perfect score. Joan Benoit Samuelson wins the first Olympic women's marathon. Connie Carpenter-Phinney wins the first Olympic gold medal ever awarded for cycling and becomes the first woman to compete in both the Winter and Summer Olympics (she competed in 1972 in speed skating).

1988
Summer Games: Seoul, South Korea; Winter Games: Calgary, Alberta, Canada
Swimmer Kristin Otto, of the German Democratic Republic, wins six gold medals, the most medals ever won at one Games by a female swimmer. In the Winter Games, figure skater Debi Thomas becomes the first African American to win an Olympic medal in ice skating. Track and field Olympian Jackie Joyner-Kersee becomes the first woman to win *The Sporting News* Man of the Year Award.

1992
Summer Games: Barcelona, Spain
At thirteen, Fu Mingxia of China becomes the second-youngest person to win an individual gold medal when she wins the platform diving event.

1994
Winter Games: Lillehammer, Norway
In the Winter Olympics, speed skater Bonnie Blair becomes the first American woman to win five gold medals.

1996
Summer Games: Atlanta, Georgia, United States
Softball debuts; Dot Richardson hits the first home run in Olympic softball history and the American women win the first-ever softball gold. The U.S. women gymnasts take their first Olympic team gold. Nova Peris-Kneebone becomes the first Aboriginal woman to win Olympic gold, as part of the field hockey team. Women's soccer also debuts, and the U.S. wins the gold medal.

1998

Winter Games: Nagano, Japan

Fifteen-year-old Tara Lipinski becomes the youngest athlete to win a gold medal at the Winter Games. Women's ice hockey is introduced for the first time.

2000

Summer Games: Sydney, Australia

Marion Jones earns more Olympic medals (three gold and two bronze) than any other female track athlete in a single Olympics. Cathy Freeman becomes the first Aboriginal woman to win an individual Olympic medal and the first Aboriginal woman to win a gold medal, in the 400 meter. Fu Mingxia wins the three-meter springboard title to become the first female diver to win gold medals in three different Olympic Games. The modern pentathlon for women is contested for the first time.

2002

Winter Games: Salt Lake City, Utah, United States

Short track speedskater Yang Yang is the first Chinese athlete, male or female, to win a gold medal at the Winter Games. Vonetta Flowers and Jill Bakkan become the first ever winners of an Olympic gold medal in two-woman bobsled, and Flowers becomes the first black athlete to earn Winter gold. Ice skater Naomi Lang is the first Native American female athlete to participate in the Olympic Winter Games.

2004

Summer Games: Athens, Greece

Women's wrestling is introduced, with twenty-one nations qualifying to send wrestlers to the games. Nineteen-year-old Mariel Zagunis becomes the first U.S. fencer (of either gender) to win a gold medal in one hundred years.

2006

Winter Games: Turin, Italy

Claudia Pechstein becomes the first female Winter Olympian to win medals in five consecutive Olympics (1992–2006), and is the most successful German Winter Olympian of all time, with five gold medals, two silver, and two bronze. Croatia's Janica Kostelic becomes the first woman to win four golds in alpine skiing (the other three she won in 2002). Tanith Belbin, along with her partner Benjamin Agosto, wins the silver medal for ice dancing—the first medal for the United States in ice dancing in 30 years. Tanja Poutiainen earns the first medal in alpine skiing for Finland when she wins silver in the giant slalom. The Swedish team wins women's curling and become the first curling team to ever hold Olympic, World, and European titles at the same time.

How to Negotiate a Salary

for dog-walking, errand-running, babysitting—or anything!

Let us never negotiate out of fear, but let us never fear to negotiate.
—John F. Kennedy, Inaugural Address, 1961.

T HE WORD "negotiate" comes from the Latin word *negotiari,* meaning "to trade." When you negotiate something, you are essentially asking for someone to trade you something, and making a case for why that would be a good idea. There are several steps to a successful negotiation: preparation, presentation, contemplation, and sealing the deal.

Preparation

Define your goals. Do you want a higher salary? Do you want more hours? Do you want to be paid extra for overtime? Narrowing down what it is you want will help you approach the task of asking for it.

Do your research. Find out what the going rate is in your neighborhood for the work you do—how much do your friends get paid for the same work? Does the amount they get depend on the level of responsibility they have? Once you know the answers to these questions, you'll know the facts about what other people are paid, and you'll be better prepared to ask for what you want.

Presentation

Plan what you're going to say and how you're going to say it.

Begin with lower-priority requests, if possible, and work your way up to the big ones. (When you get to the big request, you can trade off some of the lower-priority requests if necessary.)

Accentuate the positive. This is not the time for modesty—emphasize your accomplishments and abilities and point out why it is you deserve what you are asking for. Smile, be confident, and be friendly.

Contemplation

Listen. Sometimes the most important part of a conversation is the part when you're not talking. When it's time for the other person to respond, listen carefully to what he or she has to say.

Think. You may be presented with a counteroffer—an offer made in response to your offer. You don't have to respond to a counteroffer right away. You can take your time and think about it, even if that means not giving your answer for a few days.

Sealing the Deal

Sign on the dotted line. Once both parties have reached an agreement, it's a good idea to put that final offer in writing, and have both of you sign the document. This will prevent any future misunderstandings or miscommunications about what was actually agreed upon during your negotiation. Still, sometimes a good old-fashioned handshake will do.

Common Mistakes

Not preparing. Make sure you have done your research and know what you are talking about. If you're not sure, postpone the negotiation until you've had time to get ready.

Trying to win at all costs. Arguing or using intimidating behavior is going to hinder rather than help the negotiation process. Remember, the central process of negotiation is discussion with others to reach an agreement or compromise. It's a dialogue, not a monologue.

Talking too much. Listen carefully to what the other person has to say, and when it's your turn to speak, be direct and to the point.

Trying to be someone you're not. The key in negotiation is to be comfortable. If you are trying to act "tough" because you think it will make the discussion go your way, you may be sadly disappointed. Being the most confident version of yourself is better than trying to be the kind of person you think you should be in order to win.

TIPS

Even though it might make you nervous to ask for something, whether it's a higher salary or more responsibility, it's important to try to maintain an open and confident attitude. You want to make the person you're negotiating with want to say yes to you—and it's very hard to say no to a smiling, friendly person. Some people call this technique to "disarm with charm." But whether or not you're good at being "charming," try to smile, look people directly in the eye, and concentrate on not speaking too fast. Remember, this is just a conversation! You have those all the time. (Also, the people you're negotiating with may expect you to be nervous or insecure about the negotiation process—so acting comfortable and confident may catch them off guard and make them even more likely to say yes to your request.)

Public Speaking

IF YOU WOULD RATHER DIE than speak in public, you're in good company: glossophobia (fear of speaking in public, or "stage fright") affects as much as 75 percent of the population. But speaking in front of a group doesn't have to be nerve-racking, especially if you practice before you do it. Public speaking shares many of the principles of a good negotiation: Preparation, Practice, and Presenting—with the confidence to "seal the deal."

PREPARE

Know what you're going to say
Write out your speech, and practice saying it aloud. You don't necessarily need to memorize it, but you should know it well enough so that if you had to talk without your notes, you could pull it off.

Know who you're going to say it to
Knowing your audience is good advice no matter what you are performing. If you know you will be giving a speech in your history class, that's going to inform your material much differently than if you were giving a toast at your dad's 50th birthday party. You want to adapt your speech to fit the people you are speaking to. That way nobody gets bored, and what you say will be a good match for your audience.

Know where you're going to say it
It's a good idea to familiarize yourself with the place where you'll be speaking, if you can. Is it a big room or a small one? Will you have to speak loud and project, or will there be a microphone that you will have to adjust? Is there a lectern or a chair, or will you be able to move around while you talk? When you have some information about where you'll be, you'll know what to expect before you get there, and that will help cut down on your nerves once it's showtime.

PRACTICE

Visualize
Most of the fear we have around public speaking isn't about talking in front of people, but about doing something potentially embarrassing in front of people. To combat this, practice imagining yourself giving your speech and doing a great job. Walk yourself through it in your head, from beginning to end, giving yourself a chance to visualize yourself doing well instead of living out your worst fears.

Realize
Make it real by practicing your speech ahead of time—by yourself, in front of your family, in front of your friends, the family pets, whoever you can get to be an audience for you. It's a good idea to either write out your speech on notecards or print it out in a very big font so that you can quickly look down, see what you need to say, and look back up to say it. Practicing delivering your speech so that it becomes routine will stand you in good stead when you start to feel unnerved onstage

or in front of the class. Practicing with an audience is also a chance to realize that your audience wants you to succeed. People want to hear what you have to say, and they want you to do well.

Exercise

If you are waiting around while others speak before you, it is helpful to step outside the room just before you speak to calm yourself down with deep-breathing exercises, breathing in slowly through your nose and breathing out through your mouth. If you're too nervous to breathe, you might channel that energy into a quick set of jumping jacks, or shaking out your arms and legs. Then take some deep breaths to feel calm and centered. This is something you can do in practice and in performance.

PRESENT

It's not about you

Remember as you begin your presentation, it's about your speech, not about you. It's helpful to concentrate on the message—not the medium. That way instead of thinking about all the different ways things could go wrong as you deliver your talk, you focus yourself on the content of your talk and about getting those points across.

It's all about you

Whether or not you crumble out of nervousness or do fantastically well thanks to sheer nerve is completely up to you—in other words, it is in your control. When you're incredibly nervous, you have the opportunity to harness that energy and transform it into vitality and enthusiasm. Take a deep breath and dive in!

It's all good

No matter how you do, it is always good in the sense that every time you speak in public, you gain experience. Use this to build your sense of self-confidence: if you've done well, you now have proof for the next time around that you can do well. And if nerves have gotten the best of you, you now have proof that the worst has happened and you've survived. Either way, you know that you've done it— you've spoken in public once, and you can do it again. This confidence-building is crucial, because having confidence is the key to speaking well.

> ### QUICK TIPS
> **Keep it short and sweet.**
> **Slow down:** Don't talk too fast.
> **Look up!** If it's too scary to look at the audience in the front row, look at the people in the back of the room.
> **Smile:** Look confident, even if you don't feel confident.
> **Pretend:** Pull a "Brady Bunch," where you imagine everyone in the audience is sitting there in their underwear. Find a friendly face in the audience and pretend you're only talking to that person.
> **Practice:** Join the debate team, dare yourself to speak up in class, give a speech in front of a mirror. The more opportunities you have to speak in public, the easier it gets.
> **Biggest asset:** Self-confidence. Act as though you have a right to be there—because you do.

Telling Ghost Stories

SO: YOU'VE PITCHED YOUR TENT, set up your campfire, and toasted your s'mores. Or maybe you've made a sleep-over fort at your best friend's house, played Truth or Dare and Bloody Mary, and gotten out the flashlights and sleeping bags. What next? Two words: Ghost stories.

Everybody loves a scary story, especially late at night around a flickering campfire, or in the dark of an unfamiliar living room with a small flashlight illuminating your face. And you may have noticed, if you've been on a few camp-outs or sleepovers, that many of these stories have similar themes: a ghost out for revenge or literally haunted by grief; a lonely road or abandoned house; an element of shock or surprise; and just enough true-life details to make it all seem believable in the dead of night.

Some stories involve real people and places—and supposedly real sightings—like the ghost of Queen Anne Boleyn, second wife of King Henry VIII, who is said to haunt both the Tower of London, where she was imprisoned and beheaded in 1536, and the Hever Castle in Kent, her childhood home and the setting of her first encounter with the king who would later sentence her to death. Other stories are about more anonymous ghosts—regular people who lived in the not-too-distant past and had believably scary things happen to them. And don't discount the shock value of a good old urban legend—supposedly real stories of supposedly real people who had scary things happen to them: the woman who died of spider bites after a spider nested in her hair; the man who picked up a hitchhiker only to discover that she was a ghost haunting the highway where she had been killed in a car wreck 40 years before; the girl who died when her shrink-to-fit jeans shrunk so much while she wore them that she was crushed by their constricting force.

Whichever kind of story you choose to tell, here are some tips for making up good ones, and telling them right.

ELEMENTS OF A GHOST STORY

Mix and match these common elements to make your own ghost story.

Common characters	Common ghost features	Common ghost motivations	Common settings	Common situations
☠ A young girl	☠ Able to be sensed by animals and children	☠ Ghost needs to find an object or person they left behind	☠ Your house	☠ Going out alone at night
☠ An old woman			☠ An abandoned mine	☠ Being alone in a spooky place
☠ A camper	☠ Haunting the place where they died	☠ Ghost needs to warn the main character about something	☠ A graveyard	
☠ A person driving alone			☠ The woods	☠ Getting trapped in a haunted house overnight
☠ Two friends who think they're braver than they are	☠ Appearing at night and vanishing by dawn	☠ Ghost needs to deliver a comforting message to the main character	☠ Your local scary place (cranky neighbor's house, the old creek, etc.)	☠ Picking up a hitchhiker
☠ A person from your city's past	☠ Playful or prankish— playing music or moving things to scare people	☠ Ghost is out for revenge	☠ A long, empty hallway	☠ Disregarding a ghost's warning or a local legend
☠ A distant relative			☠ A castle	☠ Triggering events that summon a ghost
☠ A hitchhiker			☠ Any isolated, spooky place	

Don't forget to use spooky ghost story words, like graveyard, curse, legend, bone-chilling, creepy, ominous, deadly, mysterious, eerie, grisly, gruesome, blood-curdling . . . anything that adds to the scary mood.

Using realistic details can make your story even spookier—having the main character be a girl who used to go to your school years ago, or having the story take place in your town, or down the street from your house, lends the tale an air of believability that draws your listeners in. Sometimes it's helpful to have a friend in on the story—so that when you end your story with something like, "The girl was never found" (said in a somber, dramatic voice, of course), your friend can scream out, "I'm here!!!!" and make everyone else shriek.

TELLING IT RIGHT

Make sure you prepare—practice ahead of time, and coordinate with a friend if you're going to be using a buddy for maximum scaring. When you tell your story, speak slowly, in a serious voice, and look at everyone you're speaking to. Make sure to take your audience into consideration: if there are little sisters or younger girls there, you might want to save the super-scary stuff for after they're asleep. And even if your crowd is a bit older, seriously scary stories can make for some sleepless nights. It's fun to make yourself a little scared, but if a listener finds your tale too frightening, it's also okay to turn on the light and remind everyone that it's just a story.

> **Some famous ghost stories in classic literature:**
>
> Edgar Allen Poe's
> *The Tell Tale Heart* (1843)
> Washington Irving's
> *The Legend of Sleepy Hollow* (1820)
> W.W. Jacobs'
> *The Monkey's Paw* (1902)
> Charles Dickens'
> *A Christmas Carol* (1843)
> Oscar Wilde's
> *The Canterville Ghost* (1887)
> Shakespeare's *Hamlet* (1602)

OR IS IT??????

In this passage from Act I, Scene V, of the play *Hamlet*, we witness one of the spookiest scenes in all of Shakespeare: Hamlet is confronted by the ghost of his father, the former King of Denmark, who tries to tell Hamlet that he was murdered by his own brother.

ACT I. SCENE V

GHOST
I am thy father's spirit,
Doom'd for a certain term to walk the night,
And for the day confined to fast in fires,
Till the foul crimes done in my days of nature
Are burnt and purged away. But that I am
*   forbid*
To tell the secrets of my prison-house,
I could a tale unfold whose lightest word
Would harrow up thy soul, freeze thy young
*   blood,*
Make thy two eyes, like stars, start from their
*   spheres,*
Thy knotted and combined locks to part
And each particular hair to stand on end,
Like quills upon the fretful porpentine:
But this eternal blazon must not be

To ears of flesh and blood. List, list, O, list!
If thou didst ever thy dear father love—

HAMLET
O God!

GHOST
Revenge his foul and most unnatural murder.

HAMLET
Murder!

GHOST
Murder most foul, as in the best it is;
But this most foul, strange and unnatural.

HAMLET
Haste me to know't, that I, with wings as
*   swift*

As meditation or the thoughts of love,
May sweep to my revenge.

GHOST
I find thee apt;
And duller shouldst thou be than the fat weed
That roots itself in ease on Lethe wharf,
Wouldst thou not stir in this. Now, Hamlet,
    hear:
'Tis given out that, sleeping in my orchard,
A serpent stung me; so the whole ear of
    Denmark
Is by a forged process of my death
Rankly abused: but know, thou noble youth,
The serpent that did sting thy father's life
Now wears his crown.

HAMLET
O my prophetic soul! My uncle!

GHOST
Ay, that incestuous, that adulterate beast,
With witchcraft of his wit, with traitorous
    gifts,—
O wicked wit and gifts, that have the power
So to seduce!—won to his shameful lust
The will of my most seeming-virtuous queen:
O Hamlet, what a falling-off was there!
From me, whose love was of that dignity
That it went hand in hand even with the vow

I made to her in marriage, and to decline
Upon a wretch whose natural gifts were poor
To those of mine!
But virtue, as it never will be moved,
Though lewdness court it in a shape of heaven,
So lust, though to a radiant angel link'd,
Will sate itself in a celestial bed,
And prey on garbage.
But, soft! methinks I scent the morning air;
Brief let me be. Sleeping within my orchard,
My custom always of the afternoon,
Upon my secure hour thy uncle stole,
With juice of cursed hebenon in a vial,
And in the porches of my ears did pour
The leperous distilment; whose effect
Holds such an enmity with blood of man
That swift as quicksilver it courses through
The natural gates and alleys of the body,
And with a sudden vigour doth posset
And curd, like eager droppings into milk,
The thin and wholesome blood: so did it mine;
And a most instant tetter bark'd about,
Most lazar-like, with vile and loathsome crust,
All my smooth body.
Thus was I, sleeping, by a brother's hand
Of life, of crown, of queen, at once dispatch'd:
Cut off even in the blossoms of my sin,
Unhousel'd, disappointed, unanel'd,
No reckoning made, but sent to my account
With all my imperfections on my head:
O, horrible! O, horrible! most horrible!
If thou hast nature in thee, bear it not;
Let not the royal bed of Denmark be
A couch for luxury and damned incest.
But, howsoever thou pursuest this act,
Taint not thy mind, nor let thy soul contrive
Against thy mother aught: leave her to heaven
And to those thorns that in her bosom lodge,
To prick and sting her. Fare thee well at once!
The glow-worm shows the matin to be near,
And 'gins to pale his uneffectual fire:
Adieu, adieu! Hamlet, remember me.

How to Change a Tire

CHANGING A TIRE is one of those life skills that never seem essential until the moment you need it. This is good thing to learn even if you are a ways off from having your driver's license.

1. The car should be parked on level ground, out of danger's way, with the engine off and the parking brake on. Ask everyone to hop out of the car to make it lighter.

2. Check to make sure you have all the necessary equipment: a functioning spare tire, a tire jack, and a cross wrench. If you are missing any of these you will unfortunately have to wait for the tow truck.

3. If you have tire blocks, put them under the other tires to keep the car in place. Medium-sized rocks work too.

4. Start to loosen the lug nuts; these are the nuts that keep the hubcap on. Not all cars have hubcaps, but look and you'll see what needs to be loosened. Put the lug wrench on each lug nut. Remember "righty-tighty, lefty-loosey" to guide you which way to turn the lug wrench.

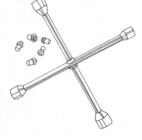

If your car's lug nuts were last tightened with a hydraulic lug nut tightener in a mechanic's shop, they will be very tight. Jump on the cross wrench. Get everyone in your family to jump on the cross wrench and in any other way work the lug nuts free. Some very organized people keep a length of hollow pipe in their car, which can be attached to the cross wrench for extra leverage. If you have it, WD-40 also helps. Some people swear that in a pinch, pouring cola over the lug nuts will do the trick. Caution: don't take the nuts all the way off, just loosen them.

5. The jack will keep the car up and off the ground while the tire is changed. Each car has a slightly different way to do this, so consult the manual if it's nearby. In general, there's a solid metal plate on the car frame, in front of back tire frame and just behind the front tire. Once you've found this, the cool part begins, in which you raise the car.

Put the jack right under the metal plate, and start pumping. The car will lift off the ground. From time to time make sure that the jack stays connected to the metal plate. Stop pumping when the car tire is 6-8 inches off the ground.

6. Now you can remove the lug nuts entirely. Stash them somewhere safe. Grab the tire and pull it toward you. It will be dirty. You can clean up after.

7. Pick up the spare tire and align its holes with the bolts. Push the spare onto the tire bolts until it absolutely stops. Replace the lug nuts and tighten, but not all the way.

8. Carefully pump down the jack to lower the car, stopping when all four tires are back on the ground.

9. Now tighten the lug nuts. Don't tighten them around the circle; instead, tighten the first, then tighten the nut across from it, and continue on from there. You're done.

Make Your Own Quill Pen

THE MAIN INGREDIENT in a quill pen is, of course, the quill. As not all of us live in close proximity to turkeys, crows, or geese, it may be necessary to ask your local poultry farmer for a spare feather. In a pinch, you can try an art supply store or a calligraphy studio. Wherever you find your feather, it's best to get more than one, just in case. The other tools you'll need are a sharp knife or razor, a cutting board, and a pencil.

MAKING THE QUILL

Hold the tip of the quill in boiling water for a minute or two to soften it up so that it can be cut without splitting or breaking off. (It should become soft and somewhat pliable, like your fingernails after a hot bath.) You may also strip some of the feathers off to make room for your hand to hold the quill.

For this you will need adult supervision. Use the knife to slice horizontally across the end of the quill. This angled cut should begin about an inch from the end of the shaft on the underside of the quill.

Make a second cut at a steeper angle, about a half-inch from the end, to shape the nib (the "point" of the pen). Clean out the hollow part, scraping out any fluff of fuzz from inside the quill.

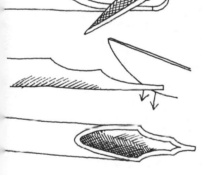

Use the knife to make a slit in the middle of the nib.

Use your pencil to open the slit slightly by pressing up gently from underneath. Lay the nib on a cutting board and slice the tip off so that it is square. At this point you may refine the nib by further cutting down the angled sides or using fine sandpaper to gently smooth out rough edges.

USING YOUR QUILL PEN

It's a good idea to practice on newsprint or water-color paper before moving on to fancier papers. You may want to pencil in some lines or margins as guides before you begin, but this is not required. Dip your quill into the ink you've bought, and then begin to write on your paper. Try not to drench your quill with the ink—the nib should be saturated just enough to write a few letters at a time. Otherwise you'll get blots, drips, and splats. Writing with a quill pen is a leisurely task; the ink takes a while to dry, and the nib will need re-dipping every word or so. Depending on the angle of your nib and the way you hold your pen, your quill will make thin lines as well as thick lines, so feel free to experiment. Practice by writing your favorite sentence—a famous quote or favorite saying—over and over until you can write it without any blots or errors.

Hiking

IN THE 1920s, work began to create and protect a system of National Scenic Trails in the United States. As a result, the 3,100-mile Continental Divide Trail runs from Canada to Mexico, with stops at Yellowstone and National Glacier Parks. The Appalachian Trail can be hiked from Georgia all the way to Maine. And the glorious Pacific Crest Trail winds through the top of the Sierra Nevada range and hits over 13,000 feet above sea level. These are the prized wilderness trails that hikers dream of.

The wilderness is the ideal locale for pulling yourself across outcroppings of bedrock, trudging through leaves, or nimbly hopping over a stream. There are glorious discoveries to be made on smaller and more ordinary trails closer to home. All you need are your sneakers, some water, a map, a compass, and a sense of adventure.

1. Head to a Trail Head

Most trail heads—that's the beginning of the trail—have a posted map to view what the hike entails. The map describes clues, like colorful marks on trees, signs, and places where other trails cut in, that will help you keep track of your location.

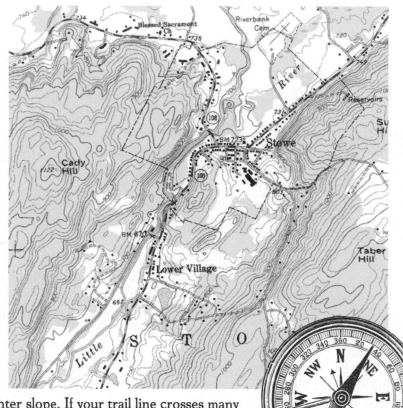

Topo (topography) lines—the mysterious squiggly lines on the map—show elevation. Trace your finger along each line, look at the lines alongside, and you'll start to see peaks and troughs. Each continuous topo line is the same elevation. Lines that lay close together indicate a steeply rising terrain. Lines spread farther apart signal a lighter slope. If your trail line crosses many topo lines, you're in for a steep walk. A trail that follows the curve of topo lines is taking a single altitude, and the walking is relatively flat.

Getting lost and finding your way home is part of the journey and a compass should help you figure out how to get back on the path. Match the dial on the compass so it reads north wherever the needle points, and turn the map, too, to line up with the compass' north. Start early in the day and bring a whistle along if you're worried.

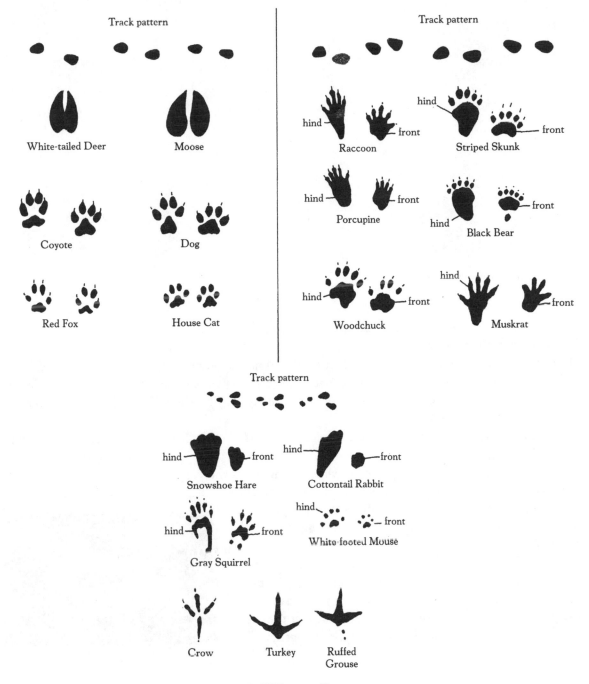

Track pattern

White-tailed Deer

Moose

Coyote

Dog

Red Fox

House Cat

Track pattern

Raccoon — hind, front

Striped Skunk — hind, front

Porcupine — hind, front

Black Bear — hind, front

Woodchuck — hind, front

Muskrat — hind, front

Track pattern

Snowshoe Hare — hind, front

Cottontail Rabbit — hind, front

Gray Squirrel — hind, front

White-footed Mouse — hind, front

Crow

Turkey

Ruffed Grouse

2. What to Do

In one sense, hiking is just walking on a footpath that often angles up, but in the wilderness. If you look closely at the trees you should be able to see how they are different from one another. With a good guide to identification you will be able to figure out the various trees by leaves, bark, and fruit. You can also see life at its smallest by turning over rocks and digging into streams. You may want to try to figure out which animals have passed by the trail by identifying their tracks and scat (droppings).

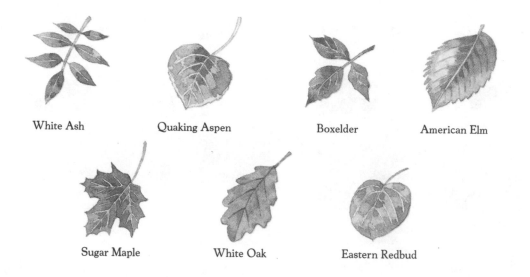

White Ash   Quaking Aspen   Boxelder   American Elm

Sugar Maple   White Oak   Eastern Redbud

3. What to Look Out For

Once upon a time, mythology has it that children were given shovels and machetes, sent out after breakfast, and told to clear their own trails and not come home for dinner until six o'clock. While clearing a trail makes an inspiring metaphor, we can't advise it for two reasons. First, most wilderness is now protected, and we hikers are asked to stay on the trail and leave the homes of animals and plants untrodden.

Second, many woods are filled with poison ivy, and there's little worse than coming home from a hike with set of small dots on your arm, ready to erupt into the worst round of five-day itching you can imagine. "Leaves of three, let them be" is the watch-out-for-poison-ivy mantra. There are many well-behaved three-leaved plants out there, but poison ivy takes so many forms and seasonal colors that the best advice is to stay far from for all three-leaved plants—on the ground, vining up trees, and hanging from overhead.

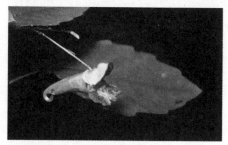

If you run aground of poison ivy, nature is there to help you. Look immediately for jewelweed, also called forget-me-not. It often grows nearby poison ivy and especially loves creek beds. Break open the stem and rub the jewelweed's juice onto your skin as an antidote against the poison ivy.

Jewelweed

4. How to Make a Walking Stick

A walking stick should only be fashioned from a fallen branch, not pulled from a tree, and should reach from the ground to your shoulder. First, use your Swiss Army knife to remove the bark and whittle away extra branches and spurs. Then sand it down until the stick is smooth to touch, and finally just shine it with a little linseed oil.

Greek and Latin Root Words

MANY ENGLISH WORDS have their origins in Latin and Greek. Knowing a word's roots, prefixes, or suffixes, can be your clue to its meaning—even if you don't understand it at first glance.

A word's "root" is the part of the word that carries the main component of meaning. Adding a prefix to the beginning of the root word, or a suffix to the end of it, can add other layers of meaning, but the core concept of the word is in its root. Here is a chart of Greek and Latin root words, their meanings, and some examples (the Greek terms are in *italic*).

Greek and Latin roots	Meaning	English examples
-anthrop-	human	anthropology
-arch-/-archi-	ancient	archetype
-aster-/-astra-	star	astronomy, astral
-audi-	hear	audible
-bene-	good	benefit
-bio-	life	biography
-brev-	short	abbreviation
-chron-/-chrono-	time	anachronism, chronicle
-dem-	people	democracy, demagogue
-derm-	skin	dermatologist
-dict-	to say	dictate, predict
-duc-	to lead; to take	produce, reduce
-fer-	carry	transfer
-fix-	fasten	affix, fixative
-gen-	kind, type; birth	generation

Greek and Latin roots	Meaning	English examples
-geo-	earth	geography, geology
-graph-	write	graphic
-gress-	to walk	progress
-hydr-/hydro-	water	hydrate
-ject-	to throw	eject, project
-jur/just-	law	jury, justice
-log/logue-	word, thought	dialogue, monologue
-luc-	light	lucid, luculent
-manu-	hand	manual
-meter/metr-	measure	thermometer
-morph-	form	amorphous
-neg-	no	negative
-ocu-	eye	ocular
-olig-	few	oligarchy
-op/oper-	work	operation
-osteo-	bone	osteoporosis
-path-	feeling, suffering	empathic, sympathy
-pel-	to drive	compel, dispel,
-pend-	to hang	depend, pendulum
-philo-/-phil-	love	philanthropy, philosophy

Greek and Latin roots	Meaning	English examples
-phon-	sound	polyphonic, phonetics
-phys-	body; nature	physical
-pod-	foot	podiatrist
-port-	to carry	export, support
-proto-	first	prototype
-pseudo-	false	pseudonym
-scrib-/-script-	to write	describe, transcribe
-sect-	cut	dissect
-sol-	alone	solitary, solo
-struct-	build	construct
-tact-	touch	contact, tactile
-tele-	far off	telephone
-tract-	to pull, drag, draw	attract, contract, extract
-ter/terr-	earth	territory
-vac-	empty	vacant, vacuous
-ver-	truth	verify
-verb-	word	verbal
-vert-	to turn	convert, revert
-vid/vis-	see	video, visualize

A prefix is a word part added to the beginning of a root word to change its meaning. Here are some Greek and Latin prefixes, their meanings, and examples.

Greek and Latin prefixes	Meaning	English examples
a-/an-	without; not	amoral, atypical
ad-	to	addict
amb-/ambi-	both	ambidextrous
ante-	before	antecedent
anti-/ant-	opposite	antifreeze, antacid
auto-	self	autobiography, autopilot
bi-/bi-	two	bipedal
bio-	life	biology
centi-	hundred	centimeter, century
circum-	around	circumvent, circumnavigate
con-	with	concert
co-	together	coauthor
de-	off; from; down	depart, defrost
deci-	ten	decimeter, decade
di-	two	diameter
dis-	opposite; not	disable, discomfort
e-/ex-; ec-/ex-	out	exit, exegesis
hyper-	too much	hyperactive, hypersensitive
hypo-	too little	hypoactive

Greek and Latin prefixes	Meaning	English examples
in-	not	invalid
inter-	between	interstate, international
intra-	within	intramurals
macro-	large	macrobiologist
micro-	small	microscope
milli-	thousand	millipede
mis-	bad	misnomer
mon-/mono-	one; single	monochrome
nano-	billion	nanosecond
neo-	new; recent	neophyte, neonate
non-	not	nonstop
omni-	all	omniscient
pan-	all	panorama
para-	alongside	paralegal
per-	throughout	pervade
peri-	all around	periscope
poly-	many	polygon
post-	after	postpone
pre-	before	precede, prepare
pro-	forward	protest

Greek and Latin prefixes	Meaning	English examples
re-	again; backward	rearrange, rewind
retro-	back	retrograde
sub-	under	submarine, subway
super-	more than	supermarket
sym-	together	symbol, symbiotic
syn-	with	synchronize
thermo-/therm-	heat	thermal, thermometer
trans-	across, beyond, through	transatlantic
un-	not	unwilling

A suffix is a word part added to the end of a root word to change its meaning. Here are some Greek and Latin suffixes, their meanings, and examples.

Greek and Latin suffixes	Meaning	English examples
-able/-ible	capable or worthy of	likable, flexible
-al	relating to	maternal
-algia	pain	myalgia, neuralgia
-arium	place of	aquarium, terrarium
-ation	action or process	civilization, strangulation
-dom	quality; state	freedom
-fy/-ify	to make or cause to become	purify, humidify

Greek and Latin suffixes	Meaning	English examples
-gram	something written or drawn	cardiogram, telegram
-graph	something written or drawn; an instrument for writing, drawing, or recording	monograph, phonograph
-ic	relating to	poetic
-ile	quality; state	juvenile
-ism	the act, state, or theory of	criticism, optimism
-ist	one who practices	biologist, cyclist
-ize	to cause to be or to become	legalize, modernize
-logue/-log	speech; to speak	dialogue, travelogue
-logy/-ology	the study of	biology, dermatology
-ment	action or process	entertainment, amazement
-meter/-metry	measuring device; to measure	geometry, kilometer, perimeter
-oid	like or resembling; shape or form	humanoid, trapezoid
-ous	quality; state	nebulousa
-phile	loving	audiophile, Francophile
-phobe/-phobia	an intense fear of a specific thing; a person who fears that thing	agoraphobe, agoraphobia, xenophobe, xenophobia
-phone	sound; device that receives or emits sound; speaker of a language	telephone, Francophone
-ty/-ity	quality; state	certainty, frailty, similarity
-tion	quality; state	preservation
-ular	relating to	cellular

Now that you know roots, prefixes, and suffixes, you can figure out what new words mean—and your can mix and match word parts from the charts to make your own words, like hyperlogophobia!

Paper Flowers and Capillary Action

YOU WILL NEED

❀ A piece of paper (notebook paper is fine)

❀ A pencil

❀ Scissors

❀ A large bowl or dish of water

TO MAKE YOUR PAPER FLOWER, draw a large circle on your piece of paper, and then draw triangle-shaped petals all around it. Cut out the shape and close the triangle parts down on top of the paper. Place your closed paper flower on the surface of the water in your dish or bowl, and watch what happens: your flower will blossom, thanks to something called capillary action. Capillary action, or capillary motion, is the ability of one thing to pull another thing inside it—think of sponges or paper towels and how they soak up spills. When your paper flower is placed in water, the paper begins drawing the water in through capillary action. As the paper fibers swell with water, the folded petals unfurl.

Capillary action isn't a phenomenon restricted just to science experiments or wiping counters—it happens every day in our bodies, with the circulation of our blood and even the draining of constantly produced tears from our eyes. And some modern fabrics use capillary action to draw sweat away from skin. You can try this experiment with other kinds of paper to see how capillary action works with different materials, from construction paper and watercolor paper to tracing paper and tissue paper.

Cootie Catchers
(Origami fortune tellers)

AS WE ALL KNOW, cooties are invisible, communicable germs that can infect anyone who is touched by someone who has them. This makes sense with what we know about the word "cooties," which comes to us from the Malay word *kutu*, meaning "lice." But how did a folded-paper fortune-telling device become associated with cooties?

Playground lore has it that cooties, which often lie mysteriously dormant until recess, can only be eradicated in one of two ways: either the infected person can touch another person and transfer the cooties, or a pincer-like piece of folded paper can be used to catch the cooties and then throw them away. As cooties are usually associated with persons of the opposite sex, and as history has given girls numerous rituals for divining their futures in love and marriage, it makes sense that a cootie catcher might evolve into an origami fortune-telling game used to both reveal a girl's future and to protect her from it.

Of course, when you design your own cootie catcher, you can make it say anything you want, and the fortunes it tells might have nothing to do with anyone who may or may not have cooties.

FOLDING INSTRUCTIONS

If you have any size of square-shaped paper handy, use that. If you don't, take regular letter-sized paper, fold the bottom of the paper up to make a triangle, crease the edge, and cut off the strip above the triangle. When you open the triangle, you'll have a perfect square with a crease diagonally down the middle.

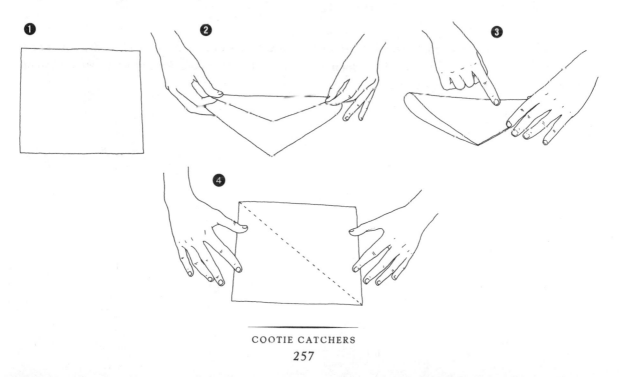

Fold the square into a triangle again, this time the opposite way, crease the edge, then unfold. You now have a square with an X folded into it.

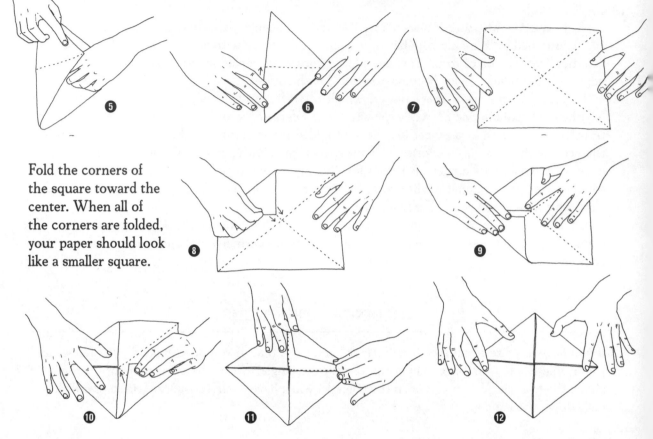

Fold the corners of the square toward the center. When all of the corners are folded, your paper should look like a smaller square.

Turn your paper over so that the folded sides face down, then fold the corners of the square toward the center again. When the four corners are folded, your paper should be an even smaller square, composed of triangles. Number these triangles one through eight.

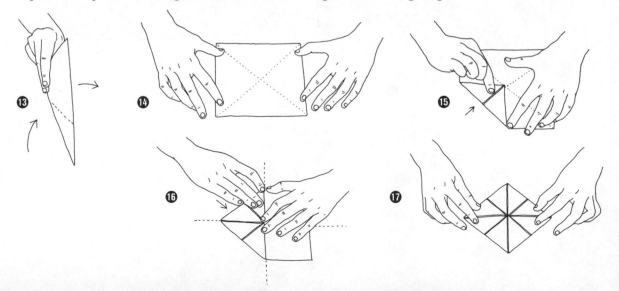

Now fold the square vertically, crease it, and open it back up. Fold it horizontally, crease it, and open it up again. The numbered triangle side should be facing you.

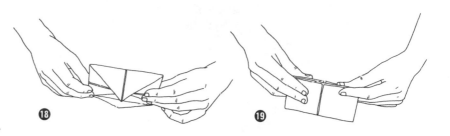

Lift up the flaps and write a fortune or message on each triangle inside, then close the flaps again. Flip the square over and color each of the triangles a different color.

Turn the square back over so the number side is facing up and fold it in half, towards you. Slip your thumbs and index fingers under the flaps and pinch them together to make the cootie catcher's edges come together. When you open your fingers, you should see the numbered triangles inside; when you close them, you should see the colored triangles outside.

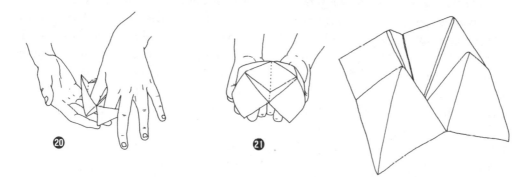

PLAYING INSTRUCTIONS

Find a friend who wants their fortune told. Have them choose a color from the outer triangles, then open and close the cootie catcher (up and down and side to side), moving once for each letter in the color they've picked, until it's all spelled out. Then have your friend choose a number from the inner triangles. Move the cootie catcher open and closed that many times. Then have your friend select one more number from the inner triangles. Lift up the corresponding flap and read the fortune inside. (This can be fun stuff like: "You will be a famous singer," "You will build a scooter with your mom," "You will beat your friends in a game of four-square...")

Jacks

JACKS, ALONG WITH MARBLES, is one of the oldest games in the world. Store-bought jacks are a bunch of six-pointed star-shaped objects, with a ball to bounce as we scoop them up, but in its early form the game was played with whatever was at hand—stones, small animal bones, or even crumpled-up paper.

Players decide who goes first by "flipping" or using any rhyming game to determine the first player. Flipping means tossing jacks in the air and trying to catch as many as you can on the back of your hand. The player who catches the most gets to go first.

To begin play, toss the ten jacks onto the playing surface. Then bounce the ball in the air, pick up one jack using your throwing hand, and catch the ball in the hand holding the jack before the ball bounces. (Place the jack you've collected in your other hand or off to the side before you try to pick up another one.) Do this again, picking up one jack at a time without the ball bouncing twice, until you've picked up all ten jacks. This is "onesies." Once you've done that successfully, move on to "twosies": scatter the ten jacks again, and this time pick up two jacks at a time. Do this until you've picked up all ten jacks. Continue to "threesies," where you pick up the jacks three at a time, "foursies," four at a time, and on all the way to "tensies."

(When there are "leftovers"—one jack in "threesies," two jacks in "foursies"—you pick them up individually. If you pick them up before you've picked up the groups, that is known as "putting the cart before the horse," and you must call "cart" as you pick up the individual "leftover" jacks. "Threesies" has three groups of three and one jack in the "cart"; "Foursies" has two groups of four and two jacks in the "cart"; etc.)

Your turn is over when you don't pick up the correct number of jacks, you miss the ball, or the ball bounces. When it's your turn again, start up where you left off—if you lost your turn on "twosies," start at twosies. The winner is the player who is able to successfully pick up the largest number of jacks.

TIPS AND VARIATIONS

Usually, only one hand may be used to throw the ball and pick up the jacks, but play can be simplified to allow two hands. You can also make it more difficult by only allowing players to use their "bad" hands (right hand for left-handed players, left hand for right-handed players).

OTHER JACKS LINGO

Kissies
When two jacks are touching. They can be separated by calling "Kissies!" while a player moves them apart.

Fancies
Complicated ways of picking up the jacks, like not being allowed to touch the jacks you don't pick up.

Around the World
Toss the ball, circle the ball with your hand, and then pick up jacks before the ball bounces.

Cats in the Well
Make a loose fist with the thumb and first finger of your non-throwing hand. The jacks you pick up ("cats") are dropped through the opening (the "well").

Eggs in the Basket, or Picking Cherries
Toss the ball, pick up the jacks, and transfer the jacks to your other hand before catching the ball.

Pigs in the Pen
Make an arch with the thumb and first finger of your non-throwing hand. Then toss the ball, flick a jack through the arch, and then catch the ball.

Pigs over the Fence
Make a "fence" with your non-throwing hand by putting your hand on its side, thumb facing up. Toss the ball, transfer the jacks to other side of your "fence," and catch the ball.

PICKING WHO'S IT

Rhymes to determine who goes first can be used for any game, from jacks to tag to board games to truth or dare. Here are some fun schoolyard ways of figuring out who gets to be first.

Eeny, Meeny, Miny, Moe

(Point at each player for each word said; whoever lands on "it" goes first. OR whoever lands on "it" is out, and you start again until there is only one person left who is not "it." That person gets to go first.)

Eeny, meeny, miny, moe
Catch a tiger by the toe
If he hollers let him go,
Eeny, meeny, miny, moe.
My mother said to pick the very best one
And you are not it.

Bubblegum, Bubblegum in a Dish

(On "wish," the player says a number, which is then counted out. The player on whom the last number falls is It, and gets to go first)

Bubblegum, bubblegum in a dish
How many pieces do you wish?

Skunk in the Barnyard

(Players each put one foot in a circle. A foot is pointed at for each word said, and the foot on "you!" is considered "out." Repeat until there is only one foot left. That player goes first.)

Skunk in the barnyard, pee-you!
Who put it in there, not you!

One Potato

(Players put their fists in a circle. The "potato peeler" puts her fist on the players fists as she says the words. Whoever lands on "more" removes her fist. The last player left goes first.)

One potato, two potato
One potato, two potato, three potato, four.
Five potato, six potato, seven potato,
more.

Queens of the Ancient World V
Zenobia, Queen of the East

IN THE THIRD CENTURY AD, Zenobia of Palmyra was the famed Queen of the East. According to the author of *Historia Augusta,* she had long black hair and warm brown skin, piercing dark eyes and a lyrical, strong voice. Known for her boldness, determination, and fairness as a leader, she was just in her twenties when she built and ruled an empire that covered most of what is now the Middle East.

Zenobia was born around 240 AD at Palmyra, a sparkling, palm-tree-filled paradise deep in the desert of Syria (now the ruins of Tadmor, about 150 miles northeast of Damascus). Her father was a tribal ruler who had enticed her mother from Egypt to this prosperous and cosmopolitan trading outpost.

Zenobia's full given name was Iulia Aurelia Zenobia. "Iulia" was a popular girl's name in Rome, which, even though it was far away, ruled the Syrian desert. "Aurelia" meant that her family were Roman citizens, an important honor. "Zenobia" came from her family's Aramaic tribe. Historians know that by the age of eighteen, she had already married the governor of Palmyra, a man named Odainat (known in Latin as Septimius Odaenathus). Then she changed her name to Septimia Zenobia, to match his.

ZENOBIA, QUEEN OF THE EAST

As wife to the land's governor, Zenobia was well educated, and her court was filled with philosophers and poets. Many an evening was spent lingering over sumptuous meals, talking about Homer and Plato, making speeches, and laughing at riddles and wit. The peace was disturbed in 260, however, when the Persian king, Shapur, tried to take Syria from the Romans. As allies of Rome, the Palmyrans guarded the frontier where the Roman Empire met the Persian, so Odainat and Zenobia prepared for combat.

The emperor of Rome, Valerian, faced rebellion everywhere—to the west, north, and now to the east. His troops were dispirited, but nonetheless he marched them to battle. The Persians had superior strength and fighting skills, so they easily routed the weary Roman soldiers. Valerian and Shapur agreed to meet at the city of Edessa and negotiate terms. When Valerian showed up, the Persians ambushed him and took him into captivity.

That's when two Roman messengers urged their horses across the desert sand to Palmyra, bringing the terrible news of Valerian's capture. Odainat and Zenobia were ready. Side by side, the couple donned armor, saddled their horses, and led the army of Palmyra against the Persians, in search of Valerian.

While Odainat was a courageous and daring warrior, ancient writers tell us Zenobia was even more so, and praised her battle skills, including her exceptional way with the troops. She rallied them, kept them inspired, and at times even handed off her horse to march for miles with the foot soldiers. Unfortunately, the Persians killed Valerian before Odainat and Zenobia could save him, but the couple's brave leadership earned them the complete respect of the Palmyran army and people.

Was it odd for these troops to see a woman in front, her long black hair streaming out from beneath her helmet? The ancient cultures of Greece and Rome often portrayed the deity of war as a woman, and female Victory statues graced nearly every city. In fact, the Palmyran soldiers followed Zenobia to battle again and again in the following years.

In 267 AD, seven years after their first battle together, Zenobia's husband Odainat was assassinated. The royal line fell to Zenobia's toddler son, Vaballathus, who was clearly too young to rule. Zenobia, then 27 years old, became queen in his stead. She dreamed of an empire of Palmyra and prepared the troops for a battle of independence.

The Romans were busy in Europe defending themselves from the Goths, Zenobia knew, so she attacked the Roman province of Egypt. The Egyptians, too, were distracted, off battling pirates in the Mediterranean Sea. She conquered them, and then went to conquer cities in Arabia, Palestine, and Syria. By 269, she declared her empire's independence from Rome and minted new coins with her image and the word "REGINA"—Queen.

Historians tell us that Zenobia ruled tolerantly as Queen of the East, drawing on the Palmyran traditions of hospitality and openness to treat all people with fairness, including the pagans, Jews, and Christians of her empire. She opened new trade routes and met with Christian bishops and other leaders of the cities she conquered.

As Zenobia grew her Palmyran empire, armies threatened the larger Roman Empire on all sides. The new Roman emperor, Aurelian, was battling the Goth and Visigoth tribes in northern Europe. When his messengers arrived with news of Queen Zenobia's expanding kingdom, Aurelian set off for Egypt, determined to win the territory back, and then to Turkey (which in ancient times was called Asia Minor). After these small victories, he prepared to attack Antioch, a city in northern Syria that Zenobia now ruled.

Zenobia had never faced the vast legions of the mighty Roman army. She could have given up and returned to the Roman fold, but decided instead to take a last stand and save the heart of her hard-earned empire. She assembled the troops along one side of the north-flowing Orontes River. Her soldiers fought all day, Zenobia along with them. Then, as the sun dipped toward the western horizon, the tired soldiers, bleary and water-starved after a long day, fell into a trap, in which the Romans massacred them from all sides.

Zenobia managed to escape with seventy thousand soldiers and retreated to the city of Emesa. They found a hill and, under cover of night, climbed to the top and lay in wait, ready to rain down arrows on the Roman soldiers. The Romans, though, pulled out their colorful shields, held high overhead, each shield meeting the next to cover the men and protect them from the Palmyrans' arrows and darts. In this formation, the Romans pushed forward up the hill. When they reached the Palmyran marksmen, they moved their shields forward and down, and attacked.

Thousands of troops died on the battlefield. Zenobia herself barely escaped and even her trusted horse fell in the battle. She commandeered a camel and turned the slow beast toward the sandy hinterlands of the Syrian desert, with hopes that the plodding animal could take her one hundred miles east to Persia, where she would be safe from Rome.

"I promise you life if you surrender," Aurelian wrote to her. Zenobia had other plans, but it was Aurelian's turn for victory. He lay siege to her beloved Palmyra and sent his best soldiers on horseback to capture the fallen paradise's fugitive queen. As she neared the Euphrates River, so close to freedom, the emperor's horsemen reached Zenobia and captured her.

The remainder of Zenobia's life is shrouded in myth. Where one ancient historian reports that she died in captivity, another writes that Aurelian took her to Rome. It is said that in 274, Zenobia was wrapped in chains of gold and made to walk down Rome's main boulevard as Aurelian celebrated his triumph over the many tribes he had battled. Still another tale suggests that some time later, Zenobia was released. In her absence, Palmyra had rebelled against Rome once more and had been crushed. Some tales hold that with no home to return to, Zenobia lived the rest of her life not far from Rome, in Tivoli.

Japanese T-Shirt Folding

Folding clothes has never been this much fun. What you need: a short-sleeved t-shirt and just a little patience.

Step 1: On a nice wide surface, lay a T-shirt flat in front of you, right side up, and with the collar part closest to you.

Step 2: With your right hand, use your thumb and forefinger to pinch the edge of the fabric about an inch or two to the right of the collar (about halfway between the edge of the collar and the edge of the shoulder seam).

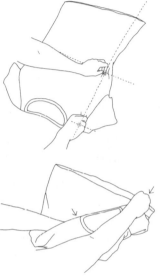

Step 3: Still holding the fabric with your right thumb and forefinger, take your left hand and draw an imaginary straight line from where you're pinching with your right hand to about the middle of the shirt (halfway between the top and the bottom). Pinch that with your left hand thumb and forefinger, making sure to get both sides of the fabric.

Step 4: Still pinching the fabric, bring your right hand over your left hand so that you are folding the shirt in half, the collar part touching the bottom part. With your right hand, grab both the original place where you were pinching and the very bottom of the shirt along the same imaginary line.

Step 5: This step is the most crucial part of the whole endeavor—it has the potential to be the place where it all goes wrong, or the moment where all the magic happens. So: Your right hand, the hand farthest away from you, should be pinching the top and the bottom of the T-shirt, and your left hand, the hand closest to you, should still be pinching the shirt in the middle. Lift both hands up directly, picking up the shirt, then—still with your thumbs and forefingers pinching the shirt in those two spots—pull your hands away from each other. (Your right hand moves to the right, your left hand moves to the left.)

Step 6. Your right and left hands should be in front of you, still pinching the shirt, and the shirt should be hanging down. Gently swing the shirt away from you and lay it on the table without letting go. Bring your right and left hands simultaneously away from you so that the fabric folds over to cover the sleeve of the shirt. Let go of the fabric and you should see the shirt folded in a perfect rectangle.

Step 7: Marvel at the glory of your awesomely folded T-shirt!

States, Statehood, Capitals, Flowers, and Trees—plus Canada!

Statehood of the original 13 colonies: Connecticut, Delaware, Georgia, Maryland, Massachusetts, New Hampshire, New Jersey, New York, North Carolina, Pennsylvania, Rhode Island, South Carolina, Virginia—1776

Fourteenth State: Vermont, March 4, 1791

Forty-ninth and Fiftieth States: Alaska, January 3, 1959; Hawaii, August 21, 1959

Union States in the American Civil War: California, Connecticut, Delaware, Illinois, Indiana, Iowa, Kansas, Kentucky*, Maine, Maryland, Massachusetts, Michigan, Minnesota, Missouri*, Nevada, New Hampshire, New Jersey, New York, Ohio, Oregon, Pennsylvania, Rhode Island, Vermont, West Virginia, Wisconsin

(* Missouri and Kentucky did not secede, but a rival government, or rump group, proclaimed secession within both of these states)

Confederate States in the American Civil War: South Carolina, Mississippi, Florida, Alabama, Georgia, Louisiana, Texas, Virginia, Arkansas, North Carolina, Tennessee

National Plant: Rose (Official since October 7, 1986)

National Tree: Oak

National Bird: Bald Eagle

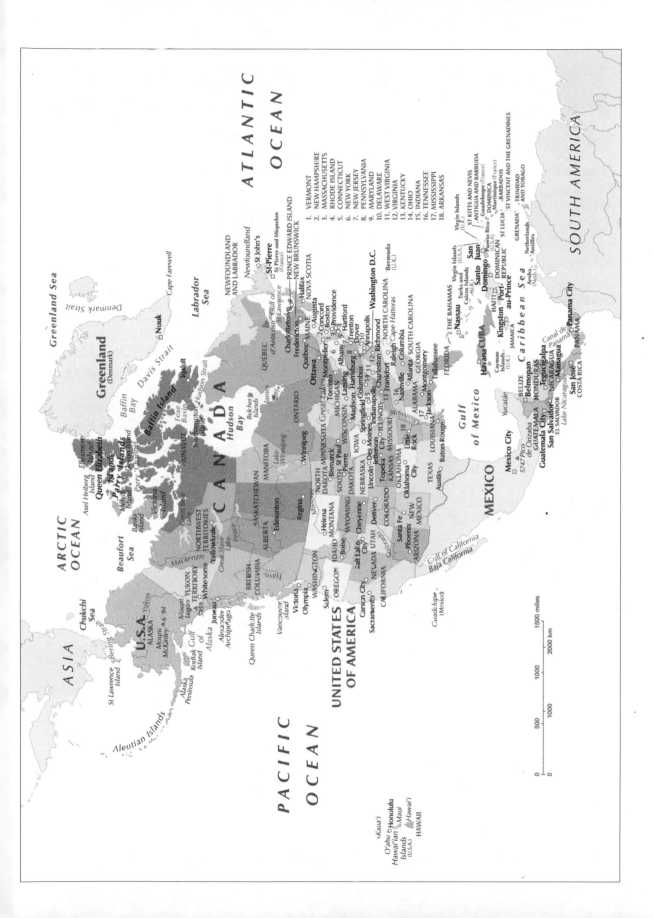

State	Date of statehood	Capital	State Flower	State Tree
Alabama	1819	Montgomery	Camellia	Longleaf Pine
Alaska	1959	Juneau	Forget-Me-Not	Sitka Spruce
Arizona	1912	Phoenix	Saguaro Cactus Blossom	Palo verde
Arkansas	1836	Little Rock	Apple Blossom	Loblolly Pine
California	1850	Sacramento	California Poppy	California Redwoods
Colorado	1876	Denver	Rocky Mountain Columbine	Colorado Blue Spruce
Connecticut	1776	Hartford	Mountain Laurel	Charter White Oak
Delaware	1776	Dover	Peach Blossom	American Holly
Florida	1845	Tallahassee	Orange Blossom	Sabal Palmetto
Georgia	1776	Atlanta	Cherokee Rose	Live Oak
Hawaii	1959	Honolulu	Hawaiian Hibiscus (ma'o hau hele)	Kukui Nut Tree
Idaho	1890	Boise	Mock Orange	Western White Pine
Illinois	1818	Springfield	Violet	White Oak
Indiana	1816	Indianapolis	Peony	Tulip-tree
Iowa	1846	Des Moines	Wild Prairie Rose	Oak
Kansas	1861	Topeka	Sunflower	Cottonwood

State	Date of statehood	Capital	State Flower	State Tree
Kentucky	1792	Frankfort	Goldenrod	Tulip Poplar
Louisiana	1812	Baton Rouge	Magnolia	Bald Cypress
Maine	1820	Augusta	White Pine Cone and Tassel	Eastern White Pine
Maryland	1776	Annapolis	Black-Eyed Susan	White Oak
Massachusetts	1776	Boston	Mayflower	American Elm
Michigan	1837	Lansing	Apple Blossom	Eastern White Pine
Minnesota	1858	Saint Paul	Pink and White Lady's Slipper	Red Pine
Mississippi	1817	Jackson	Magnolia	Magnolia
Missouri	1821	Jefferson City	White Hawthorn Blossom	Flowering Dogwood
Montana	1889	Helena	Bitterroot	Ponderosa Pine
Nebraska	1867	Lincoln	Goldenrod	Cottonwood
Nevada	1864	Carson City	Sagebrush	Single-Leaf Pinyon
New Hampshire	1776	Concord	Purple Lilac	American White Birch
New Jersey	1776	Trenton	Violet	Northern Red Oak
New Mexico	1912	Santa Fe	Yucca Flower	Pinyon
New York	1776	Albany	Rose	Sugar Maple

State	Date of statehood	Capital	State Flower	State Tree
North Carolina	1776	Raleigh	American Dogwood	Longleaf Pine
North Dakota	1889	Bismarck	Wild Prairie Rose	American Elm
Ohio	1803	Columbus	Scarlet Carnation	Ohio Buckeye
Oklahoma	1907	Oklahoma City	Oklahoma Rose	Eastern Redbud
Oregon	1859	Salem	Oregon Grape	Douglas Fir
Pennsylvania	1776	Harrisburg	Mountain Laurel	Eastern Hemlock
Rhode Island	1776	Providence	Violet	Red Maple
South Carolina	1776	Columbia	Yellow Jessamine	Cabbage Palmetto
South Dakota	1889	Pierre	Pasque Flower	Black Hills Spruce
Tennessee	1796	Nashville	Iris	Tulip Poplar
Texas	1845	Austin	Bluebonnet	Pecan
Utah	1896	Salt Lake City	Sego Lily	Blue Spruce
Vermont	1791	Montpelier	Red Clover	Sugar Maple
Virginia	1776	Richmond	American Dogwood	Flowering Dogwood
Washington	1889	Olympia	Coast Rhododendron	Western Hemlock
West Virginia	1863	Charleston	Rhododendron	Sugar Maple

State	Date of statehood	Capital	State Flower	State Tree
Wisconsin	1848	Madison	Wood Violet	Sugar Maple
Wyoming	1890	Cheyenne	Indian Paintbrush	Plains Cottonwood

SEVEN THINGS YOU PROBABLY DIDN'T KNOW ABOUT CANADA

1. A Canadian invented basketball. (James Naismith, a physical education instructor from Almonte, Ontario, came up with the game in 1891 while working at the YMCA International Training School in Springfield, Massachusetts.)

2. Parts of Canada are located further to the south than parts of the US. (Toronto is further south than much of New England and the northern Midwest.)

3. Canadians celebrate Thanksgiving on the second Monday in October, not in November.

4. Canadians do not have $1 and $2 bills. Instead, they use coins, known unabashedly as Loonies ($1) and Toonies ($2).

5. America actually invaded Canada twice, in 1775 and 1812, and was rebuffed both times.

6. Canada has 10 provinces and three territories. The provinces are Alberta, British Columbia, Manitoba, New Brunswick, Newfoundland and Labrador, Nova Scotia, Ontario, Prince Edward Island, Quebec, and Saskatchewan. The three territories are the Northwest Territories, Nunavut, and Yukon. Nunavut was the last territory to be added, in 1999.

7. The languages most spoken in Canada are English, French, and Chinese. New Brunswick is the only officially bilingual province (English and French), and in Quebec, French is the official governmental language.

Make Your Own Paper

ANCIENT EGYPTIANS wrote on paper made from papyrus plants and parchment, which was made from stretched and dried skins of calves, goats, and sheep. In China, early paper was made with silk, bark from mulberry trees, and other plant fibers. Today, paper is mostly made from wood fibers, though specialty paper is made from linen, cotton, and even synthetic materials like latex. But the most basic technique for making paper is essentially the same today as it was in ancient times, and you can try it out right in your own home.

To make your own paper, you'll need:

- Recycled paper (such as newspaper, magazines, toilet paper, paper bags, notebook paper, construction paper, tissue paper, napkins)

- A sponge

- Wire mesh screen (an old door or window screen)

- A wood frame (you can use an old picture frame, or you can build a frame yourself using four pieces of wood and some nails)

- Plastic basin or tub (should be large enough to fit your frame)

- A blender

- Felt, blotting paper, flannel, or other absorbent fabric (newsprint will work in a pinch)

- Stapler

- Liquid starch

- Rolling pin

- Iron

Tear your paper into small pieces and fill the blender halfway full with it. Add warm water until the blender is full. Blend the paper and water for about 30 seconds, starting at low speed and then gradually increasing. Blend until you get a smooth, well-blended pulp with no chunks or bits of paper.

Use your screen and wood frame to make what's called a mold. Stretch the screen over the frame as tightly as possible and use a stapler to affix it. Trim off any excess. Now is also a good time to lay out the felt or blotting paper that you will use later. Place it next to your basin so that it will be ready when you need it.

Fill up the basin or tub about halfway full with water. Add your blender full of pulp. Make two more blenders of pulp and add these to the basin. Stir the water and pulp in the basin—feel free to use your hands—and then stir in two teaspoons of liquid starch. Mix well, then submerge your mold (the screen and wood frame) into the basin, with the screen side on the bottom. Move the mold from side to side until the pulp settles on top of it evenly.

Carefully raise the mold out of the water and hold it above the basin while the water drains. The pulp mixture should be in a uniform layer across the screen. (If there are holes, or if the pulp is not lying evenly, submerge the mold again and give it another try.) Press down on it gently to squeeze out the moisture, and use a sponge to soak up excess water from the bottom of the screen.

After the mold stops dripping, flip the screen paper-side down onto your felt, flannel, or other blotting material. Press out any moisture with the sponge and then carefully lift the mold, leaving the wet sheet of paper on the fabric. Use your hands to press out bubbles or other slight imperfections.

Place another piece of blotting material on top of the paper and use a rolling pin to squeeze out the moisture. Now your handmade sheet of paper needs to dry. Find a good spot and let it sit for a few hours. You can also use an iron (on a medium setting) to encourage the drying process; just make sure to iron the paper through the blotting material, not directly on the paper itself. When the paper is fully dry, carefully remove the top cloth and then peel off the paper. Now you are all set to begin using your handmade paper for whatever you desire.

Books That Will Change Your Life

WE PRESENT these titles for your reading pleasure, knowing there are endless books beyond this list to discover and love, too. We know you will read them in your own fashion and at your own pace.

20 GIRL CLASSICS

- *A Wrinkle in Time* by Madeleine L'Engle, and her other books too.
- *Anne of Green Gables* (and *Emily of New Moon*) by L.M. Montgomery
- *Behind Rebel Lines: The Incredible Story of Emma Edmonds, Civil War Spy* by Seymour Reit
- *Bridge to Terabithia* by Katherine Paterson
- *Caddie Woodlawn* (and the sequel, *Magical Melons*) by Carol Ryrie Brink
- *Charlotte's Web* by E.B. White
- *The Famous Five,* a series by Enid Blyton, with Dick, Ann, Julian, George (a girl!), and her dog Timothy.
- *From the Mixed-Up Files of Mrs. Basil E. Frankweiler* by E.L. Konigsburg
- *Harriet the Spy* by Louise Fitzhugh
- *The Illyrian Adventure* series by Lloyd Alexander
- *The Little Princess* (and *The Secret Garden*) by Frances Hodgson Burnett
- *Keep Climbing, Girls* by Beah H. Richards
- *Little Women* and *Jo's Boys* by Louisa May Alcott
- *Little House on the Prairie* by Laura Ingalls Wilder—the entire series.
- *Lizzie Bright* (and *The Buckminster Boy*) by Gary Schmidt
- *Mandy* by Julie Andrews
- *Matilda* (and *The BFG*) by Roald Dahl. Actually, make that anything by Roald Dahl.
- *Miss Happiness and Miss Flower* by Rumer Godden
- *Pippi Longstocking* by Astrid Lindgren
- *Ramona* by Beverly Cleary (the series)

OTHER FAVORITES

- *Alice's Adventures in Wonderland* and *Through the Looking Glass* by Lewis Carroll
- *Amazing Grace* by Mary Hoffman
- *All of a Kind Family* by Sydney Taylor
- *The Borrowers* by Mary Norton
- *Call of the Wild* by Jack London
- *The Chronicles of Narnia* by C.S. Lewis. Seven classic novels from the 1950s, including the most famous, *The Lion, the Witch, and the Wardrobe*
- *The Good Earth* by Pearl S. Buck

- *Great Expectations* by Charles Dickens
- *Harry Potter* by J.K. Rowling. All seven, in time, and as you grow.
- *The Hobbit* and *The Lord of the Rings* by J.R.R. Tolkien
- *The Hoboken Chicken Emergency* and other madcap stories by Daniel Pinkwater
- *Island of the Blue Dolphins,* by Scott O'Dell, about a girl Robinson Crusoe. When you're done, read the original *Robinson Crusoe* by Daniel Defoe.
- *Jane Eyre* by Charlotte Brontë
- *Johnny Tremain* by Esther Forbes
- *The Little Prince* by Antoine de Saint-Exupery
- *Marjorie Morningstar* by Herman Wouk
- *Mary Poppins* by P.L. Travers
- *Mrs. Frisby and the Rats of NIMH,* by Robert C. O'Brien
- *My Side of the Mountain* and *Julie of the Wolves* by Jean Craighead George
- *Out of the Dust* by Karen Hesse
- *The Phantom Tollbooth* by Norton Juster. Yes, another boy-hero-rescues-the-princesses plot (though here the princesses are Rhyme and Reason), but a great book nonetheless.
- *Pride and Prejudice* by Jane Austen
- *Treasure Island* by Robert Louis Stevenson
- *A Tree Groes in Brooklyn* by Betty Smith
- *The True Confessions of Charlotte Doyle* by Avi
- *Winnie the Pooh* by A.A. Milne. The original books, and the poems.
- *The Witch of Blackbird Pond* by Elizabeth George Speare
- *Wuthering Heights* by Emily Brontë
- *The Wonderful Wizard of Oz* by Frank Baum

SCIENCE FICTION AND FANTASY BOOKS

- Lloyd Alexander's *The Chronicles of Prydain*
- Isaac Asimov's *Foundation* and *Robot* series
- Ray Bradbury's *Dandelion Wine* and *Fahrenheit 451*
- Orson Scott Card's *Ender's Game* and all the books in the Ender series
- Susan Cooper's *The Dark is Rising* sequence
- Lois Lowry's *The Giver, Gathering Blue,* and *Messenger*
- Ursula K. LeGuin's *The Tombs of Atuan* and her *Earthsea* trilogy
- Anne McCaffrey's *Dragonsong* trilogy
- Robin McKinley's *The Blue Sword* and *The Hero and the Crown*
- Philip Pullman's *His Dark Materials*

CLASSIC GIRL-AND-HER-HORSE BOOKS

- *Black Beauty* by Anna Sewell
- *Misty of Chincoteague* by Marguerite Henry
- *My Friend Flicka* by Mary O'Hara
- *National Velvet* by Enid Bagnold
- *The Girl Who Loved Wild Horses* by Paul Goble

MYTHOLOGIES AND FAIRY TALES

- *Bullfinch's Mythology* is a start. Some might say it's for grown-ups, but read a few lines to yourself out loud and you'll see whether or not it works for you.
- *The Complete Hans Christian Andersen Fairy Tales* by Hans Christian Andersen
- *One Thousand and One Arabian Nights*
- *The Complete Grimm's Fairy Tales* by Brothers Grimm
- *The Adventures of Robin Hood*
- *The Once and Future King* by T.H. White, about King Arthur's Court.
- *Beauty: A Retelling of the Story of Beauty and the Beast* by Robin McKinley
- *The Odyssey* by Homer

OLD-FASHIONED GIRL-DETECTIVE SERIES

- *Nancy Drew* by Carolyn Keene. Starting with *The Secret of the Old Clock,* all the mysteries in River Heights end in Nancy's lap, and with her girlfriends George and Bess at her side, she always finds the secret passageways to solve them. The series began in the 1920s, and was revised twice, in the 1950s and the 2000s, each time becoming slightly less intrepid.

- *Trixie Belden.* An even better girl detective series is the *Trixie Belden* books, featuring Trixie, a teenaged, freckle-faced tomboy from upstate New York whose down-to-earth nature, pluck, and quick thinking aid her in solving mysteries with her friends Honey and Jim. Julie Campbell started the series in 1948 and wrote the first six books; after that the books were written by a series of writers using the pseudonym Kathryn Kenny.

NONFICTION

When we were young and bored, our parents told us, "Go read the dictionary!" We did, and look where it got us. One should never underestimate the pleasure to be found flipping through a dictionary, an encyclopedia, or an old science book.

Miscellanea

AS WE REACH the end, there are some additional things one really should know, and here they are, in no particular order.

1. Skipping Stones. Find a rock as close to smooth, flat, and round as you can. Hold it flattest-side down, index finger curled around one edge, and throw it sidearm, low and parallel to the water, snapping the wrist at the last possible moment before you let go to give it some spin. The stone should hit the water at a low, 20 degree angle or so. Keep practicing till the stone bounces off the water a few times.

2. Steering a Sled. We'll tell you here in case you do not know: it's opposite to how you steer a bicycle or a car, and akin to a kayak or canoe. Lean left to go right. Lean right to go left.

3. Flying a Kite. Toss the kite into the wind, or run with the kite behind you until the wind catches it, then unhurriedly let the string out. If the kite swoops, pull on the string. Extra ribbons on the tail help to stabilize, and they are pretty too. Make sure there's enough wind, then practice so the string in your hand feels like second nature.

4. Water Balloons. To fill, attach the mouth of the balloon to the water faucet (or use an adapter that comes with many packages of water balloons), and—this is key—keep the faucet on low so the water pressure doesn't send the balloon into outer space. Once the water balloon smashes to the ground, clean up the colorful scraps, since when the fun's over, the balloon remnants turn into trash.

5. Lanyards. Making lanyards (flat plastic thread box-stitched into a loop, bar, or creative shape) has been a treasured summertime activity. Lanyard strings were once extremely precious, and people who knew all the box stitch variations were popular and in high demand.

Nowadays, lanyard, or gimp, as some people call it, is more plentiful. It's also more cheaply made, and doesn't hold together as well when you cross it over in mysterious ways and pull it tight.

6. Cat's Cradle. Now here's an old-fashioned girl activity worth preserving. This two-person game of creating various figures with one string loop may actually be the oldest and most widely known game in the history of humanity.

Russians call it "the game of string," and Chinese call it "catch cradle." British geographer Alfred Wallace tried to teach the game to children in Borneo in the 1800s, only to have them show him new variations he had never seen. And Kenyan anthropologist Louis Leakey used it in the early 1900s to connect with African tribes.

It's pretty much impossible to describe the intricate movements of cat's cradle on paper without a lot of pictures. And it's better to learn from someone in person anyway. So find a girl who knows and have her show you.

7. Ping-Pong. Forget nudging your parents for a horse; ask for a ping-pong table instead. Have a good supply of those air-filled white balls ready for when they lodge in the crevices between storage boxes that have been stacked high against the basement walls to make space for the ping-pong table. If you're alone you can fold one of the table sides to vertical and push it against a wall to practice.

8. Harmonica. Invaluable for nights by the campfire when the embers are low, the camp songs are done, and nearly everyone has fallen asleep. Hold with your thumb and first finger. Blow breath into it, and draw it back through the holes. Experiment with sound. Flapping the other fingers up and down while you blow or draw will create a wavery vibrato.

9. Snowshoeing. The best sport for winter, because you don't need a ski lift to get you up the hill. Just strap a pair of snowshoes on over your boots and head outdoors.

10. Temperature Conversions. To convert Celsius to Fahrenheit, multiply by 9, divide by 5, and add 32. To convert temperatures the other way, from Fahrenheit to Celsius, subtract 32, divide by 9, and multiply by 5.

11. Bicycle Wheelies. Whether yours is a tough mountain bike or a ladylike pastel blue number with tassels out the handlebars and a basket, you'll want to know how to pop a wheelie.

Once you're at speed, lean forward, hands grabbing the handlebars, and then shift your body weight slightly up and backward. That should be enough to lift the front wheel off the ground, whether you're doing show-offs on the street in front of your house, or trying to get your bike over tree stumps on a rugged trail.

12. Handball. It sounds ridiculously boring but it's not. Find a clean wall with no windows, or another flat surface, and bounce a pink rubber ball against it, open-handed. It's the best way possible to discover what your hands can do, and to learn about angles of reflection. Play alone or with friends, rotating in when someone misses the ball.

13. Take Things Apart. Old televisions and fax machines, a cell phone that no longer works, or a computer that's ten years out of date and living its final years in the back shed: no discarded machine should go undismantled. Teensy-tiny drivers and hex keys can unlock the smallest screws, so grab a hammer and whatever does the trick and see what's inside. That's how the world's best engineers learned what they know.

14. Time Capsules. This girlhood of yours is filled with days to remember. Make a scrapbook if you like, but really, any old box will do—an antique tin, a shoebox, or a box hammered together from plywood and nails. Keep your mementos, letters, ticket stubs, the list of dreams scribbled on a napkin, a picture of your best friends, and the poem or phrase you thought up last night before bed. Stow this box of inspiration somewhere safe, keep adding to it, and don't look at it for twenty years.

15. Words to Live By. Be brave and walk with confidence. And remember, in the words of Amelia Earhart, "Adventure is worthwhile in itself."

Daring Book for Girls Badges

This book wouldn't be complete without some Daring Girl badges, which you can print out at our website: www.daringbookforgirls.com

SPORTS AND GAMES

GIRL LORE

ADVENTURE

WORLD KNOWLEDGE

LIFE SKILLS

ARTS AND LITERATURE

ILLUSTRATION CREDITS

8: *Woman Having Her Palm Read,* courtesy the Picture Collection, The Branch Libraries, The New York Public Library, Astor, Lenox and Tilden Foundations

22: Princess Sarah Culberson, courtesy of Sarah Culberson

41: *Mausoleum of Halicarnassus* by Martin Heemskerck © Bettmann/CORBIS

56: Moai statues Photograph © Tim Waters www.flickr.com/photos/tim-waters

96: Coins of Salome Alexandria's reign, © jewishencyclopedia.com

123: Amelia Earhart, Library of Congress

124: Alexandra David-Néel. Mary Evans Picture Library/Alamy

126: Freya Stark, Popperfoto/Alamy

126: Florence Baker. Classic Image/Alamy

136: Mrs. John Adams (Abigail Smith), the Emmet Collection, Miriam and Ira D. Wallach Division of Art, The New York Public Library, Astor, Lenox and Tilden Foundations

149: Hedy Lamarr, courtesy of MGM

150: Josephine Baker, Library of Congress

160: Antonius et Cleopatra, the Print Collection, Miriam and Ira D. Wallach Division of Art, The New York Public Library, Astor, Lenox and Tilden Foundations

167–173: Scooter plans inspired by and adapted from Les Kenny of www.buildeazy.com, a website featuring building projects for kids and adults. Used with permission.

176: © iStockphoto.com/Douglas Allen

205: Florence Nightingale, Library of Congress

205: Clara Barton, Library of Congress

246: Topographic map: USGS

248: Jewelweed, Robert H. Mohlenbrock @ USDA-NRCS PLANTS Database / USDA SCS. 1989. Midwest wetland flora: Field office illustrated guide to plant species. Midwest National Technical Center, Lincoln, NE.

262: *Queen Zenobia Addressing Her Soldiers,* by Giovanni Battista Tiepolo, c. 1730, Samuel H. Kress Collection. Image courtesy of the Board of Trustees, National Gallery of Art, Washington, DC.

Acknowledgments

With thanks to our agents, Laura Gross and Sam Stoloff; Phil Friedman, Matthew Benjamin, Stephanie Meyers, and everyone at HarperCollins and The Stonesong Press. And to Molly Ashodian and her friends, Barbara Card Atkinson, Rob Baird, Samira Baird, Dana Barron, Gil Binenbaum, Nate Binenbaum, Steve and Nurit Binenbaum, Rona Binenbaum, the Bromley-Zimmerman family, Sarah Brown, Bill Buchanan, Elin Buchanan, Emi Buchanan, Jessie Buchanan, Shannon Buchanan, Betsy Busch, Stacy DeBroff, Katie Dolgenos, Asha Dornfest, Ann Douglas, Eileen Flanagan, Marcus Geduld, the Goldman-Hersh family, Kay Gormley, Sarah Heady, the Larrabee-O'Donovan family, Jack's Marine, Jane Butler Kahle, Megan Pincus Kajitani, Les Kenny, Killian's Hardware, Andy Lamas, Jen Lawrence, Sara Lorimer, Rachel Marcus, Molly Masyr, Metafilter (especially the women of Ask Metafilter), Jim Miller, Tracy Miller, Marjorie Osterhout, Myra and Dan Peskowitz, Deborah Rickards, Rittenhouse Lumber, Carol Sime, Lisa Suggitt of rollergirl. ca, Alexis Seabrook, Kate Scantlebury, Tom Sugrue, Carrie Szalay, and Felicia Sullivan. Appreciation to everyone who offered advice and inspiration, and to daring girls everywhere.